How to win any pub quiz

John Smith

GUINNESS PUBLISHING

Design: John Mitchell

Cover: Electric Echo

Illustrations: Peter Harper

The Work Copyright © John Smith 1995

The right of John Smith to be identified as Author of this Work has been
asserted in accordance with the Copyright, Design & Patents Act 1988.

First published in 1993 by Guinness Publishing
  Revised edition 1995
    Reprint 10 9 8 7 6 5 4 3 2 1 0

Typeset in Great Britain by
Ace Filmsetting Ltd, Frome, Somerset
Printed and bound in Great Britain by
Cox & Wyman Ltd

A catalogue record for this book is available from the British Library

ISBN 0-85112-645-6

Contents

Preface

Things have changed little since the publication of *How to Win Any Pub Quiz* in September 1993. The successful quiz player is still the person who can store fact after fact, and later recall those facts from memory. If anything has changed it is the quality of question-setting. Many quizzes are now set by question setters with inadequate reference sources and little idea of what makes for an interesting and enjoyable evening. The result is that more and more questions are being recycled, rehashed or reworded by unimaginative setters. People are still asking questions about capital cities, the Beaufort scale and national flags (some of them are still getting them wrong!).

The response to the first edition of this book was generally very favourable, but some reviewers misunderstood my intentions. The book was not written for the "Brain of Britain" contestant, nor would it help you very much on "Round Britain Quiz". It was written for the person who regularly plays in a quiz at their local pub or club, or who likes to pit their wits against contestants on TV quiz programmes. (Just try watching a quiz programme with a copy of this book; your performance will improve considerably.)

I would like to take this opportunity to thank those who were kind enough to write to me with their comments and suggestions after reading the first edition, they have been most helpful. I have included some of their suggestions in this enlarged edition together with updates on some sections.

This book does not set out to answer every question that you will be asked in a quiz but it will cover many of them. I have listed below a few further general rules that should always be kept in mind when attempting to win pub quizzes.

1   Keep fully abreast of current affairs, the names of tin-pot dictators and ministerial mistresses are a favourite source for questions.
2   Do not be an intellectual snob about TV soap operas.
3   Keep abreast of the singles and album charts.

4   Commit to memory the winners of recent sporting events.

5   Always make a note of the breed of the Supreme Champion at Crufts.

6   Only ever give a surname as an answer. A wrongly remembered forename will almost certainly cost you the point. Yes, sometimes a question master will specify the need for a first name as he asks the question – this can sometimes be a great help; you then know he is looking for one of a pair of brothers or perhaps simply one of two people in the same sphere who share a surname.

7   In many team versus team quizzes the order of questions changes with team A taking the first question of a pair in the first half and team B going in first in the second half. If this is not the case and the order of questions remains fixed, always "bat" second. A close, but incorrect answer from the opposition can sometimes help.

8   Try not to upset question masters; no matter how vague or dimwitted they may appear. They will *always* get you back. Many question masters don't like being corrected on their pronunciation or inability to recognise Roman numerals. Don't embarrass them by asking "Do you mean a *British* prime minister?". They may not know themselves, and they will certainly resent their ignorance being exposed to public view. Keep your mouth shut and use common sense.

9   Never, ever give more information than is asked for. You may be tempted to add "Of course Sam Cooke's original version was better", but you will look pretty stupid if the opposition is then asked who recorded the song in 1961; wouldn't be Sam Cooke, would it?

These last two points can cause conflict when you come up against the aforementioned inadequate question setter, who asks you where Napoleon was born. Does he want the country, the island or the city? You pays your money and you takes your chance.

10 If you play in the type of quiz where teams mark each other's papers, cultivate a reputation for generosity in marking (especially if the paper you are marking stands not a snowball's chance in hell of beating yours). You will find that other teams will reciprocate.
    One great England batsman had a reputation for "walking" – a real sportsman. Umpires hadn't so much as thought about the appeal

before he was half-way to the pavilion, tucking his bat under his arm. Such was his reputation that if he stood at the crease, with a sympathetic smile and a gentle shake of the head, the umpire naturally assumed that he hadn't "nicked it". (Of course, nobody twigged that he walked when his team was 280 for three and had two hours in which to score 30 runs. He always seemed to stay at the crease when he was the last recognised batter left and 40 runs were required in eight overs!)

You too can earn such a useful reputation by marking wisely and well.

11 In a team versus team quiz never, never try and help your own thought processes along by speaking aloud. Simply by saying "Oh! I can see his face!" gives a clue. The answer is male.

I do hope these tips and this revised edition bring you quizzing success.

Author biography

John Smith

John Smith has been a full-time question-setter and researcher for over ten years. His television credits include: Quiz Night, Fifteen-to-One, Masterteam, Every Second Counts, *and, most recently, as a member of the small team of setters for the revived* University Challenge.

He started playing in quizzes at the age of ten (which was so long ago there weren't any history questions!) and has now been playing in quiz leagues in the north west for almost twenty years.

He started 'hustling' for quiz prizes about fifteen years ago, but eventually realised that turning gamekeeper could be more profitable than poaching. So he started setting questions for pub quizzes in 1981, partly for the enjoyment and partly because he was becoming fed up with hearing the same boring questions around the quiz circuit.

John continues playing in his local quiz league but gave up competing in general pub quizzes some years ago, mainly out of frustration at badly phrased questions and wrong answers.

His own specialist areas of expertise are soccer (particularly Liverpool F.C.), popular music of the 1950s and 60s and Sherlock Holmes.

John lives with his long-suffering wife and family in Cheshire and continues to play (with some frustration) in his local pub quiz league.

Abbreviations

A fully comprehensive list of abbreviations would run to many pages. However, many abbreviations listed in authoritative works are either never asked in quiz competitions or are so glaringly obvious to the quiz player that we need not list them here. Consequently this list does not include such abbreviations as ERD (Emergency Reserve Decoration) or BA (Bachelor of Arts). Please refer to the Chemicals Section for abbreviations for chemical elements.

ABM	Anti-ballistic Missile Defence System
ACAS	Advisory, Conciliation and Arbitration Service
AFV	Armoured Fighting Vehicle
AGM	Air to Ground Missile
AH	Anno Hegirae (in the year of the Hegira)
AIDS	Acquired Immune Deficiency Syndrome
ANC	African National Congress
ANZAC	Australian and New Zealand Army Corps
APEX	Association of Professional Executive Clerical and Computer Staffs
ASA	Advertising Standards Authority and also Amateur Swimming Association
ASH	Action on Smoking and Health
ASLEF	Associated Society of Locomotive Engineers and Firemen
ASTMS	Association of Scientific, Technical and Managerial Staffs
ATC	Air Training Corps
AUT	Association of University Teachers
AVR	Army Volunteer Reserve
BAFTA	British Academy of Film and Television Arts
Bart	Baronet
BCh(D)	Bachelor of Dental Surgery
BCL	Bachelor of Civil Law
BDS	Bachelor of Dental Surgery
BECTU	Broadcasting, Entertainment and Cinematograph Technicians Union
BEM	British Empire Medal
BIM	British Institute of Management

BLitt	Bachelor of Letters
BSI	British Standards Institution
Bt	Baronet
CB	Companion, Order of the Bath
CBE	Commander, Order of the British Empire
CDS	Chief of Defence Staff
CFC	Chlorofluorocarbon
CGM	Conspicuous Gallantry Medal
CGS	Chief of General Staff
CH	Companion of Honour
CIA	Central Intelligence Agency
CM	Chirurgiae Magister (Master of Surgery)
CMEA	Council for Mutual Economic Assistance
CMG	Companion, Order of St Michael and St George
CPRE	Council for the Protection of Rural England
CRE	Council for Racial Equality
CVO	Commander, Royal Victorian Order
DBE	Dame Commander, Order of the British Empire
dc	Direct current·
DC	District of Columbia
DCB	Dame Commander, Order of the Bath
DCh	Doctor Chirurgiae (Doctor of Surgery)
DCL	Doctor of Civil Law
DCM	Distinguished Conduct Medal
DCMG	Dame Commander, Order of St Michael and St George
DD	Doctor of Divinity
DDS	Doctor of Dental Surgery
DDT	Dichlorodiphenyltrichloroethane
DFC	Distinguished Flying Cross
DFM	Distinguished Flying Medal
DLitt	Doctor of Letters
DNA	Deoxyribonucleic acid
DSC	Distinguished Service Cross
DSM	Distinguished Service Medal
ECG	Electrocardiogram
ECU	European Currency Unit

EEG	Electroencephalogram
EFTA	European Free Trade Association
eg	Exempli gratia
EMS	European Monetary System
ENEA	European Nuclear Energy Agency
ERM	Exchange Rate Mechanism
ERNIE	Electronic Random Number Indicator Equipment
ESA	European Space Agency
ESP	Extra-sensory perception
ETA	Euzkadi ta Askatasuna (Basque Separatist Movement)
Et alibi	And elsewhere
et seq	Et sequentia (and the following)
FANY	First Aid Nursing Yeomanry
FCCA	Fellow of the Chartered Association of Certified Accountants
FCIA	Fellow of the Corporation of Insurance Agents
FCIB	Fellow of the Chartered Institute of Bankers or Fellow of the Corporation of Insurance Brokers
FCIS	Fellow of the Institute of Chartered Secretaries and Administrators
FCMA	Fellow of the Chartered Institute of Management Accountants
FGS	Fellow of the Geological Society
FHS	Fellow of the Heraldry Society
FICE	Fellow of the Institution of Civil Engineers
FIEE	Fellow of the Institution of Electrical Engineers
FIFA	International Association Football Federation
FIS	Fellow of the Institution of Statisticians
FLA	Fellow, Library Association
FLS	Fellow, Linnean Society
FM	Frequency modulation
FRAM	Fellow, Royal Academy of Music
FRAS	Fellow, Royal Astronomical Society
FRBS	Fellow, Royal Botanical Society
FRCGP	Fellow, Royal College of General Practitioners
FRCM	Fellow, Royal College of Music

FRCOG	Fellow, Royal College of Obstetricians and Gynaecologists
FRCP	Fellow, Royal College of Physicians
FRCS	Fellow, Royal College of Surgeons
FRGS	Fellow, Royal Geographical Society
FRHS	Fellow, Royal Horticultural Society
FRIBA	Fellow, Royal Institute of British Architects
FRICS	Fellow, Royal Institution of Chartered Surveyors
FRS	Fellow, Royal Society
FRSA	Fellow, Royal Society of Arts
FRSC	Fellow, Royal Society of Chemistry
FZS	Fellow, Zoological Society
GATT	General Agreement on Tariffs and Trade
GBE	Dame/Knight Grand Cross, Order of the British Empire
GCB	Dame/Knight Grand Cross, Order of the Bath
GCHQ	Government Communications Headquarters
GCVO	Dame/Knight, Royal Victorian Order
GPMU	Graphical Paper and Media Union
HAC	Honourable Artillery Company
HCF	Highest common factor
HIV	Human Immunodeficiency Virus
HOLMES	Home Office Large Major Enquiry System (Police computer system)
HWM	High water mark
IAEA	International Atomic Energy Agency
IATA	International Air Transport Association
Ibid	Ibidem (in the same place)
IBRD	International Bank for Reconstruction and Development
ICAO	International Civil Aviation Organisation
ICBM	Inter-continental Ballistic Missile
Id	Idem (the same)
ie	Id est (that is)
IEA	International Energy Agency
ILEA	Inner London Education Authority
IMF	International Monetary Fund

INLA	Irish National Liberation Army
INRI	Iesus Nazarenus Rex Iudaeorum (Jesus of Nazareth, King of the Jews)
IQ	Intelligence Quotient
K *(in music)*	Köchel numeration (classification of Mozart's works)
KBE	Knight Commander, Order of the British Empire
KCB	Knight Commander, Order of the Bath
KCVO	Knight Commander, Royal Victorian Order
KGB	Soviet Committee of State Security
kWh	kilowatt-hour
LCM	Lowest common multiple
LLB	Bachelor of Laws
LLD	Doctor of Laws
LLM	Master of Laws
Lsd	Librae solidi denarii (£.s.d.)
MBA	Master of Business Administration
MBE	Member, Order of the British Empire
MCC	Marylebone Cricket Club
MCh	Master of Surgery
MDS	Master of Dental Surgery
mega	One million times
micro	One-millionth part
milli	One-thousandth part
MIRAS	Mortgage Interest Relief at Source
MLR	Minimum Lending Rate
MS	Master of Surgery; manuscript (plural MSS)
NAAFI	Navy, Army and Air Force Institutes
NALGO	National and Local Government Officers' Association
NASA	National Aeronautics and Space Administration
NAS/UWT	National Association of School Masters/Union of Women Teachers
NEDC	National Economic Development Council
NFU	National Farmers' Union
NP	Notary Public
NSPCC	National Society for the Prevention of Cruelty to Children
NUCPS	National Union of Civil and Public Servants

NUJ	National Union of Journalists
OAPEC	Organisation of Arab Petroleum-Exporting Countries
OAS	Organisation of American States
OAU	Organisation of African Unity
OBE	Officer, Order of the British Empire
OECD	Organisation for Economic Co-operation and Development
Ofgas	Office of Gas Supply
Oftel	Office of Telecommunications
OM	Order of Merit
OPCS	Office of Population, Censuses and Surveys
OPEC	Organisation of Petroleum-Exporting Countries
OS	Ordnance Survey (or Old Style when relating to a calendar)
PLA	Port of London Authority
PLC	Public Limited Company
PLO	Palestine Liberation Organisation
pp	Per procurationem (by proxy)
PPS	Parliamentary Private Secretary
Pro tem	Pro tempore (for the time being)
PS	Post scriptum (postscript)
PSBR	Public Sector Borrowing Requirement
PSV	Public Service Vehicle
QARANC	Queen Alexandra's Royal Army Nursing Corps
QARNNS	Queen Alexandra's Royal Naval Nursing Service
QED	Quod erat demonstrandum (which was to be proved)
QGM	Queen's Gallantry Medal
QMG	Quartermaster General
QPM	Queen's Police Medal
QSO	Quasi-stellar object (quasar)
quango	Quasi-autonomous non-governmental organisation
qv	Quod vide (which see)
RAM	Royal Academy of Music
RAMC	Royal Army Medical Corps
RBA	Royal Society of British Artists
RCM	Royal College of Music
REME	Royal Electrical and Mechanical Engineers

RGS	Royal Geographical Society
RHA	Regional Health Authority
RHS	Royal Horticultural Society or Royal Humane Society
RMT	National Union of Rail, Maritime and Transport Workers
RNIB	Royal National Institute for the Blind
RNID	Royal National Institute for the Deaf
RNLI	Royal National Lifeboat Institution
RNR	Royal Naval Reserve
RNVR	Royal Naval Volunteer Reserve
ROC	Royal Observer Corps
RoSPA	Royal Society for the Prevention of Accidents
RSPB	Royal Society for the Protection of Birds
RSVP	Répondez s'il vous plait (reply please)
RYS	Royal Yacht Squadron
SCM	State Certified Midwife
SDLP	Social Democratic and Labour Party
SDP	Social Democratic Party
SEN	State Enrolled Nurse
SERPS	State Earnings Related Pension Scheme
SI	Système Internationale (d'Unités) (International System of Units)
Sic	So written
SOGAT	Society of Graphical and Allied Trades
SPQR	Senatus Populusque Romanus (the Senate and People of Rome)
SSP	Statutory Sick Pay
STD	Subscriber Trunk Dialling
SWAPO	South West African People's Organisation
TCCB	Test and County Cricket Board
TES	Times Educational Supplement
TGWU	Transport and General Workers Union
TLS	Times Literary Supplement
TNT	Trinitrotoluene
TT	Tuberculin Tested
UAE	United Arab Emirates
UCATT	Union of Construction, Allied Trades and Technicians

UCCA	Universities' Central Council on Admissions
UDI	Unilateral Declaration of Independence
UDM	Union of Democratic Mineworkers
UDR	Ulster Defence Regiment
UEFA	Union of European Football Associations
UFC	Universities' Funding Council
UHF	Ultra High Frequency
UKAEA	United Kingdom Atomic Energy Authority
UNESCO	United Nations Educational Scientific and Cultural Organisation
UNICEF	United Nations International Children's Emergency Fund
UNIDO	United Nations Industrial Development Organisation
Unita	National Union for the Total Independence of Angola
USDAW	Union of Shop, Distributive and Allied Workers
VASCAR	Visual average speed computer and recorder
VHF	Very High Frequency
VSO	Voluntary Service Overseas
VTOL	Vertical Take-off and Landing (Aircraft)
WCC	World Council of Churches
WEA	Workers' Educational Association
WEU	West European Union
WFTU	World Federation of Trade Unions
WHO	World Health Organisation
WRAC	Women's Royal Army Corps
WRAF	Women's Royal Air Force
WRNS	Women's Royal Naval Service
WRVS	Women's Royal Voluntary Service
ZANU	Zimbabwe African National Union

Advertising Slogans

Advertising slogans (particularly those used on TV) are a rich source of questions for quiz-setters. The power of advertising should not be underestimated – many phrases originally used in campaigns have slipped easily into the language ("Nice one Cyril") and most of us are subjected to hours of slogans every week. Old, obsolete slogans find favour with question-setters and many of them are included in this list; however, I have also listed some of the more recent ones that I have heard in quizzes. The following should help you give a good impression of a couch potato.

Access	Take the waiting out of wanting *and* Your flexible friend (*or should it be fiend?*)
American Express	Don't leave home without it
Audi	Vorsprung durch technik
Avis	We try harder
Bernard Matthews products	They're bootiful
Birds Eye Peas	Fresh as the moment when the pod went "pop"!
Bristol	Today's cigarette
British Airways	The world's favourite airline
British Caledonian	Never forget, you have a choice
British Gas (privatisation)	If you see Sid, tell him
Brut	Splash it all over
Camay	You'll look a little lovelier each day
Campari	"Nice 'ere i'nit" *and* "Nah, from Luton Airport"
Carlsberg	Probably the best lager in the world
Consulate	Cool as a mountain stream (*an old favourite*)
Courage	It's what your right arm's for
Domestos	Kills all known germs
Double Diamond	Works wonders
Esso	Put a tiger in your tank
Fairy Snow	Forces grey out, forces white in
Flash	Cuts cleaning time in half

Frosties	They're grrrreat!
Fry's Turkish Delight	Full of Eastern promise
Halifax	Get a little Xtra help
Harmony Hair Spray	That girl is/isn't using Harmony hairspray
Harp	Time for a sharp exit
Heineken	Refreshes the parts other beers cannot reach
Homepride	Graded grains make finer flour
Mackeson	Looks good, tastes good, and by golly, it does you good
Maltesers	With the less fattening centres
Martini	The bright one, the right one
Midland	The listening bank
Mr Kipling	Makes exceedingly good cakes
National Airlines	"I'm . . . , fly me"
Omo	Adds brightness to cleanness and whiteness
1001	Cleans a big, big carpet for less than half-a-crown
Oxo	Gives a meal man appeal (*hardly politically correct in today's climate*)
PAL	Prolongs active life
Pepsodent	You'll wonder where the yellow went when you brush your teeth with Pepsodent
Players	It's the tobacco that counts
Rael Brook Toplin	The shirt you don't iron
Remington	"I was so impressed, I bought the company"
Roses	Grow on you
St Bruno	Patron saint of pipe-smokers
Senior Service	Satisfy
Smarties	Whatalotigot *and* Buy some for Lulu
Strand	You're never alone with a Strand (*a real favourite*)
Surf	Hold it up to the light, not a stain and shining bright

Tide	Gets your clothes deep down clean
Trebor Mints	A minty bit stronger
TSB	The bank that likes to say Yes
Volvo	Tested by dummies, driven by the intelligent
Wonderloaf	Nice one, Cyril (*supposedly devised by Peter Mayle of* A Year in Provence *fame*)
Woodbine	The great little cigarette
Woolwich	We are/I am with the Woolwich
Yellow Pages	Let your fingers do the walking

Aeroplane Flights

December 1903   First powered flight by the Wright Brothers at Kitty Hawk, North Carolina

November 1906   First aeroplane flight in Europe by Alberto Santos-Dumant, near Paris

October 1908   First aeroplane flight in Britain by Samuel Cody

April 1909   First aeroplane flight by a British Citizen (J. T. C. Moore-Brabazon) (Lord Brabazon)

July 1909   First crossing of English Channel by Louis Bleriot in a Bleriot Monoplane

June 1919   First nonstop aeroplane flight across the Atlantic by Captain John Alcock and Lt. Arthur Brown in a Vickers Vimy from Newfoundland to Co. Galway, Ireland

Nov/Dec 1919   First flight from Britain to Australia by Cptn. Ross Smith and Lt. Keith Smith

May 1927   First nonstop solo Trans Atlantic flight by Cptn. Charles Lindbergh of the USA in a Ryan Monoplane (duration 33½ hours) from Long Island, New York to Le Bourget, Paris

May/June 1928   First Trans Pacific flight (from San Francisco to Brisbane) by Cptn. C. K. Smith and C. T. P. Ulm

July 1933   First solo circumnavigation of the world (from New York to New York) by Wiley Post in a Lockheed Vega. Flight time of 115½ hours.

August 1939   First turbojet test flight by Flt. Cptn. Erich Warsitz in a HE178 in Germany

October 1947   First supersonic flight by Cptn. Charles E. Yeager in a Bell XS-1 in California

March 1949   First nonstop round the world flight completed by Cptn. James Gallagher from Carswell Air Force Base, Texas, in a Boeing B-50 Super Fortress. Time taken 94 hours

July 1949   First flight of a turbojet-powered airliner, the
                       de Havilland Comet 1
October 1958   First Trans Atlantic passenger service to be
                       flown by a turbojet-powered airliner. The de
                       Havilland Comet 4
December 1968   First flight of the Soviet supersonic airliner, the
                       Tupolev TU-144
February 1969   First flight of the Boeing 747 Jumbo Jet
March 1969   First flight of the BAC/Aerospatiale Concorde
January 1976   First scheduled supersonic passenger airline
                       flights inaugurated by Air France and
                       British Airways. The Air France route was from
                       Paris to Rio de Janeiro and the British Airways
                       route from London Heathrow to Bahrain
June 1979   First crossing of the English Channel by a
                       manpowered aircraft. The Gossamer
                       Albatross piloted by Bryan Allen took 2hrs
                       49mins for the flight

Airlines

The national airlines of many countries are obvious by the name, eg Air France, British Airways, etc, but here are some frequently asked airlines and their countries.

Argentina	Aerolineas
Brazil	VARIG
Belgium	Sabena
Colombia	ACES
Czech Republic	CSA
Japan	JAL (Japanese Airlines)
Japan	ANA (All Nippon Airways)
Netherlands	KLM
Paraguay	LAP
Poland	LOT
Portugal	TAP
Denmark/Norway/Sweden	SAS
Venezuela	VIASA

Airports

"Which city is served by (x) airport?" is a frequent question. There are thousands of airports around the world but here are some which have always been popular with question setters.

Arlanda	Stockholm
Barajas	Madrid
Benito Juarez	Mexico City
Bergamo	Milan
Bromma	Stockholm
Cannon International	Reno
Capodichino	Naples
Cristoforo Colombo (Christopher Columbus)	Genoa
Dum Dum	Calcutta
Ferihegy	Budapest
Findel	Luxembourg
Fornebu	Oslo
Galileo Galilei	Pisa ·
Hanedi	Tokyo
Hopkins	Cleveland
Jan Smuts	Johannesburg
J F Kennedy	*(Look out for this one)* La Paz
Jomo Kenyatta	Nairobi
Kimpo	Seoul
Lambert	St Louis
Leonardo Da Vinci	Rome
Lester B Pearson	Toronto
Linate	Milan
Lindbergh	San Diego
Logan	Boston
Louis Botha	Durban
McCarran	Las Vegas
McCoy	Orlando
Marco Polo	Venice
Mirabel	Montreal
O'Hare	Chicago
Okecie	Warsaw

Queen Alia	Amman
Riem	Munich
Schipol	Amsterdam
Schwechat	Vienna
Simon Bolivar	Caracas
Sky Harbour	Phoenix
Stapleton	Denver
Will Rogers	Oklahoma City
William B Hartsfield	Atlanta

Alphabet (Greek)

A common source of questions, is "Which letter of the Greek alphabet is the equivalent to 'o' or 'p' or 's'?" Here is a list.

Alpha	a	**Nu**	n
Beta	b	**Xi**	x
Gamma	g	**Omicron**	o
Delta	d	**Pi**	p
Epsilon	e	**Rho**	r
Zeta	z	**Sigma**	s
Eta	e	**Tau**	t
Theta	th	**Upsilon**	u
Iota	i	**Phi**	ph
Kappa	k	**Chi**	kh
Lambda	l	**Psi**	ps
Mu	m	**Omega**	o

American Football Teams

Fifteen years ago you would never have been asked in which American city a certain football team plays, but such questions now seem to occur in every other quiz. The following is a list of American cities and the names of the American Football team that play there.

Atlanta	Atlanta Falcons
Buffalo	Buffalo Bills
Chicago	Chicago Bears
Cincinnati	Cincinnati Bengals
Cleveland	Cleveland Browns
Dallas	Dallas Cowboys
Denver	Denver Broncos
Detroit	Detroit Lions
Foxboro	New England Patriots
Green Bay	Green Bay Packers
Houston	Houston Oilers
Indianapolis	Indianapolis Colts
Kansas City	Kansas City Chiefs
Los Angeles	Los Angeles Raiders
	Los Angeles Rams
Miami	Miami Dolphins
Minnesota	Minnesota Vikings
New Orleans	New Orleans Saints
New York	New York Jets
	New York Giants
Philadelphia	Philadelphia Eagles
Phoenix	Phoenix Cardinals
Pittsburgh	Pittsburgh Steelers
San Diego	San Diego Chargers
San Francisco	San Francisco 49ers
Seattle	Seattle Seahawks
Tampa	Tampa Bay Buccaneers
Washington	Washington Redskins

American Presidents

Yet another subject from the other side of the Atlantic that seems to be very popular in British quizzes. For some reason the middle names of American presidents seem to be popular with the question setters, so all the 20th Century presidents are listed here with their full names.

1	George Washington	1789–1797
2	John Adams	1797–1801
3	Thomas Jefferson	1801–1809
4	James Madison	1809–1817
5	James Monroe	1817–1825
6	John Quincy Adams	1825–1829
7	Andrew Jackson	1829–1837
8	Martin van Buren	1837–1841
9	William H. Harrison†	1841–1841
10	John Tyler	1841–1845
11	James K. Polk	1845–1849
12	Zachary Taylor†	1849–1850
13	Millard Fillmore	1850–1853
14	Franklin Pierce	1853–1857
15	James Buchanan	1857–1861
16	Abraham Lincoln*	1861–1865
17	Andrew Johnson	1865–1869
18	Ulysses Simpson Grant	1869–1877
19	Rutherford B. Hayes	1877–1881
20	James A. Garfield*	1881–1881
21	Chester A. Arthur	1881–1885
22	Grover Cleveland	1885–1889
23	Benjamin Harrison	1889–1893
24	Grover Cleveland	1893–1897
25	William McKinley*	1897–1901
26	Theodore Roosevelt	1901–1909
27	William Howard Taft	1909–1913
28	Woodrow Wilson	1913–1921
29	Warren Gamaliel Harding†	1921–1923
30	John Calvin Coolidge	1923–1929
31	Herbert Clark Hoover	1929–1933

32	**Franklin Delano Roosevelt†**	1933–1945
33	**Harry S Truman**	1945–1953
	(*There is much conjecture to what the 'S' stood for. It probably stood for nothing at all.*)	
34	**Dwight David Eisenhower**	1953–1961
35	**John Fitzgerald Kennedy***	1961–1963
36	**Lyndon Baines Johnson**	1963–1969
37	**Richard Milhous Nixon**	1969–1974
38	**Gerald Rudolph Ford**	1974–1977
39	**James Earl Carter**	1977–1981
40	**Ronald Wilson Reagan**	1981–1989
41	**George Herbert Walker Bush**	1989–1993
42	**William Jefferson Clinton**	1993–

* Assassinated whilst in office
† Died of natural causes whilst in office

American States
State Capitals and Nicknames

Real old chestnuts these! The capitals and nicknames of American states have always occurred in quizzes with a regularity out of all proportion to the importance of the subject. For many years it almost seemed compulsory to have a question on an American state capital in any quiz. Anyway here they are.

State	State Capital	Nicknames
Alabama	Montgomery	Heart of Dixie, Cotton State, Yellow Hammer State
Alaska	Juneau	The Last Frontier, Land of the Midnight Sun
Arizona	Phoenix	Grand Canyon State, Apache State
Arkansas	Little Rock	Land of Opportunity, Wonder State, Bear State
California	Sacramento	Golden State
Colorado	Denver	Centennial State
Connecticut	Hartford	Constitution State, Nutmeg State
Delaware	Dover	First State, Diamond State
Florida	Tallahassee	Sunshine State, Peninsula State
Georgia	Atlanta	Empire State of the South, Peach State
Hawaii	Honolulu	Aloha State
Idaho	Boise City	Gem State, Gem of the Mountains
Illinois	Springfield	Prairie State
Indiana	Indianapolis	Hoosier State
Iowa	Des Moines	Hawkeye State
Kansas	Topeka	Sunflower State, Jayhawk State
Kentucky	Frankfort	Bluegrass State
Louisiana	Baton Rouge	Pelican State, Creole State, Sugar State, Bayou State
Maine	Augusta	Pine Tree State

State	State Capital	Nickname
Maryland	Annapolis	Old Line State, Free State
Massachusetts	Boston	Bay State, Old Colony State
Michigan	Lansing	Wolverine State
Minnesota	St Paul	North Star State, Gopher State
Mississippi	Jackson	Magnolia State
Missouri	Jefferson City	Show Me State
Montana	Helena	Treasure State
Nebraska	Lincoln	Cornhusker State, Beef State Tree Planters State
Nevada	Carson City	Sagebrush State Silver State Battle Born State
New Hampshire	Concord	Granite State
New Jersey	Trenton	Garden State
New Mexico	Santa Fe	Land of Enchantment Sunshine State
New York	Albany	Empire State
North Carolina	Raleigh	Tar Heel State Old North State
North Dakota	Bismarck	Sioux State Flickertale State
Ohio	Columbus	Buckeye State
Oklahoma	Oklahoma City	Sooner State
Oregon	Salem	Beaver State
Pennsylvania	Harrisburg	Keystone State
Rhode Island	Providence	Little Rhody
South Carolina	Columbia	Palmetto State
South Dakota	Pierre	Cayote State Sunshine State
Tennessee	Nashville	Volunteer State
Texas	Austin	Lone Star State
Utah	Salt Lake City	Beehive State
Vermont	Montpelier	Green Mountain State
Virginia	Richmond	The Old Dominion Cavalier State

State	State Capital	Nickname
Washington	Olympia	Evergreen State
		Chinook State
West Virginia	Charleston	Mountain State
		Panhandle State
Wisconsin	Madison	Badger State
Wyoming	Cheyenne	Equality State

Animals – Scientific Classification

Great care should be taken here. Many question setters confuse the terms order, class, family and species. Perhaps the following example will help.

Mammals are a *class* of animals. Within that class are *orders* – for example, Carnivora which includes cats, dogs and bears. Cats belong to the *family* Felidae, but there are many *species* of cat.

Of course, it will not help you at all if the question setter has confused the terms or simply thrown in the word family when he means species.

Detailed questions on species are usually confined to mammals; beyond mammals, orders and classes are firm favourites. The following list excludes some obvious orders such as crocodilia and primates, although you can still trip up by thinking that man belongs to the order Mammalia and not the order Primates.

Class	Orders	
Insects	Coleoptera	Beetles, weevils
	Diptera	Flies
	Hymenoptera	Bees, wasps, ants
	Lepidoptera	Butterflies, moths
	Orthoptera	Grasshoppers, locusts, cockroaches
	Siphonaptera	Fleas
Arachnids	Araneae	Spiders
	Aricina	Mites, ticks
	Chilopoda	Centipedes
	Diplopoda	Millipedes

Class	Orders	
Fish	Anguilliformes	Eels
	Selachii	Sharks
Amphibians	Anura	Frogs (Ranidae family), toads (Bufonidae family)
	Chelonia	Turtles, tortoises
Reptiles	Lacertilia	Lizards
	Ophidia	Snakes
Birds	Passeriformes	Perching birds
Mammals	Artiodactyla	Cows, goats, deer, giraffe, sheep
	Cetacea	Whales, dolphins, porpoises
	Edentata	Anteaters, armadillos, sloths
	Insectivora	Shrews, hedgehogs, moles
	Lagomorpha	Rabbits, hares
	Marsupialia	Pouched mammals
	Monotremata	Egg-laying mammals
	Perissodactyla	Horses, zebras, rhino
	Pinnipedia	Seals, walruses
	Rodentia	Rats, mice. (Some of these are sometimes confused with insectivora and vice versa.)

Now a little more detail on some families of mammals within orders of mammals

Order	Families	
Artiodactyla	Suidae	Pigs
	Cervidae	Deer
	Bovidae	Cattle, antelopes
Carnivora	Felidae	Cats
	Canidae	Dogs
	Ursidae	Bears
Insectivora	Erinaceidae	Hedgehogs
	Talpidae	Moles
Rodentia	Sciuridae	Squirrels
	Muridae	Rats, mice

Animals – Scientific Names

Sometimes these questions are put in a very straightforward manner, for example "Which animal has the scientific name 'Meles meles'?" but you will occasionally come across the sort of question in which the quiz setter tries to display his or her erudition, eg "Who wrote an opera about a kleptomaniac Pica pica?" The questions almost invariably relate to native British animals. The following is a list of the most frequently asked.

Mammals	*Scientific Name*
Badger	Meles meles
Cat (wild)	Felis sylvestris
Deer (fallow)	Dama dama
Deer (red)	Cervus elaphus
Dormouse	Muscardinus avellenarius
Fox	Vulpes vulpes
Goat	Capra hircus (the species most common in Britain)
Hare	Lepus Europaeus
Hedgehog	Erinaceus Europaeus
Mink	Mustela lutreola (European mink)
	Mustela vison (American mink)
Mole	Talpa Europaea
Mouse (harvest)	Micronys minutus
Mouse (house)	Mus musculus
Otter	Lutra lutra
Rabbit	Oryctolagus cuniculus (beware of the pronunciation of this one)
Shrew (Pygmy)	Sorex minutus
Squirrel (grey)	Sciurus carolinensis
Squirrel (red)	Sciurus vulgaris
Stoat	Mustela erminea
Vole (water)	Arvicola terrestris
Vole (field)	Microtus agrestis
Weasel	Mustela nivalis
Wolf	Canis lupus

Birds	Scientific Name
Blackbird	Turdus merula
Crow (carrion)	Corvus corone corone
Crow (hooded)	Corvus corone cornix
Cuckoo	Cuculus canorus
Goose (barnacle)	Branta leucopsis
Goose (brent)	Branta bernicla
Goose (greylag)	Anser anser
Goldcrest	Regulus regulus
Goldfinch	Carduelis carduelis
Heron	Ardea cinerea
Jay	Garrulus glandarius
Jackdaw	Corvus monedula
Kestrel	Falco tinnunculus
Kingfisher	Alcedoatthis
Lapwing	Vanellus vanellus
Linnet	Acanthis cannabina
Mallard	Anas platyrhynchos
Martin (house)	Delichon urbica
Martin (sand)	Riparia riparia
Merlin	Falco columbarius
Nightjar	Caprimultus europaeus
Owl (barn)	Tyto alba
Owl (snowy)	Nyctea scandica
Owl (tawny)	Strix aluco
Pigeon (blue rock)	Columba lavia
Puffin	Fratercula arctica
Raven	Corvus corax
Robin	Erithacus rubecula
Skylark	Aluad arvensis
Sparrow (house)	Passer domesticus
Sparrow (tree)	Passer montanus
Starling	Sturnus vulgaris
Swallow	Hirundo rustica
Swan (mute)	Cygnus olor
Swan (whooper)	Cygnus cygnus
Swift	Apus apus

Birds	Scientific Name
Thrush (song)	Turdus musicus
Thrush (missel)	Turdus viscivorus
Wren	Troglodytes troglodytes
Woodpecker (green or yaffle)	Picus viridis

Others	Scientific Name
Eel	Anguilla anguilla
Frog	Rana temporaria
Grass Snake	Natrix natrix
Lizard (common)	Lacerta vivipara
Lizard (sand)	Lacerta agalis
Slow Worm	Anguis fragilias
Toad	Bufo bufo
Toad (natterjack)	Bufo calamita

Apostles

The Twelve Apostles (with one replacement)

Andrew
Bartholomew
James the Great
James the Less
John
Judas Iscariot
Jude
Matthew
Matthias (The man who replaced Judas)
Peter
Philip
Simon
Thomas

Architectural Terms

The difficulty with this section is knowing what to include and what to leave out. An explanation of the most frequently asked terms is listed here in alphabetical order.

Acanthus	A representation of leaves or plants usually found at the top of a column.
Bailey	The area within the outer walls of a castle.
Barbican	A fortified entrance or gateway.
Buttress	The vertical support built against the outer wall of a building.
Campanile	A bell-tower.
Capital	The top of a column, usually featuring mouldings or carvings.
Cartouch	Ornamental stonework resembling a scroll of paper.
Caryatid	A column carved or constructed in the form of a female figure.
Console	An ornamental supporting bracket.
Cupola	A domed roof surmounting a square tower.
Dado	The lower part of a wall. Usually decorated or painted in a different style from that part of the wall above.
Gargoyle	A water spout, usually carved in the form of some imp or grotesque creature.
Gazebo	A summer-house situated in a garden.
Hypocaust	An underground room in Roman architecture which contained a furness; providing an early form of central heating.
Keystone	Central wedge-shaped stone on top of an arch.
Lancet window	A narrow, pointed window.
Mansard roof	A roof pitched at two angles, the lower part being much steeper than the other part.
Merlon	The 'teeth' of battlements.
Mezzanine floor	An intermediate floor between ground and first floor level.

Motte   A mound built within castle walls.

Mullion   The vertical bar in a window.

Oriel window   Bay window on an upper floor, supported by projecting stonework.

Pediment   The low pitched gable in classical architecture usually supported by posts.

Pier   Vertical masonry support for a wall arch.

Rotunda   A circular dome-roofed building.

Rustication   External stoneware with the surface left rough.

Spandrel   The triangular space underneath a staircase.

Stucco   External plasterwork on a building made to resemble stone.

Transom   The horizontal bar in a window.

Venetian window A triple window with the central window arched.

Orders of Architecture: The three Greek orders of architecture were Doric, Ionic and Corinthian, Doric being the most simplistic and Corinthian the most stylised. The two orders added by the Romans at a later date were Tuscan, which was a form of Doric, and Composite which was a mixture of Ionic and Corinthian.

Armed Forces

Relative Ranks

A popular subject for quiz questions, eg "What is the naval equivalent of the army rank of major?"

Royal Navy	*Army*	*Royal Air Force*
Admiral of the Fleet	Field Marshal	Marshal of the RAF
Admiral	General	Air Chief Marshal
Vice Admiral	Lieutenant General	Air Marshal
Rear Admiral	Major General	Air Vice Marshal
Commodore	Brigadier	Air Commodore
Captain	Colonel	Group Captain
Commander	Lieutenant Colonel	Wing Commander
Lieutenant Commander	Major	Squadron Leader
Lieutenant	Captain	Flight Lieutenant
Sub-Lieutenant	Lieutenant	Flying Officer
Acting Sub-Lieutenant	Second Lieutenant	Pilot Officer

Parts of a suit of armour

One of those topics which crop up in quizzes that have no relevance to the 20th Century. Usually they come in the form of "Where will you find a couter and a poleyn?". Always worth knowing which bits go where.

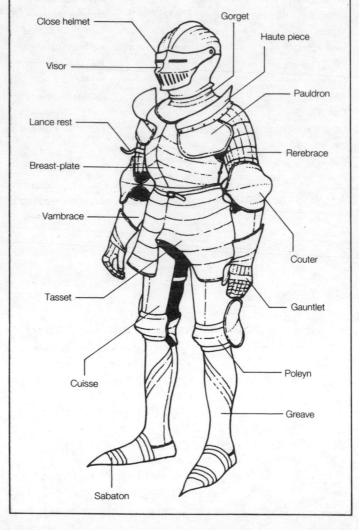

Close helmet

Visor

Lance rest

Breast-plate

Vambrace

Tasset

Cuisse

Sabaton

Gorget

Haute piece

Pauldron

Rerebrace

Couter

Gauntlet

Poleyn

Greave

....

Assassinations

Another popular subject which reveals the average quiz setter's obsession with violence and murder. An assassination is the murder of a major religious or political figure. It is not the murder of a celebrity (eg John Lennon) nor is it the judicial killing of a prominent figure, no matter how dubious the circumstances which surrounded the judicial proceedings. The following is a list of "popular" assassinations.

Date	Victim	
48 BC	**Pompey the Great**	Murdered in Egypt.
44 BC	**Julius Caesar**	Stabbed to death in the Senate House in Rome.
AD 41	**Caligula**	Murdered by an officer of his own imperial bodyguard.
AD 54	**Claudius I**	Died after eating mushrooms poisoned by his wife, Agrippina.
1100	**William II (William Rufus)**	Killed by an arrow whilst hunting in the New Forest. The arrow was fired by Walter Tirrel. This may or may not have been an accident.
1170	**Thomas Becket**	Archbishop of Canterbury murdered in his own cathedral by knights acting on behalf of King Henry II.
1437	**James I of Scotland**	Murdered by a group led by Sir Robert Graham.
1478	**George, Duke of Clarence**	Brother of Edward IV and Richard III. Drowned in a vat of Malmsey wine in the Tower of London.
1520	**Montezuma II**	Last Emperor of the Aztecs, stoned to death by his own people probably at the instigation of the Spanish.
1567	**Henry, Lord Darnley**	Second husband of Mary Queen of Scots and father of James VI of Scotland (James I of England) killed in an explosion at Kirk O'Field,

Date	Victim	
		a house in Edinburgh; probably at the instigation of Bothwell (and possibly Mary herself).
1793	**Jean-Paul Marat**	French revolutionary leader. Stabbed to death in a bath by Charlotte Corday.
1812	**Spencer Perceval**	The only British Prime Minister to be assassinated. Shot whilst entering the House of Commons by John Bellingham.
1865	**Abraham Lincoln US President**	Shot by John Wilkes Booth at Ford's Theater, Washington (he was watching the play Our American Cousin).
1881	**Tsar Alexander II of Russia**	Killed in a bomb blast by Nihilists.
1881	**James Garfield US President**	Shot by Charles J. Guiteau at a railway station in Washington on 2nd July. He died 10 weeks later.
1901	**William McKinley US President**	Shot by an anarchist, Leon Czolgosz, on 6th September in Buffalo in New York. He died eight days later.
1914	**Archduke Francis Ferdinand**	Heir to the Imperial Austria/ Hungarian throne (also his wife, the Duchess of Hohenburg), shot whilst visiting Sarajevo on 28th June. The assassin was Gavrillo Princep, a student and supposedly a member of the subversive Black Hand Gang.
1916	**Grigory Rasputin**	Russian monk and mystic. Murdered in Moscow by a group of courtiers led by Prince Yusupof.

Date	Victim	
1918	**Tsar Nicholas II of Russia, his wife the Tsarina Alexandra, their son Czarevitch Alexis and their daughters Olga, Tatiana, Maria and Anastasia**	Executed by firing squad at Ekaterinburg.
1934	**Engelbert Dollfuss Chancellor of Austria**	Shot by Austrian Nazis in Vienna.
1940	**Leon Trotsky**	Exiled Soviet revolutionary, murdered by Ramon Mercador near Mexico City.
1948	**Mohandas K. Gandhi**	Shot by Nathuran Godse on September 17th in New Delhi.
1963	**John F. Kennedy President of the USA**	Shot by Lee Harvey Oswald on 22nd November in Dallas, Texas. Oswald was murdered by nightclub owner Jack Ruby while awaiting trial.
1966	**Hendrik Verwoerd S. African Prime Minister**	Stabbed to death in the South African Parliament by a parliamentary messenger Dimitri Tsafendas on September 6th.
1968	**Rev. Dr Martin Luther King Jnr.**	Shot by James Earl Ray in Memphis, Tennessee on April 4th. Ray was arrested at Heathrow Airport and sentenced to 99 years imprisonment.
1968	**Robert F. Kennedy US Senator**	Shot in the kitchen area of the Ambassador Hotel, Los Angeles, by Sirhan Sirhan (5th June).

Date	Victim	
1975	**Sheik Mujibur Rahman Bangledesh President**	Killed in an Army coup.
1979	**Lord Louis Mountbatten**	Murdered when a bomb exploded in his small fishing boat off the coast of County Sligo, Ireland.
1981	**Anwar al Sadat President of Egypt**	Shot by members of his own armed forces as he reviewed a military march past in Cairo.
1986	**Olof Palme Prime Minister of Sweden**	Shot in a Stockholm street returning from a visit to the cinema.
1988	**Zia ul Haq President of Pakistan**	The plane carrying him exploded in mid-air shortly after take-off.

....

Australian States

It is rather surprising how many people are ignorant of the state capitals of Australian States. So here they are:

New South Wales	Sydney
Queensland	Brisbane
South Australia	Adelaide
Tasmania	Hobart
Victoria	Melbourne
Western Australia	Perth
Northern Territory	Darwin

Bandleaders – Signature Tunes

Modern musicians don't have signature tunes, but at one time all major bands and artists had them. Not many of them crop up in quizzes but the following are worth remembering.

Louis Armstrong	When it's Sleepytime down South
Count Basie	One o'clock Jump
Bing Crosby	When the Blue of the Night Meets the Gold of the Day
Bob Crosby	Summertime
Tommy Dorsey	I'm Getting Sentimental Over You
Duke Ellington	Take the A Train
Benny Goodman	Let's Dance (*opening*)
	Goodbye (*closing*)
Woody Herman	Woodchopper's Ball
Earl Hines	Deep Forest
Joe Loss	In the Mood
Glenn Miller	Moonlight Serenade
Jack Payne	Say it with Music
Artie Shaw	Nightmare
George Shearing	Lullaby of Broadway
Paul Whiteman	Rhapsody in Blue

} *Don't confuse these two*

Baseball Teams

These do not occur with the regularity of American Football teams but they still do crop up in quiz questions.

Atlanta	Atlanta Braves
Baltimore	Baltimore Orioles
Boston	Boston Red Sox
Los Angeles	California Angels
Chicago	Chicago Cubs
	Chicago White Sox
Cincinnati	Cincinnati Reds
Cleveland	Cleveland Indians
Detroit	Detroit Tigers
Houston	Houston Astros
Kansas City	Kansas City Royals
Los Angeles	Los Angeles Dodgers
Milwaukee	Milwaukee Brewers
Minnesota	Minnesota Twins
Montreal	Montreal Expos
New York	New York Yankees
	New York Mets
Oakland	Oakland Athletics
Philadelphia	Philadelphia Phillies
Pittsburgh	Pittsburgh Pirates
San Diego	San Diego Padres
San Francisco	San Francisco Giants
St Louis	St Louis Cardinals
Seattle	Seattle Mariners
Arlington	Texas Rangers
Toronto	Toronto Blue Jays

Battles

This subject is not quite as popular as it once was. However, the questions do still occur with some regularity. Whole libraries have been written on the history of warfare and battles but this brief list covers the engagements which are most frequently asked in quizzes.

31 BC	**Battle of Actium;** Roman Fleet under Octavian defeated a Roman Egyptian Fleet led by Mark Antony and Cleopatra.
1415	**Agincourt;** English Army under Henry V defeated larger French Army under the command of the Constable of France.
1944/45	**Ardennes Offensive;** Allied Forces under Eisenhower and Montgomery repelled a German offensive led by Von Rundstedt.
1805	**Austerlitz;** French Army led by Napoleon Bonaparte defeated a combined Austrian/Russian force led by Kutuzov.
1854	**Balaclava;** British under the command of Lord Raglan repulsed a Russian attack led by Prince Menshikov *(Charge of the Light Brigade took place during this battle).*
1314	**Bannockburn;** Scottish force under Robert the Bruce defeated a much larger English Army led by Edward II.
1704	**Blenheim;** Combined British and Austrian force led by Marlborough defeated a French and Bavarian Army under the command of Marshal Tallard.
1812	**Borodino;** French Army under the command of Napoleon Bonaparte defeated the Russians commanded by Kutuzov.
1485	**Bosworth Field;** Henry Tudor's much smaller force defeated the Army of Richard III *(the last occasion an English Monarch died on the battlefield).*

1690	**Battle of the Boyne;** Anglo-Dutch Army under William III defeated a Catholic Army under the command of James II.
216 BC	**Battle of Cannae;** Carthaginian Army led by Hannibal defeated a much larger Roman force led by Varro and Paulus.
1797	**Cape St Vincent;** Small British Fleet led by Sir John Jervis defeated larger Spanish force under the command of Don Juan de Langara.
451	**Battle of Chalons;** Roman and Visigoth allies under Flavius Aetius and Theodoric defeated the Huns under Attila.
1346	**Crecy;** English Army commanded by Edward III defeated a French Army led by Philip VI.
1746	**Culloden;** Royalist Army led by the Duke of Cumberland defeated the Jacobite force under the command of Prince Charles Edward Stuart.
6 June 1944	**D Day;** Allied Forces under the overall command of General Eisenhower successfully breached German defences on the Normandy coast.
1954	**Dien Bien Phu;** Overwhelming Vietnamese force under General Giap defeated a French force under the command of Colonel de Castries.
1942	**El Alamein;** British Eighth Army under Montgomery defeated German and Italian forces led by Rommel.
1513	**Flodden Field;** English Army led by the Earl of Surrey defeated a much larger Scottish force led by James IV *(James became the last British Monarch to die in battle)*.
1915/16	**Gallipoli Landings;** Allied forces under Hamilton (and later Monro) repulsed by Turkish force led by General Von Sanders.
1863	**Gettysburg;** Union Army of the Potomac led by General Meade defeated the Confederate Army of General Robert E. Lee.

1066	**Hastings (or more properly Senlac Hill);** Norman forces led by Duke William of Normandy defeated Harold Godwineson's Saxon Army.
1854	**Inkerman;** Anglo-French force under Lord Raglan and General Pelissier defeated a Russian force under the command of Prince Menshikov.
1916	**Jutland;** British Fleet under Admiral Jellicoe forced the German Fleet under Scheer to withdraw to their bases.
1571	**Lepanto;** Defeat of Turkish Navy by combined Spanish and Venetian forces.
1813	**Leipzig;** Huge Russian, Austrian, Prussian force under the command of Schwarzenberg defeated a smaller force of French under the command of Napoleon Bonaparte.
1876	**Little Big Horn;** Huge Allied Indian Army led by Crazy Horse completely destroyed a Force of 264 of the US Seventh Cavalry led by Lt. Col. George Armstrong Custer.
1709	**Malplaquet;** Allied English Army under Marlborough defeated a French force led by Marshal Villars.
490 BC	**Marathon;** Greek force led by Callimachus and Miltiades defeated a Persian force under the command of Artaphrenes and Datis.
1800	**Marengo;** French Army led by Napoleon Bonaparte defeated the Austrians under the command of General Melas.
1644	**Marston Moor;** Parliamentary Army under the command of the Earl of Manchester defeated the Royalist force led by Prince Rupert.
1914	**Mons;** BEF slowed the advance of German First Army led by Von Kluck.
1645	**Naseby;** Parliamentary Army led by Fairfax defeated the Royalist Army under the command of Prince Rupert.

1815	**New Orleans;** American forces under Jackson defeated the British Army led by General Pakenham.
1798	**Battle of the Nile;** British Fleet under Nelson defeated a French Fleet under the command of Brueys.
1898	**Omdurman;** British and Egyptian force led by Kitchener defeated much larger Sudanese Army under the command of Kalifa Abdullah.
1917	**Passchendaele;** Inconclusive Allied offensive also known as "The Third Battle of Ypres".
1941	**Pearl Harbor;** 360 Japanese planes at the command of Admiral Nagumo devastated the US Pacific Fleet.
42 BC	**Philippi;** Army led by Antony and Octavian defeated a force led by Brutus and Cassius.
1757	**Plassey;** Small British force led by Clive defeated huge Indian Army under the command of Siraj ud Daula.
1356	**Poitiers;** English force under the command of Edward the Black Prince defeated much larger French force commanded by King John II.
1798	**Battle of the Pyramids;** French force under Napoleon Bonaparte defeated much larger Egyptian Army led by Murad Bey.
1706	**Ramillies;** British and Allied Army under the command of Marlborough defeated French Army led by Marshal Villeroi.
1879	**Rorke's Drift;** 140 British troops repelled attacks by 4,000 Zulus led by Cetewayo.
1782	**The Saints;** British Fleet under Admiral Rodney defeated a French Fleet led by Comte de Grasse.
1455	**St Albans;** First battle of the War of the Roses. Yorkist victory over Lancastrian forces.
1812	**Salamanca;** British and Allied Forces under Wellington defeated a French Army led by Marmont.

1916	**Somme;** Anglo-French offensive which failed to break through German lines.
1588	**Spanish Armada;** 121 English ships under the command of Lord Howard of Effingham defeated 130 Spanish ships commanded by the Duke of Medina Sidonia.
Aug1942– Feb1943	**Stalingrad;** German Sixth Army under General von Paulus lay siege to the city but were forced to surrender to the Russian Army commanded by Marshal Zhukov.
480 BC	**Thermopylae;** 100,000 Persians under the command of Xerxes defeated a small Greek Army led by Leonidas.
732	**Tours;** Frankish Army under the command of Charles Martel defeated a Moslem Army under the command of Abd-er Rahman, thus repulsing the Moslem incursion into Europe.
1805	**Trafalgar;** 27 British ships under the command of Admiral Lord Nelson defeated a Franco-Spanish fleet commanded by Villeneuve.
1916	**Verdun;** French Army under the command of Marshal Petain withstood advances by the German Fifth Army and mounted successful counter-attacks.
1808	**Vimeiro;** British force under Wellesley (later the Duke of Wellington) defeated a French Army led by Junot.
1813	**Vitoria;** British and Allied force led by Wellington defeated a French Army led by Joseph Bonaparte.
1815	**Waterloo;** Anglo-Prussian Army led by Wellington and Blücher defeated the French force commanded by Napoleon Bonaparte.
1651	**Worcester;** Parliamentarian force led by Cromwell defeated a smaller Royalist Army under the command of Charles II.
202 BC	**Zama;** Roman Army led by Scipio defeated the Carthaginian force led by Hannibal.

Beaufort Scale

The Beaufort Scale takes its name from Admiral Sir Francis Beaufort who originally devised the scale in 1805.

Scale No.	Wind Force	mph
0	Calm	1
1	Light air	1–3
2	Slight breeze	4–7
3	Gentle breeze	8–12
4	Moderate breeze	13–18
5	Fresh breeze	19–24
6	Strong breeze	25–31
7	High wind	32–38
8	Gale	39–46
9	Strong gale	47–54
10	Whole gale	55–63
11	Storm	64–72
12	Hurricane	73–82
13	Hurricane	83–92
14	Hurricane	93–103
15	Hurricane	104–114
16	Hurricane	115–125
17	Hurricane	126–136

Bible

There are 39 books in the Old Testament of the Holy Bible and there are 27 in the New Testament. Obviously the Bible can be used as a source for many questions in quizzes. This section, however, confines itself to listing the books of the Bible (in the order in which they occur) and the number of chapters contained in each book.

Old Testament

Name of Book	Number of Chapters
Genesis	50
Exodus	40
Leviticus	27
Numbers	36
Deuteronomy	34
Joshua	24
Judges	21
Ruth	4
First Book of Samuel	31
Second Book of Samuel	24
First Book of Kings	22
Second Book of Kings	25
First Book of Chronicles	29
Second Book of Chronicles	36
Ezra	10
Nehemiah	13
Esther	10
Job	42
Psalms	150
Proverbs	31
Ecclesiastes	12
Song of Solomon	8
Isaiah	66
Jeremiah	52
Lamentations	5
Ezekiel	48
Daniel	12

Name of Book	Number of Chapters
Hosea	14
Joel	3
Amos	9
Obadiah	1
Jonah	4
Micah	7
Nahum	3
Habakkuk	3
Zephaniah	3
Haggai	2
Zechariah	14
Malachi	4

New Testament

Name of Book	Number of Chapters
Matthew	28
Mark	16
Luke	24
John	21
The Acts of The Apostles	28
Romans	16
First Corinthians	16
Second Corinthians	13
Galatians	6
Ephesians	6
Philippians	4
Colossians	4
First Thessalonians	5
Second Thessalonians	3
First Timothy	6
Second Timothy	4
Titus	3
Philemon	1
Hebrews	13

Name of Book	Number of Chapters
James	5
First Peter	5
Second Peter	3
First John	5
Second John	1
Third John	1
Jude	1
Revelation of St John the Divine	22

Births and Deaths - Famous People

Questions relating to the births and deaths of famous people can come in a variety of forms: "Give a year in the life of X", "In which year did 'Y' die?", "Which of the following was born first...", "Give one year when both 'X' and 'Y' were alive". The great difficulty in compiling this list has been in deciding who should and who should not be included, so a note of explanation is required.

Excluded from this list are English and British monarchs since the Norman Conquest, British prime ministers, and presidents of the United States, these are dealt with in other sections of the book. I have also excluded from this list anybody who was alive during the 20th Century (because they are hardly likely to occur in the "Give one year in the life of" type of question). I have tried to include in the list those people who, although they may be famous, most of us have difficulty in placing at the correct point in history.

Pre-Christian Era

Cyrus the Great	Persian king	c 600–529 BC
Buddha	Indian founder of Buddhism	c 563–483 BC
Darius	Persian king	c 558–486 BC
Confucius	Chinese philosopher	c 551–479 BC
Pythagoras	Greek mathematician	c 528–500 BC
Themistocles	Greek statesman	c 527–460 BC

Xerxes	Persian King	c 519–465 BC
Sophocles	Greek dramatist and poet	c 496–406 BC
Pericles	Athenian statesman	c 495–429 BC
Socrates	Greek philosopher	c 470–399 BC
Hippocrates	Greek physician sometimes known as the father of medicine	c 460–377 BC
Plato	Greek philosopher	c 427–347 BC
Aristotle	Greek philosopher	c 384–322 BC
Alexander the Great	Macedonian emperor	356–323 BC
Archimedes	Greek mathematician and inventor	c 287–212 BC
Hannibal	Carthaginian general	247–183 BC
Cicero	Roman politician and philosopher	106–43 BC
Julius Caesar	Roman emperor	100–44 BC
Mark Antony	Roman military leader	c 82–30 BC
Virgil	Roman poet	70–19 BC
Cleopatra	Egyptian queen	69–30 BC
Horace	Roman poet and satirist	65–8 BC
Augustus Caesar	First Roman emperor	63 BC–14 AD
Ovid	Roman poet	43 BC–17 AD
Tiberius	Second Roman emperor	42 BC–37 AD
Claudius	Roman emperor	10 BC–54 AD

From the Birth of Christ to the 13th Century

Nero	Roman emperor	37–68
Hadrian	Roman emperor	76–138
Diocletian	Roman emperor	245–313
Constantine the Great	Roman emperor	c 280–337
Attila the Hun		c 406–453
St Augustine	Founder of Christianity in Britain	550–605
Mohammed	Prophet and founder of Islam	570–632

Bede	Historian and theologian	673–735
Charlemagne	Frankish king	742–814
Alfred the Great	English king	849–899
Ethelred the Unready	English king	968–1016
Canute	English king	c 994–1035
Macbeth	Scottish king	c 1005–1057
El Cid	Spanish warrior	1040–1099
Omar Khayyam	Persian poet	c 1050–1120
Thomas Becket	Archbishop of Canterbury	1118–1170
Genghis Khan	Mongol warrior leader	1167–1227
St Francis of Assisi	Patron Saint of Italy	c 1182–1226
Kublai Khan	Mongol warrior leader	1216–1294

13th Century

Thomas Aquinas	Religious philosopher and theologian	1225–1274
Marco Polo	Venetian merchant and explorer	c 1254–1324
Alighieri Dante	Italian poet	1265–1321
Giotto	Italian painter	1266–1337
Sir William Wallace	Scottish patriot and soldier	1272–1305
Robert the Bruce	Scottish king	1274–1329

14th Century

Giovanni Boccaccio	Italian writer and poet	1313–1375
William Langland	English poet	c 1332–1400
Tamerlane	Mongol emperor	c 1336–1405
Geoffrey Chaucer	English poet	1340–1400
Dick Whittington	Merchant and Lord Mayor of London	1358–1423
Jan Van Eyck	Dutch artist	1390–1441
Johannes Gutenberg	German printing pioneer	1398–1468
Henry the Navigator	Portuguese prince	1394–1460
Thomas à Kempis	German theologian	1380–1471

15th Century

Joan of Arc	French military leader and saint	1412–1431
Tomas de Torquemada	Founder of the Spanish Inquisition	c 1420–1498
William Caxton	English printing pioneer	1422–1491
John Cabot	Venetian explorer	c 1425–1500
Giovani Bellini	Venetian painter	1430–1516
Sir Thomas Malory	English writer	c 1430–1471
Ivan the Great	Tsar of Russia	1440–1505
Alessandro Botticelli	Italian artist	1445–1510
Leonardo da Vinci	Artist, mathematician, inventor	1452–1519
Heironymous Bosch	Dutch artist	1450–1516
Bartholomeu Dias	Portuguese explorer	1450–1500
Desiderius Erasmus	Dutch theologian	c 1466–1536
Albrecht Dürer	German artist	1469–1524
Namak	Indian teacher and founder of Sikhism	1469–1538
Francisco Pizarro	Spanish conquistador	c 1470–1541
Vasco da Gama	Portuguese explorer	1471–1528
Nicolaus Copernicus	Polish astronomer	1473–1543
Michelangelo	Italian painter and sculptor	1475–1564
Thomas Wolsey	English churchman and politician	1475–1530
John Cabot	Genoese explorer	c 1425–1500
Sebastian Cabot	(Son of John) English explorer	c 1476–1557
Thomas More	English philosopher, politician and theologian	1478–1535
Lucretia Borgia	Italian aristocrat and reputed poisoner	1480–1519
Ferdinand Magellan	Portuguese explorer	1480–1521
Montezuma II	Aztec emperor	1480–1520

Martin Luther	German monk and leader of the Reformation	1483–1546
Raphael	Italian artist	1483–1520
Ulrich Zwingli	Swiss religious reformer	1484–1531
Hernando Cortes	Spanish explorer and military leader	1485–1547
Titian	Italian artist	1487–1576
Thomas Cranmer	English churchman	1489–1586
Jacques Cartier	French explorer	1491–1557
St Ignatius of Loyola	Founder of the Jesuit Order	1491–1556
William Tyndale	Priest and translator of the Bible into English	c 1492–1536
Antonio Correggio	Italian painter	1494–1534
Francois Rabelais	French physician and philosopher	c 1494–1553
Hans Holbein	German painter	1497–1543

16th Century

Benvenuto Cellini	Italian artist	1500–1571
Nostradamus	French astrologer	1503–1566
John Knox	Scottish religious reformer	1505–1572
St Francis Xavier	Spanish missionary	1506–1552
Andrea Palladio	Italian architect	1508–1580
John Calvin	French theologian and religious reformer	1509–1564
Gerhardus Mercator	Flemish cartographer	1512–1594
Jacopo Tintoretto	Venetian painter	1518–1594
Catherine de Medici	Queen of France	1519–1589
Pieter Brueghel	Dutch artist	c 1525–1569
Ivan the Terrible	First Tsar of Russia	1530–1584
Sir Humphrey Gilbert	English explorer and navigator	1539–1583
El Greco	Cretan-born artist	1541–1614
Miguel Cervantes	Spanish writer	1547–1616

Nicholas Hilliard	English artist	1547–1619
Boris Godunov	Russian Tsar	c 1552–1605
Sir Walter Raleigh	English explorer, writer and philosopher	c 1552–1618
Edmund Spenser	English poet	1552–1599
Francis Bacon	English writer and philosopher	1561–1626
Galileo Galilei	Italian astronomer and scientist	1564–1642
Christopher Marlowe	English dramatist and poet	1564–1593
William Shakespeare	Dramatist and poet	1564–1616
Johannes Kepler	German astronomer	1571–1530
John Donne	English writer and poet	c 1572–1631
Michelangelo Caravaggio	Italian artist	1573–1610
Inigo Jones	English architect	1573–1652
Ben Jonson	English poet and dramatist	1573–1637
Sir Peter Paul Rubens	Flemish painter	1577–1640
William Harvey	English physician and discoverer of the circulation of blood	1578–1657
Frans Hals	Dutch portrait painter	1580–1666
Orlando Gibbons	English musician and composer	1583–1625
Duc de Richelieu	French cardinal	1585–1642
Georges de la Tour	French artist	1593–1652
Nicholas Poussin	French artist	1594–1665
René Descartes	French philosopher	c 1596–1650
Gianlorenzo Bernini	Italian artist	1598–1680
Sir Anthony Van Dyke	Dutch artist	1599–1641
Diego Velasquez	Spanish painter	1599–1660

17th Century

Cardinal Jules Mazarin	French statesman	1602–1661
Abel Tasman	Dutch navigator	1603–1659
Rembrandt	Dutch painter	1606–1669
John Milton	English poet	1608–1674
Evangelista Torricelli	Italian physicist	1608–1647
Sir Peter Lely	Dutch artist	1618–1680
John Evelyn	English Diarist	1620–1706
George Fox	Founder of the Quakers	1624–1691
Andrew Marvell	English poet and political writer	1621–1678
Jean Baptiste Molière	French playwright	1622–1673
Blaise Pascal	French scientist, mathematician and philosopher	1623–1662
Robert Boyle	Irish chemist and physicist	1627–1691
John Bunyan	English preacher and author	1628–1688
Samuel Pepys	English diarist	1633–1703
Louis XIV (The Sun King)	King of France	1638–1715
John Dryden	English poet, dramatist and essayist	1631–1700
Jan Vermeer	Dutch artist	1632–1675
Sir Christopher Wren	English architect	1632–1723
Sir Isaac Newton	English scientist	1642–1727
William Penn	English Quaker and founder of the State of Pennsylvania	c 1644–1718
Antonio Stradivari	Italian musical instrument maker	1645–1737
Captain William Kidd	English privateer	1645–1701
John Churchill	First Duke of Marlborough English military leader	1650–1722

Edmund Halley	English astronomer	1656–1742
Daniel Defoe	English novelist	1660–1731
Sir John Vanburgh	English architect	1664–1726
Thomas Newcomen	British steam engine pioneer	1663–1729
Jonathan Swift	Irish novelist, essayist and poet	1667–1745
Joseph Addison	English poet and essayist	1672–1719
Peter the Great	Russian Tsar	1672–1725
Abraham Darby	Engineer and pioneer of the Industrial Revolution	1678–1717
Johann Sebastian Bach	German composer	1685–1750
George Friedrich Handel	German composer	1685–1759
Gabriel Fahrenheit	German physicist	1686–1736
Alexander Pope	English poet	1688–1744
Voltaire	French philosopher and writer	1694–1778
Antonio Canaletto	Venetian artist	1697–1768
William Hogarth	English artist	1697–1764

18th Century

Anders Celsius	Swedish astronomer and physicist	1701–1744
John Wesley	Founder of Methodism	1703–1791
Henry Fielding	English novelist	1707–1754
Frederick the Great	Prussian king	1712–1786
Jean-Jacques Rousseau	French writer and philosopher	1712–1778
Lancelot (Capability) Brown	English landscape gardener	1715–1783
Thomas Grey	English poet	1716–1771
Sir David Garrick	English actor manager	1717–1779
Horace Walpole	English writer	1717–1799

James Hargreaves	English weaver and textile engineer	c 1720–1778
Tobias Smollett	Scottish novelist	1721–1771
Sir Joshua Reynolds	English artist	1723–1792
Adam Smith	English economist	1723–1790
Emmanuel Kant	German philosopher	1724–1804
George Stubbs	English artist	1724–1806
Giovanni Casanova	Italian librarian and adventurer	1725–1798
Robert Clive	English soldier and colonial governor	1725–1774
Thomas Gainsborough	English artist	1727–1788
Robert Adam	Scottish architect and designer	1728–1792
Captain James Cook	English sea captain and navigator	1728–1779
Oliver Goldsmith	Irish author	1728–1774
Catherine the Great	Russian empress	1729–1796
Henry Cavendish	English chemist and physicist	1731–1810
William Cowper	English poet	1731–1800
Richard Arkwright	English inventor and industrialist	1732–1792
Franz Joseph Haydn	German composer	1732–1809
James Watt	Scottish engineer	1736–1819
Thomas Paine	English writer and political reformer	1737–1809
Sir William Herschel	English astronomer	1738–1822
James Boswell	Scottish writer and biographer of Dr Johnson	1740–1795
Marquis de Sade	French writer	1740–1814
Antoine Lavoisier	French chemist	1743–1794
Francisco Goya	Spanish artist	1746–1828
Jeremy Bentham	English philosopher and writer	1748–1832

Johann Wolfgang von Goethe	German philosopher and poet	1749–1832
Edward Jenner	English physician, pioneer of vaccinations	1749–1823
Charles James Fox	English statesman	1749–1806
Richard Brinsley Sheridan	Irish dramatist	1751–1816
Thomas Telford	Scottish engineer	1751–1834
John Nash	English architect	1752–1853
Captain William Bligh	English naval officer and colonial administrator	1754–1817
Sarah Siddons	English actress	1755–1831
Wolfgang Amadeus Mozart	Austrian composer	1756–1791
William Blake	English poet and artist	1757–1827
Horatio Nelson	English naval commander	1758–1805
Maximilien Robespierre	French revolutionary leader	1758–1794
Noah Webster	American lexicographer	1758–1843
Robert Burns	Scottish poet	1759–1796
William Wilberforce	English anti-slavery campaigner	1759–1833
Ludwig van Beethoven	German composer	1770–1827
William Wordsworth	English poet	1770–1850
Sir Walter Scott	Scottish poet and novelist	1771–1832
Richard Trevithick	English steam railway pioneer	1771–1833
Klemens Metternich	Austrian statesman	1773–1859
Robert Southey	English poet	1774–1843
Jane Austen	English novelist	1775–1817
Charles Lamb	English essayist	1775–1834
John Constable	English painter	1776–1837
Sir Humphry Davy	English chemist	1778–1829

Elizabeth Fry	Prison reformer	1780–1845
George Stephenson	English engineer, steam locomotive pioneer	1781–1848
Niccolo Paganini	Italian violin virtuoso	1782–1840
Simon Bolivar	Venezuelan revolutionary leader	1783–1830
Washington Irving	American writer	1783–1859
Jacob Grimm	German mythologists	1785–1863
Wilhelm Grimm }		1786–1859
Davy Crockett	American frontiersman	1786–1836
Lord Byron	English poet	1788–1824
Michael Faraday	English physicist	1791–1867
Gioacchino Rossini	Italian composer	1792–1868
Percy Bysshe Shelley	English poet	1792–1822
John Keats	English poet	1795–1821
Franz Peter Schubert	Austrian composer	1797–1828
Eugene Delacroix	French artist	1798–1863
Honoré de Balzac	French novelist	1799–1850
Aleksandr Pushkin	Russian writer	1799–1837

19th Century

Alexandre Dumas	French novelist	1802–1870
Victor Hugo	French poet, dramatist and novelist	1802–1885
George Sand	French novelist	1804–1876
John Stuart Mill	English philosopher and economist	1806–1873
Giuseppe Garibaldi	Italian political leader	1807–1882
Henry Wadsworth Longfellow	American poet	1807–1882
Felix Mendelssohn	German composer	1809–1847
Alfred Lord Tennyson	English poet	1809–1892
Frederick Chopin	Polish composer	1810–1849
Robert Schumann	German composer	1810–1856
Franz Liszt	Hungarian composer	1811–1886
William Makepeace Thackeray	English novelist	1811–1873

Robert Browning	English poet	1812–1889
Richard Wagner	German composer	1813–1883
Anthony Trollope	English novelist	1815–1882
Walt Whitman	American poet	1819–1892
Fyodor Dostoevsky	Russian writer	1821–1881
Gustave Flaubert	French novelist	1821–1880
Gregor Mendel	Austrian monk and scientist	1822–1884
Louis Pasteur	French chemist	1822–1895
Anton Bruckner	Austrian composer	1824–1896
Wilkie Collins	English novelist	1824–1889
Bedrich Smetana	Czech composer	1824–1884
Johann Strauss	Viennese musician and composer	1825–1899
Emily Dickinson	American poet	1830–1886
Johannes Brahms	German composer	1833–1897
Modest Mussorgsky	Russian composer	1839–1881
Piotr Ilyich Tchaikovsky	Russian composer	1840–1893
Robert Louis Stevenson	Scottish writer	1850–1894
Vincent van Gogh	Dutch artist	1853–1890

Birthstones

These are useful to know because they do crop up in questions occasionally. However, some caution must be exercised; listed here are two lists of birthstones, one relating to the calendar month and the other one relating to the zodiac sign. Occasionally question setters confuse the two.

January	Garnet	**Aries**	Ruby
February	Amethyst	**Taurus**	Topaz
March	Bloodstone	**Gemini**	Carbuncle
April	Diamond	**Cancer**	Emerald
May	Emerald	**Leo**	Sapphire
June	Agate	**Virgo**	Diamond
July	Cornelian	**Libra**	Jacinth
August	Sardonyx	**Scorpio**	Agate
September	Chrysolite	**Sagittarius**	Amethyst
October	Opal	**Capricorn**	Beryl
November	Topaz	**Aquarius**	Onyx
December	Turquoise	**Pisces**	Jasper

Bishops (Church of England)
How they Sign

Another one of those subjects which seems to take the fancy of quiz setters. It seems completely irrelevant that the Archbishop of Canterbury is George Cantuar but as the question is asked frequently, here is a list.

Canterbury	Cantuar
Carlisle	Carliol
Chester	Cestr
Chichester	Cicestr
Durham	Dunelm
Exeter	Exon
Gloucester	Gloucestr
Llandaff	Landav
London	Londin
Norwich	Norvic
Oxford	Oxon
Peterborough	Petriburg
Rochester	Roffen
Salisbury	Sarum
Winchester	Winton
York	Ebor

All other bishops sign with the English name of their diocese, eg the Bishop of Liverpool will sign Liverpool and the Bishop of Manchester will sign Manchester.

···

James Bond Films – Bond Girls and Villains

This was a glaring omission from the first edition. My apologies. Bond girls and Bond villains are a very popular source of quiz questions. They come in a number of guises: "Who played Pussy Galore?", "In which film was Donald Pleasance the villain?", etc. Here they are.

Dr No	Ursula Andress (Honeychile Rider)	Joseph Wiseman (Dr No)
From Russia With Love	Daniella Bianchi (Tatiana Romanova)	Lotte Lenya (Rosa Klebb), Robert Shaw (Red Grant)
Goldfinger	Honor Blackman (Pussy Galore)	Gert Frobe (Ulrich Goldfinger)
Thunderball	Claudine Auger (Domino)	Adolfo Celi (Emilio Largo)
You Only Live Twice	Mie Hama (Kissy Suzuki)	Donald Pleasence (Blofeld)
On Her Majesty's Secret Service	Diana Rigg (Tracy Vicenzo)	Telly Savalas (Blofeld)
Diamonds Are Forever	Jill St John (Tiffany Case), Lana Wood (Plenty O'Toole)	Charles Gray (Blofeld)
Live and Let Die	Jane Seymour (Solitaire)	Yaphet Kotto (Dr Kananga)
The Man With The Golden Gun	Britt Ekland (Mary Goodnight)	Christopher Lee (Scaramanga)
The Spy Who Loved Me	Barbara Bach (Major Anya Amasova)	Curt Jürgens (Stromberg)
Moonraker	Lois Chiles (Holly Goodhead) *(How did they get away with some of these names?)*	Michael Lonsdale (Hugo Drax)
For Your Eyes Only	Carole Bouquet (Melina)	Julian Glover (Kristatos)
Octopussy	Maud Adams (Octopussy)	Louis Jourdan (Prince Kamel Khan)

A View To A Kill	Tanya Roberts (Stacey Sutton)	Christopher Walken (Max Zorin), Grace Jones (May Day)
The Living Daylights	Maryam d'Abo (Kara Milovy)	Jeroen Krabbe (Koskov)
Licence To Kill	Carey Lowell (Pam Pouvier), Talisa Sotto (Loupe Lamora)	Robert Davi (Franz Sanchez)

James Bond Films – Title Music

A favourite theme with quiz question setters. Some of these are glaringly obvious and very easy, some are not. Here is the full list anyway.

Dr No	The James Bond Theme Written by: Monty Norman (*NOT* John Barry)
From Russia With Love	Title song performed by: Matt Monro
Goldfinger	Title song performed by: Shirley Bassey
Thunderball	Title song performed by: Tom Jones
You Only Live Twice	Title song performed by: Nancy Sinatra
On Her Majesty's Secret Service	Theme song ("All the Love in the World") performed by: Louis Armstrong
Diamonds Are Forever	Title song performed by: Shirley Bassey
Live And Let Die	Title song performed by: Paul McCartney and Wings
The Man With The Golden Gun	Title song performed by: Lulu
The Spy Who Loved Me	Title song performed by: Carly Simon

Moonraker	Title song performed by: Shirley Bassey
For Your Eyes Only	Title song performed by: Sheena Easton
Octopussy	Title song performed by: Rita Coolidge
A View To A Kill	Title song performed by: Duran Duran
The Living Daylights	Title song performed by: A-Ha
Licence To Kill	Title song performed by: Gladys Knight

Booker Prize Winners

The Booker Prize for Fiction was instigated in 1969. The following is a list of the winners and the books for which the prize was awarded.

Year	Author	Title
1969	**P. H. Newby**	Something To Answer For
1970	**Bernice Rubens**	The Elected Member
1971	**V. S. Naipaul**	In A Free State
1972	**John Berger**	G
1973	**J. G. Farrell**	The Siege Of Krishnapur
1974	**Nadine Gordimer**	The Conservationist
	Stanley Middleton	Holiday
1975	**Ruth Prawer Jhabvala**	Heat And Dust
1976	**David Storey**	Saville
1977	**Paul Scott**	Staying On
1978	**Iris Murdoch**	The Sea, The Sea
1979	**Penelope Fitzgerald**	Offshore
1980	**William Golding**	Rites Of Passage
1981	**Salman Rushdie**	Midnight's Children
1982	**Thomas Keneally**	Schindler's Ark
1983	**J. M. Coetzee**	Life And Times Of Michael K
1984	**Anita Brookner**	Hôtel du Lac
1985	**Keri Hulme**	The Bone People

1986	**Kingsley Amis**	The Old Devils
1987	**Penelope Lively**	Moon Tiger
1988	**Peter Carey**	Oscar And Lucinda
1989	**Kazuo Ishiguro**	The Remains Of The Day
1990	**A. S. Byatt**	Possession
1991	**Ben Okri**	The Famished Road
1992	**Barry Unsworth**	Sacred Hunger
	Michael Ondaatje	The English Patient
1993	**Roddy Doyle**	Paddy Clarke, Ha, Ha, Ha
1994	**James Kelman**	How Late It Was, How Late

Bottle Sizes

Although in questions these are usually referred to as champagne bottles, the sizes can pertain to any wine. Well worth committing these to memory.

Magnum	Equivalent to 2 standard bottles
Jeroboam	4 standard bottles
(sometimes called a double magnum)	
Rehoboam	6 standard bottles
Methuselah	8 standard bottles
Salmanazar	12 standard bottles
Balthazar	16 standard bottles
Nebuchadnezzar	20 standard bottles

Boxing
Boxers' Nicknames

A popular source of sporting questions. Over the years thousands of boxers have had nicknames, the following is a list of the most frequently asked.

Nickname	Real Name
Ambling Alp	Primo Carnera
Black Cloud	Larry Holmes
Boston Gob	Jack Sharkey
Brockton Blockbuster	Rocky Marciano
Bronx Bull	Jake la Motta
Brown Bomber	Joe Louis
Cincinnati Cobra	Ezzard Charles
Cinderella Man	James J. Braddock
Clones Cyclone	Barry McGuigan
Dark Destroyer	Nigel Benn
Fighting Marine	Gene Tunney
Gentleman Jim	James J. Corbett
Ghost with a Hammer in his Hand	Jimmy Wilde
Homicide Hank	Henry Armstrong
Louisville Lip	Muhammad Ali
Manassa Mauler	Jack Dempsey
Marvelous Marvin	Marvin Hagler
Michigan Assassin	Stanley Ketchel
Mighty Atom	Jimmy Wilde
Motor City Cobra	Thomas Hearns
Orchid Man	Georges Carpentier
Smokin' Joe	Joe Frazier
Stonefist	Roberto Duran
Sugar Ray	Ray Leonard or Ray Robinson
Wild Bull of the Pampas	Luis Firpo

Boxing Weight Divisions

For many years there were only nine weight divisions in professional boxing but over the last 30–40 years several intermediates have been introduced. Below is a list of the weight divisions recognised by the international controlling bodies. They are listed in descending order.

Heavyweight
Cruiserweight
Light-Heavyweight
Super-Middleweight
Middleweight
Light-Middleweight (or Super-Welterweight)
Welterweight
Super-Lightweight (or Light-Welterweight)
Lightweight
Super-Featherweight
Featherweight
Super Bantamweight (or Light Featherweight)
Bantamweight
Super Flyweight (or Light Bantamweight)
Flyweight
Light-Flyweight
Straw-weight

Breweries

Not surprisingly the geographic location of brewers is a popular subject for pub quizzes. This is a list of independent regional brewers and the town or city in which they are based:

Brewer	*Location*
Adnams & Co.	Southwold, Suffolk
Arkells	Swindon
George Bateman & Son	Skegness
Batham	Brierley Hill, West Midlands
S. A. Brain & Son	Cardiff
W. H. Brakspear & Sons	Henley-on-Thames
Cains	Liverpool
Crown Buckley	Pontyclun, Mid Glamorgan
Burtonwood	Burtonwood, Warrington
Eldridge Pope & Co.	Dorchester
Elgood & Sons	Wisbech
Everards	Leicester
Felinfoel	Llanelli
Fuller Smith & Turner	Chiswick
George Gale & Co.	Hondean, Hampshire
Gibbs, Mew	Salisbury
Greene King	Bury St Edmunds
Hall & Woodhouse	Blandford St Mary, Dorset
Hardy & Hanson	Nottingham
Harvey & Son	Lewes
Holden's	Dudley
Hook Norton	Banbury
Hoskins	Leicester
Hydes	Manchester
Joseph Holt	Manchester
Jennings	Cockermouth
King & Barnes	Horsham
J. W. Lees	Manchester
Maclay	Alloa
Marston, Thompson & Evershed	Burton-on-Trent
McMullen & Sons	Hertford

Brewer	Location
Mitchells	Lancaster
Morland	Abingdon
Morrells	Oxford
J. C. & R. H. Palmer	Bridport
Ridleys	Chelmsford
Frederick Robinson	Stockport
Shepherd Neame	Faversham
Timothy Taylor	Keighley
Daniel Thwaites	Blackburn
Ushers	Trowbridge
Vaux	Sunderland
Wadworth	Devizes
Charles Wells	Bedford
Young & Co.	Wandsworth

The Calendar – Anniversaries

It is always useful to know the exact dates on which major events took place, especially if the date of the quiz you are playing in is known in advance. Some quality newspapers do print anniversaries each day, but it is always infuriating if you cannot answer the "Which famous battle took place 500 years ago today?" type of question. Here are some worth remembering. This collection of miscellaneous facts will also stand you in good stead in any quiz.

Excluded from this list are the births of many famous people as they were rarely heralded as major events at the time.

N.B. Sources sometimes vary by a day for some of these events.

January

1st	1785	The Daily Universal Register was first published (later to become The Times)
	1958	The EEC came into being
	1959	Fidel Castro came to power in Cuba
	1973	Britain and Ireland joined the EEC
2nd	1769	The opening of the Royal Academy
	1971	The Ibrox disaster at the Rangers v Celtic match
3rd	1924	Howard Carter discovered the sarcophagus of Tutankhamun
	1959	Alaska became the forty-ninth US State
4th	1932	The Congress Party of India was declared illegal and its leader Mahatma Gandhi arrested
5th	1066	Edward the Confessor died thus setting in motion a train of events which led to the Norman Conquest
	1981	Peter Sutcliffe (the Yorkshire Ripper) was arrested and charged with murder
6th	1838	Samuel Morse demonstrated his electric telegraph system for the first time
7th	1558	England lost her last possession on the mainland of France when the French recaptured Calais

	1785	The first airborne crossing of the English Channel by Jean Pierre Blanchard and John Jeffries in a hot-air balloon
8th	1815	The Battle of New Orleans
	1959	Charles de Gaulle became President of France
9th	1799	Income Tax introduced in Britain
	1957	Anthony Eden resigned as Prime Minister
	1972	The liner Queen Elizabeth caught fire and sank in Hong Kong Harbour
10th	1645	The Archbishop of Canterbury, William Laud, was beheaded for treason
	1840	The Penny Post introduced
	1863	The London Underground railway system was opened
	1946	The first meeting of the United Nations' General Assembly in London
11th	1946	King Zog of Albania deposed
12th	1970	First Trans Atlantic flight of a Jumbo jet
13th	1893	The Independent British Labour Party formed
14th	1878	First demonstration of Bell's telephone
15th	1759	British Museum opened
16th	1780	Battle of Cape St Vincent
	1920	Prohibition introduced in the United States
	1970	Colonel Gadaffi appointed Prime Minister of Libya
17th	1912	Captain Scott reached the South Pole
18th	1778	Captain Cook discovered Hawaii and named them the Sandwich Islands
	1919	The Versailles peace conference opened
	1943	The siege of Leningrad lifted
	1963	The death of Hugh Gaitskell
19th	1966	Indira Gandhi became Prime Minister of India
	1981	American hostages released by Islamic Fundamentalists in Tehran

20th	1987	Terry Waite kidnapped in Beirut
21st	1793	Louis XVI of France executed
	1924	Death of Lenin
	1976	Inaugural flights of Concorde from London to Bahrain and from Paris to Rio de Janeiro
22nd	1901	Death of Queen Victoria
	1902	First radio transmission by Marconi
	1924	Britain's first Labour government came to power
23rd	1968	The boarding of the US spy ship Pueblo by North Koreans
24th	AD 41	Roman Emperor Caligula murdered in Rome
	1916	Conscription introduced in Britain
	1965	Death of Sir Winston Churchill
25th	1919	The League of Nations founded
	1981	Social Democrats formed by Williams, Rodgers, Jenkins and Owen
26th	1841	Hong Kong became British sovereign territory
	1885	The murder of General Gordon at Khartoum
	1886	First public demonstration of Carl Benz's motor car
27th	1926	John Logie Baird demonstrated television at the Royal Institution
	1973	American military action in Vietnam ended
28th	1547	Death of Henry VIII
	1814	Death of Charlemagne
29th	1856	The Victoria Cross instituted
30th	1933	Adolf Hitler appointed Chancellor of Germany
	1649	Execution of King Charles I
	1948	Assassination of Mahatma Gandhi
	1972	Thirteen people killed in Londonderry (Bloody Sunday)
31st	1606	Execution of Guy Fawkes
	1958	First US earth satellite launched

February

1st 1979 Ayatollah Khomeni returned to Iran after 14 years of exile in France

2nd 1943 Surrender of the German army at Stalingrad

3rd 1919 The first meeting of the League of Nations in Paris

4th 1861 Formation of the Confederacy of Southern States

1904 Russo-Japanese War began

5th 1974 US heiress Patty Hearst kidnapped

6th 1918 The Representation of the Peoples Act gave votes to married women over the age of 30

1952 Death of King George VI

1958 Munich air disaster

7th 1301 Edward II became the first English Prince of Wales

8th 1587 Mary Queen of Scots executed at Fotheringay Castle

1965 Cigarette advertising was banned on British television

1983 Derby winner Shergar was kidnapped

9th 1540 England's first recorded race meeting at Chester

10th 1567 Murder of Lord Darnley, husband of Mary Queen of Scots

1840 Marriage of Queen Victoria and Prince Albert

1942 The first official gold disc presented to Glenn Miller (for Chattanooga Choo Choo)

11th 1585 St Bernadette's vision of the Virgin at Lourdes

1990 Release of Nelson Mandella from imprisonment

12th 1553 Execution of Lady Jane Grey

	1688	Flight of James II to France. William III and Mary declared King and Queen of England
	1924	The lid of the sarcophagus of Tutankhamun removed by Howard Carter
13th	1542	Catherine Howard, fifth wife of Henry VIII executed
	1692	The Glencoe massacre
	1945	Fourteen hour blanket bombing of Dresden
	1974	Alexander Solzhenitsyn expelled from the Soviet Union
14th	1779	Murder of Captain James Cook in Hawaii
	1797	Battle of Cape St Vincent
	1929	The St Valentine's Day massacre in Chicago
	1946	Bank of England nationalised
	1989	Fatwa against Salman Rushdie issued by the Ayatollah Khomeini
15th	1942	Fall of Singapore to Japanese forces
	1971	Decimalisation of British currency
16th	1801	Resignation of Pitt the Younger as prime minister
17th	1863	International Red Cross founded in Geneva
	1958	Founding of the Campaign for Nuclear Disarmament
18th	1478	George, Duke of Clarence murdered in the Tower of London
	1678	Publication of Pilgrim's Progress
	1911	The first airmail service came into operation in India
	1930	Discovery of the planet Pluto by Clyde Tombaugh
19th	1800	Napoleon Bonaparte appointed First Consul in Paris
	1960	Birth of the Duke of York
20th	1437	Assassination of James I of Scotland
	1947	Lord Louis Mountbatten appointed Last Viceroy of India

	1962	Colonel John Glenn first American to orbit the earth (in Friendship 7)
21st	1916	Beginning of the Battle of Verdun
	1965	Murder of black muslim leader Malcolm X
22nd	1879	First ever Woolworth store opened in New York State
23rd	1821	Death of John Keats in Rome
	1836	The siege of the Alamo begins
24th	1920	National Socialist German Workers published its first manifesto
	1920	First speech by a woman MP in Britain (Lady Astor)
25th	1601	Execution of the Earl of Essex for treason
	1922	Execution of the French mass murderer Henry Landru (Bluebeard)
26th	1797	First £1 notes issued by the Bank of England
	1815	Escape of Napoleon Bonaparte from Elba
27th	1900	Founding of the Parliamentary Labour Party
	1933	Burning of the Reichstag building in Berlin
28th	1900	Relief of Ladysmith by General Buller
	1975	Moorgate train disaster
	1986	Assassination of Swedish Prime Minister Olof Palme
29th	1528	Patrick Hamilton, Scottish protestant martyr, burned at the stake
	1880	The St Gotthard tunnel between Switzerland and Italy completed

March

1st	1932	Kidnapping of the infant son of aviator Charles Lindbergh
	1959	Archbishop Makarios returned to Cyprus from exile
	1958	First overland crossing of Antarctica completed by British team led by Dr Vivian Fuchs
	1970	Rhodesia became a republic under Ian Smith
	1974	US Grand Jury ruled that President Richard Nixon was involved in the Watergate scandal
	1988	Merger of Liberal and Social Democratic parties in Britain
3rd	1974	Turkish airliner crashed near Paris, 344 killed
4th	1789	First congress of the United States convened in New York
5th	1946	Churchill made his famous Iron Curtain speech at Fulton, Missouri
	1953	Death of Joseph Stalin
6th	1836	The Alamo fell to Mexican forces
	1987	Zeebrugge disaster involving the ferry Herald of Free Enterprise
	1988	Three IRA terrorists shot dead in Gibraltar by members of the SAS
7th	1876	Alexander Graham Bell patented his telephone
	1912	Frenchman Henri Seimet became first man to fly nonstop from Paris to London
8th	1910	Baroness de Laroche, first woman to receive a pilot's licence
	1966	IRA bomb destroyed Nelson's Column in O'Connell Street, Dublin
9th	1931	Formation of the French Foreign Legion in Algeria
10th	1876	Alexander Graham Bell made the first telephone call
	1948	Death of Czech Foreign Minister Jan Masaryk

	1964	Birth of Prince Edward
11th	1682	Royal Chelsea Hospital founded
	1985	Mikhail Gorbachev appointed General Secretary of the Communist Party of the Soviet Union
	1988	The Bank of England £1 note ceased to be legal tender
12th	1945	Death of Anne Frank
	1969	Marriage of Paul McCartney to Linda Eastman
13th	1781	Discovery of the planet Uranus by Herschel
	1881	Assassination of Tsar Alexander II of Russia
	1935	Introduction of driving test in Britain
	1938	Invasion of Austria by Germany
14th	1757	Execution of Admiral Byng
	1925	First Trans Atlantic broadcast
	1953	Nikita Khrushchev appointed first Secretary of the Soviet Communist Party
15th	44 BC	Assassination of Julius Caesar
	1877	First ever Cricket Test Match between England and Australia started in Melbourne
	1917	Abdication of Tsar Nicholas II of Russia
	1949	Ending of clothes rationing in Britain
16th	1872	First FA Cup Final played (at Kennington Oval)
	1968	Mai Lai massacre in Vietnam
17th	1921	Dr Marie Stopes opened Britain's first birth control clinic
	1969	Golda Meir appointed Prime Minister of Israel
	1978	Grounding of the oil tanker Amoco Cadiz on the Britanny coast
18th	978	Assassination of King Edward the Martyr at Corfe Castle
	1584	Death of Ivan the Terrible of Russia
	1834	The Tolpuddle Martyrs sentenced to transportation
	1871	Communard uprising in Paris

	1922	Mahatma Gandhi sentenced to six years' imprisonment
	1935	30-mph speed limit introduced in Britain in built-up areas
	1949	Establishment of NATO
	1965	First space walk by cosmonaut Colonel Alexei Leonov
	1967	Grounding of the oil tanker Torrey Canyon off Land's End
	1978	Former Italian prime minister Aldo Moro kidnapped
19th	1976	Separation of Princess Margaret and Lord Snowdon
20th	1549	Thomas Seymour executed for treason
	1974	Attempted kidnap of Princess Anne in The Mall
	1976	Pattie Hearst, newspaper heiress, found guilty of armed robbery
21st	1556	Execution at the stake of Thomas Cranmer for heresy
	1960	Sharpeville massacre in South Africa
22nd	1895	First public performance of moving film
	1945	Formation of the Arab League
23rd	1933	Hitler gained absolute power in Germany
24th	1603	Death of Elizabeth I
		Union of English and Scottish crowns when James VI of Scotland acceded to the English throne
		Assassination of Paul I, Tsar of Russia
	1976	Isabel Peron deposed as President of Argentina
	1980	Murder of Archbishop Oscar Romero in San Salvador
25th	1807	Abolition of the slave trade in Britain
	1957	Signing of the Treaty of Rome by the six founder members of the EEC
26th	1827	Death of Beethoven

	1945	Death of David Lloyd George
27th	1942	Commando raid at St Nazaire
	1968	Death of Yuri Gagarin in plane crash
	1989	First democratic election for the Soviet parliament
28th	1854	Britain entered the Crimean War
	1939	Franco's forces took Madrid. End of Spanish Civil War
	1941	Battle of Cape Matapan
29th	1461	Battle of Towton
	1871	Royal Albert Hall opened
30th	1981	President Reagan shot in assassination attempt in Washington
31st	1889	Eiffel Tower opened
	1959	Dalai Lama fled Tibet
	1986	Hampton Court Palace severely damaged by fire

April

1st
1908	Formation of the Territorial Army
1918	Formation of the Royal Air Force
1948	Blockade of Berlin by Soviet troops began
1947	School leaving age raised to 15
1973	VAT introduced in the UK

2nd
1801	Battle of Copenhagen
1905	The Simplon Tunnel officially opened
1982	Invasion of the Falkland Islands by Argentina

3rd
1860	Founding of the Pony Express
1882	Jesse James shot dead
1913	Emmeline Pankhurst found guilty of inciting arson and sentenced to 3 years' imprisonment

4th
1968	Assassination of Dr Martin Luther King
1979	Execution of ex-President of Pakistan, Zulfiqar Ali Bhutto

5th
1794	Execution of French revolutionary leader Danton
1895	Arrest of Oscar Wilde at the Cadogan Hotel
1955	Sir Winston Churchill resigned as Prime Minister

6th
1199	Death of Richard I
1830	Founding of the Mormon Church
1896	First modern Olympic Games opened in Athens
1909	Commander Robert Peary became the first man to reach the North Pole
1917	United States of America entered World War I
1944	Introduction of PAYE in Britain

7th
1739	Hanging of Dick Turpin at York
1958	First "Ban The Bomb" march to Aldermaston

8th
1838	Maiden voyage of the Great Western
1904	Ratification of the Entente Cordiale

9th
1865	End of the American Civil War

10th
1974	Resignation of Golda Meir as Israeli Prime Minister

11th	1713	Treaty of Utrecht signed
	1814	Abdication of Napoleon Bonaparte
	1961	Trial of Adolf Eichmann began in Jerusalem
	1981	By-election at Fermanagh and South Tyrone won by IRA hunger striker Bobby Sands
12th	1606	The Union Flag became the official flag of Britain
	1861	Start of the American Civil War
	1945	Death of Franklin D. Roosevelt
	1961	First manned space flight (by Yuri Gagarin)
13th	1605	Death of Boris Godunov (Tsar of Russia)
	1668	First Poet Laureate appointed (John Dryden)
14th	1865	Assassination of President Abraham Lincoln
15th	1912	SS Titanic sunk on maiden voyage
16th	1746	Battle of Culloden
17th	1521	Martin Luther excommunicated
	1963	Greville Wynne charged with espionage in Moscow
	1984	WPC Yvonne Fletcher shot dead outside the Libyan People's Bureau in London
18th	1906	San Francisco earthquake
	1946	League of Nations dissolved in Geneva
	1949	The Republic of Ireland established
	1954	Colonel Nasser seized power in Egypt
19th	1775	Start of the American War of Independence
	1881	Death of Disraeli
	1961	Bay of Pigs invasion in Cuba
20th	1653	Dissolution of the Long Parliament
	1657	Spanish Fleet destroyed at Santa Cruz by Admiral Blake
21st	1509	Death of King Henry VII
	1918	Baron Manfred von Richthofen shot down in action
	1926	Birth of Her Majesty the Queen
	1960	Brasilia inaugurated as new capital of Brazil
	1989	Start of Tiananmen Square protests by Chinese students

22nd	1915	First use of poison gas by Germans at Ypres
	1983	Introduction of £1 coins in Britain
23rd	1616	Death of Shakespeare (he was also born on this day in 1564)
	1968	First British decimal coins circulated (5p and 10p)
	1984	Announcement of the discovery of AIDS virus
24th	1895	Joshua Slocum began his single-handed circumnavigation
	1949	Sweet and chocolate rationing ended in Britain
25th	1859	Work began on construction of the Suez Canal
	1916	Easter uprising in Dublin
26th	1937	Bombing of Guernica in Spanish Civil War
	1986	Chernobyl disaster
27th	1968	Abortion legalised in Britain by the Abortion Act
28th	1770	Captain James Cook landed at Botany Bay
	1789	The Mutiny on the Bounty
	1945	Assassination of Mussolini in Milan
	1969	Resignation of Charles de Gaulle as President of France
29th	1885	Women admitted to Oxford University examinations for the first time
	1945	Surrender of Germans in Italy to the Allies
30th	311	Legal recognition of Christianity in the Roman Empire
	1789	Inauguration of George Washington as first president of the USA
	1945	Suicide of Hitler
	1975	End of Vietnam War
May	1851	Opening of the Great Exhibition
1st	1931	Opening of the Empire State Building
	1960	U-2 spy plane shot down over the USSR
	1961	Betting shops legalised in Britain

	1978	First May Day Bank Holiday in Great Britain
2nd	1936	Emperor Haile Selassie fled Abyssinia in the face of Italian invasion
	1982	Sinking of the Argentinian battleship General Belgrano
3rd	1926	Start of the General Strike
	1951	Opening of the Festival of Britain
	1968	First heart transplant in Britain
4th	1780	Running of the first Derby stakes (won by Diomed)
	1979	Conservative election victory (Margaret Thatcher became Britain's first woman Prime Minister)
	1982	HMS Sheffield sunk by Exocet missile during the Falklands War
	1989	Colonel Oliver North convicted of supplying arms to the Contras
5th	1821	Death of Napoleon Bonaparte
	1980	Storming of the Iranian Embassy by SAS
6th	1626	Manhattan Island purchased by Peter Minuit
	1910	Death of King Edward VII
	1937	Hindenburg airship disaster in New Jersey
	1954	Running of the first 4-minute mile (by Roger Bannister at Oxford)
	1974	Resignation of German Chancellor Willy Brandt, because of a spy scandal
7th	1915	Torpedoing of the liner Lusitania off the Irish Coast
	1945	The final surrender of German forces (at Rheims)
8th	1961	Diplomat George Blake jailed for over 40 years for espionage
	1984	Thames Barrier opened
9th	1946	Abdication of Victor Emmanuel III of Italy
	1955	West Germany admitted to NATO

10th	1857	Start of the Indian mutiny
	1940	Churchill appointed Prime Minister on the resignation of Chamberlain
	1941	Worst day of the London blitz
	1941	Rudolf Hess landed in Scotland
	1981	Francois Mitterand elected President of France
11th	1812	Assassination of Prime Minister Spencer Perceval
	1985	Forty people killed at Bradford City football ground in a fire
12th	1926	End of the General Strike
	1949	End of the Russian blockade of Berlin
	1969	Voting age lowered to 18
13th	1981	Assassination attempt on Pope John Paul II in Rome
14th	1940	Local Defence Volunteer Force (Home Guard) formed
	1948	State of Israel proclaimed
15th	1957	Britain's first "H" bomb test
16th	1763	Dr Johnson met James Boswell for the first time
	1929	First Academy Awards ceremony
	1943	"Dambusters" raid by 617 Squadron
	1983	First use of wheel clamps in London
17th	1900	Relief of Mafeking
18th	1804	Napoleon Bonaparte proclaimed Emperor of France
19th	1536	Execution of Anne Boleyn
	1898	Death of Gladstone
	1980	Eruption of Mt. St Helens in Washington State, USA
20th	1506	Death of Christopher Columbus
	1956	USA's first "H" bomb test over Bikini Atoll
21st	1916	Introduction of British Summertime
	1927	Charles Lindbergh completed his solo Atlantic crossing

22nd	1972	First visit of an American President (Richard Nixon) to USSR
23rd	1701	Execution of Captain Kidd
	1706	Battle of Ramillies
24th	1844	First transmission of a Morse message on a US telegraph line (from Washington to Baltimore)
	1941	Sinking of HMS Hood by German battleship, Bismarck
25th	1871	Passing of the Bank Holiday Act which created public holidays at Easter, Whit and Christmas
	1951	"Disappearance" of Burgess and Maclean
26th	1865	End of the American Civil War
	1868	Last public execution in England (at Newgate Prison)
	1950	Petrol rationing ended in Britain
27th	1679	Passing of the Habeas Corpus Act
	1936	Maiden voyage of the Queen Mary
	1941	Sinking of the German battleship Bismarck
	1964	Death of Nehru
28th	1967	Completion of solo circumnavigation of the globe by Francis Chichester
	1972	Death of the Duke of Windsor
29th	1453	Fall of Constantinople to the Turks
	1660	Restoration of the monarchy. Charles II returned to London
	1871	First British bank holiday
	1953	Hillary and Tenzing reached the summit of Everest
	1985	Heysel Stadium disaster in Brussels
30th	1431	Joan of Arc burned at the stake at Rouen
	1593	Christopher Marlowe killed in a tavern brawl in London
	1959	First hovercraft flight
31st	1669	Last entry in the diary of Samuel Pepys
	1902	End of the Boer War

| 1916 | Battle of Jutland |
| 1961 | South Africa declared a republic and left the British Commonwealth |

June
1st	1946	Television licences introduced in Britain (£2)
	1957	The first Premium Bond winner drawn
2nd	1868	First Trade Union Congress convened
	1953	Coronation of HM Queen Elizabeth II
	1962	Britain's first legal casino opened in Brighton
	1964	Founding of the PLO
3rd	1937	Marriage of the Duke of Windsor to Mrs Simpson
	1956	Abolition of third class rail travel on British Railways
4th	1913	Suffragette Emily Davison threw herself under the King's horse in the Derby
	1940	Completion of the Dunkirk evacuation
	1989	Protests in Tiananmen Square, Beijing, crushed by tanks
5th	1963	Resignation of John Profumo
	1967	Six-day Arab-Israeli War began
	1968	Assassination of Senator Robert Kennedy in Los Angeles
6th	1844	YMCA founded by George Williams
	1944	D-Day. Allied invasion of Normandy
	1984	Indian troops stormed the Golden Temple at Amritsar
7th	1329	Death of Robert the Bruce
	1929	Vatican State created
		Margaret Bondfield, first woman cabinet minister (Minister of Labour)
	1942	Battle of Midway
8th	632	Death of the Prophet Mohammed
	1924	Disappearance of Mallory and Irvine near the summit of Mt. Everest
9th	1898	Britain signed a 99-year lease on Hong Kong

	1959	First atomic powered submarine launched (USS George Washington)
	1975	First live radio broadcast from the House of Commons
10th	1829	First Oxford - Cambridge boat race (at Henley)
	1921	Birth of HRH Prince Philip
11th	1940	War declared on the Allies by Italy
12th	1667	First successful blood transfusion performed by Jean Baptiste Denys
13th	1900	Beginning of the Boxer uprising in China
	1944	First V1 flying bomb attack on Britain
14th	1645	Battle of Naseby
	1800	Battle of Marengo
	1919	Alcock and Brown made the first nonstop Trans Atlantic flight
	1982	Surrender of Argentine forces in the Falklands
15th	1215	Magna Carta sealed
	1381	Killing of Wat Tyler, Kentish rebel leader
16th	1903	Formation of the Ford Motor Corporation
	1958	First yellow lines painted on British streets
	1961	Rudolph Nureyev defected to the west in Paris
	1963	Valentina Tereschkova became the first woman to travel in space
	1976	Riots in Soweto township, near Johannesburg
17th	1775	Battle of Bunker Hill
	1972	Five men arrested breaking into the Watergate building in Washington
	1982	Body of Roberto Calvi found hanging under Blackfriars Bridge
18th	1812	USA declared war on Britain
	1815	Battle of Waterloo
19th	1829	Formation of the Metropolitan Police
	1953	Execution of Russian spies Ethel and Julius Rosenberg in Sing Sing Prison
20th	1756	146 employees of the East India Company imprisoned in the "Black Hole of Calcutta"

	1819	Steamship Savannah became the first steamship to cross the Atlantic
	1837	Death of King William IV and accession of Queen Victoria to the throne
	1928	Death of explorer Roald Amundsen in a plane crash in Spitzbergen
21st	1854	First Victoria Cross won (awarded retrospectively)
	1942	Tobruk fell to Rommel
22nd	1814	First match played at the present Lords Cricket Ground
	1941	German invasion of USSR
	1979	Jeremy Thorpe found not guilty of plotting to murder Norman Scott
23rd	1757	Battle of Plassey
	1956	Nasser became president of Egypt in unopposed election
24th	1314	Battle of Bannockburn
	1859	Battle of Solferino - which led to the formation of the Red Cross
25th	1876	Battle of the Little Bighorn (Custer's last stand)
	1950	North Korea invaded South Korea precipitating the Korean War
	1953	John Christie sentenced to death for the murder of four women
26th	1917	The first American troops arrived in France under the command of General Pershing
27th	1743	Battle of Dettingen (George II became the last British monarch to lead his troops into battle)
	1905	Mutiny aboard the Russian battleship Potemkin
	1906	First Grand Prix (at Le Mans)
28th	1914	Assassination of Archduke Franz Ferdinand at Sarajevo (precipitating World War I)
	1919	Treaty of Versailles signed
29th	1966	Introduction of Barclaycard in Britain

| **30th** | 1859 | Blondin crossed the Niagara Falls on a tightrope |
| | 1894 | Tower Bridge opened to traffic |

July

1st	1837	First registration of births, deaths and marriages in Britain
	1863	Battle of Gettysburg
	1937	Introduction of 999 emergency number in Britain
	1967	First regular colour transmissions on British television
2nd	1644	Battle of Marston Moor
	1850	Death of Sir Robert Peel
	1865	Founding of the Salvation Army
	1964	Civil Rights Act in the USA signed by President Johnson
3rd	1898	Captain Joshua Slocum completed his solo circumnavigation of the globe
	1916	Beginning of the Battle of the Somme
	1976	Rescue of hostages at Entebbe Airport, Uganda, by Israeli commandos
4th	1776	US Declaration of Independence approved by the American Congress
	1848	Publication of the Communist manifesto
	1892	Keir Hardie elected first Socialist MP (Holytown, Lanarkshire)
	1943	Death of Polish prime minister Sikorski in an air crash
5th	1948	Introduction of the National Health Service
6th	1535	Execution of Sir Thomas More
	1952	Last London tram ran
	1988	Explosion aboard the Piper Alpha oil rig – over 160 men killed
7th	1982	Intruder Michael Fagan found in the Queen's bedroom
	1985	Live Aid concerts in London and Philadelphia
8th	1822	Death of Shelley

9th	1877	First Wimbledon Lawn Tennis Championships
	1938	Gas masks issued to the population in the UK
	1984	Serious damage to York Minster when it was struck by lightning
10th	1900	Paris Metro system opened
	1958	The first parking meters came into operation in London
	1985	Explosion aboard the Greenpeace ship Rainbow Warrior in Auckland Harbour
11th	1979	Return to earth of Skylab 1 after six years
12th	1910	Death of the Honourable Charles Rolls in an aeroplane crash
13th	1793	Murder of Jean Paul Marat
	1837	Queen Victoria became the first monarch to take up residence at Buckingham Palace
	1955	The hanging of Ruth Ellis (the last woman to be hanged in Great Britain)
14th	1789	Storming of the Bastille
	1865	Ascent of the Matterhorn by Edward Whymper
	1867	First demonstration of dynamite by Alfred Nobel
15th	1099	Capture of Jerusalem by Godfrey and Robert of Flanders
	1857	The massacre of Cawnpore
	1912	Introduction of Social Insurance Scheme in Britain
	1945	Blackout lifted in Britain
16th	1885	First successful treatment of rabies by Pasteur
	1918	Assassination of Tsar Nicholas II of Russia and his family
	1945	First explosion of an atomic bomb; at Los Alamos, New Mexico
17th	1841	First edition of Punch published
	1917	British Royal Family's name changed to Windsor
	1945	Potsdam Conference began
18th	64 BC	Burning of Rome

	1870	Dogma of Papal Infallibility proclaimed by the Vatican Council
	1925	Mein Kampf published
	1936	Beginning of Spanish Civil War
	1969	Chappaquidick incident involving Senator Edward Kennedy and Mary Jo Kopechne
19th	1545	The Mary Rose sank in the Solent
	1903	The first Tour de France completed
20th	1837	Opening of Euston Station (the first railway station in London)
	1944	Attempted assassination of Hitler by officers led by von Stauffenberg
21st	1798	Battle of the Pyramids
	1861	Battle of Bull Run
	1904	Completion of the trans-Siberian railway
	1969	Moon landing of Apollo 11
22nd	1812	Battle of Salamanca
	1934	Shooting of gangster John Dillinger by FBI agents
23rd	1967	Death of British cyclist Tommy Simpson while competing in the Tour de France
	1986	Marriage of Prince Andrew and Sarah Ferguson
24th	1883	Death of Captain Matthew Webb while attempting to swim the rapids above Niagara Falls
25th	1909	First crossing of the Channel by aeroplane (Louis Bleriot)
	1943	Mussolini deposed in Italy
	1959	First crossing of the English Channel by hovercraft
26th	1908	Formation of the FBI in Washington
	1952	Abdication of King Farouk of Egypt
	1956	Egyptian government nationalised the Suez Canal
	1978	Birth of Louise Brown at Oldham General Hospital (world's first test tube baby)

27th	1949	Maiden flight of the De Havilland Comet, the world's first jet airliner
	1953	End of the Korean War
	1980	Death of the Shah of Iran, in exile in Egypt
28th	1794	Execution of Robespierre
	1959	Introduction of postcodes by the Post Office (in Norwich)
29th	1588	Defeat of the Spanish Armada
	1890	Death from self-inflicted bullet wound of van Gogh
	1907	Formation of the Boy Scouts by Sir Robert Baden-Powell
	1981	Marriage of the Prince of Wales and Lady Diana Spencer
30th	1898	Death of Bismarck
	1930	First ever soccer World Cup Final (Uruguay 4 Argentina 2)
	1935	First Penguin paperback book published (Ariel, A Life of Shelley)
	1949	HMS Amethyst reached Hong Kong after running the gauntlet of Chinese communist troops in the Yangtse River
	1966	England beat West Germany 4–2 to win soccer's World Cup
31st	1910	Arrest of Dr Crippin aboard the SS Montrose
	1917	Beginning of the Battle of Passchendaele
	1919	Weimar Republic established in Germany
	1963	First ever renouncement of a peerage by a British peer (Viscount Stansgate, Anthony Wedgwood Benn)

August

1st	1714	Death of Queen Anne
	1798	Battle of the Nile
	1975	Ratification of the Helsinki Agreement on Human Rights
2nd	1100	Death of William II whilst hunting in the New Forest
	1876	Shooting of Wild Bill Hickok by Jack McCall in Deadwood
	1973	Summerland fire disaster at Douglas, Isle of Man, 30 people killed
	1990	Iraqi invasion of Kuwait
3rd	1778	Opening of La Scala Opera House in Milan
	1916	Execution of Sir Roger Casement for treason
	1926	London's first traffic lights operational at Piccadilly Circus
4th	1900	Birth of HM Queen Elizabeth, Queen Mother
	1914	Britain declared war on Germany
5th	1858	Opening of the first Trans Atlantic cable
	1891	First use of traveller's cheques
	1962	Body of Marilyn Monroe found at her Californian home
6th	1926	Gertrude Ederle became the first woman to swim the Channel
	1945	First atomic bomb dropped on Hiroshima
8th	1786	First ascent of Mont Blanc (by Michel Gabriel Piccard)
	1963	The great train robbery at Cheddington, Buckinghamshire
	1974	Resignation of US President Richard Nixon
9th	1945	Atomic bomb dropped on Nagasaki
	1969	Murder of actress Sharon Tate, wife of film director Roman Polanski, and four other people at her Hollywood home
10th	1895	First promenade concert held at the Queens Hall, London
	1897	Formation of the RAC

12th	1887	First sound recording made by Thomas Edison
	1908	First Model T Ford produced
13th	1704	Battle of Blenheim
	1961	Construction of the Berlin Wall began
	1964	Last judicial executions in Britain (Peter Allen at Walton Prison and John Walby at Strangeways)
14th	1945	Unconditional surrender of Japan thus ending World War II
	1969	Deployment of British troops in Northern Ireland
15th	1057	Death of Macbeth
	1947	Indian independence from Britain
16th	1819	Peterloo massacre in Manchester
	1977	Death of Elvis Presley
17th	1896	Discovery of gold in the Klondike
	1988	Death of President Zia ul-Haq of Pakistan in a plane crash
18th	1959	Launch of the Morris Mini by BMC
19th	1960	US spy plane pilot Gary Powers sentenced to 10 years' imprisonment by Soviet court
	1960	Summons issued against Penguin Books for planning to publish Lady Chatterley's Lover
20th	1968	Invasion of Czechoslovakia by the Soviet Union
	1989	The Marchioness pleasureboat disaster on the Thames, 51 people drowned
21st	1911	The Mona Lisa was stolen from the Louvre in Paris
	1930	Birth of Princess Margaret
	1940	Assassination of Trotsky in Mexico City
	1959	Hawaii became 50th State of the USA
	1988	Liberalisation of licensing laws in England and Wales
22nd	1485	Battle of Bosworth Field

	1642	Start of the English Civil War. Charles I raised his standard in Nottingham
	1922	Shooting of Irish Nationalist, Michael Collins
	1985	Fire disaster at Manchester Airport, 55 people killed
23rd	1914	Start of the Battle of Mons
	1926	Death of Rudolph Valentino
24th	AD 79	Eruption of Mount Vesuvius burying the cities of Pompeii and Herculaneum
	1572	St Bartholomew's Day massacre in Paris
	1942	Death of the Duke of Kent when his plane crashed
25th	1875	Captain Webb became the first man to swim the English Channel
	1919	First scheduled international air service inaugurated (between London and Paris)
	1944	Liberation of Paris
26th	1346	Battle of Crécy
	1920	19th Amendment to the US Constitution gave women the vote in federal elections
	1936	First transmission of BBC television programmes
27th	1883	Eruption of the volcano Krakatoa
	1967	Suicide of former Beatles' manager Brian Epstein
	1979	Murder of Lord Louis Mountbatten by the IRA
28th	1963	Civil Rights rally in Washington culminating in Dr Martin Luther King's famous speech
29th	1885	First motor cycle patented by Gottlieb Daimler
	1966	The Beatles' last live concert (at Candlestick Park, San Francisco)
30th	30 BC	Suicide of Cleopatra, Egyptian Queen
	1860	First British tram became operational in Birkenhead
	1918	First ever British police strike
	1941	Beginning of the Siege of Leningrad
31st	1422	Death of Henry V
	1888	First of the "Jack the Ripper" murders

September

1st	1715	Death of Louis XVI of France
	1923	300,000 killed by an earthquake in Japan
	1930	German invasion of Poland
2nd	1666	Start of the Great Fire of London
	1945	Formal surrender of Japan on board the aircraft carrier Missouri
3rd	1658	Death of Oliver Cromwell
	1939	Britain and France declared war on Germany
4th	1870	Napoleon III of France deposed
	1965	Death of Albert Schweitzer in Gabon
5th	1920	Fatty Arbuckle charged with the murder of starlet Virginia Rappe
	1972	Slaughter of Israeli athletes at the Munich Olympic Games by the Palestinian Black September Movement
6th	1522	Completion of the first circumnavigation of the world by the Vittoria
	1852	First free lending library in Britain opened in Manchester
	1879	First British telephone exchange opened in London
	1880	First cricket Test Match in England (at the Oval)
	1966	Assassination of South African prime minister Hendrik Verwoerd
7th	1533	Birth of Elizabeth I
	1812	Battle of Borodino
	1838	Rescue of the survivors on the SS Forfarshire by Grace Darling
	1892	First world heavyweight title fight under Queensberry rules (Corbett beat Sullivan)
	1940	Beginning of the London blitz
	1943	Surrender of Italy to the allies
8th	1888	First matches of the new Football League played

	1935	Shooting of senator Huey Long of Louisiana (he died two days later)
	1944	First V2 bombs fired at London
9th	1087	Death of William the Conqueror
	1513	Battle of Flodden Field and death of James IV of Scotland
	1911	First airmail service in Britain inaugurated
	1958	Notting Hill race riots
	1975	Martina Navratilova defected to the west
	1976	Death of Mao Tse-tung
10th	1894	George Smith became the first man to be convicted of drunken driving in Britain
11th	1973	Military coup in Chile. President Allende killed
12th	1978	BBC World Service newsreader Georgi Markov stabbed with a poisoned umbrella in a London street (he died four days later)
	1878	Erection of Cleopatra's needle on the Thames embankment
	1960	Introduction of MOT vehicle testing
	1974	Haile Selassie of Ethiopia overthrown in a military coup
	1977	Death of Steve Biko in police custody in South Africa
13th	1759	Battle of Quebec
14th	1752	Adoption of the Gregorian calendar in Britain
	1812	Napoleon entered Moscow
	1854	Beginning of the Crimean War
	1868	The first recorded "hole in one" (by Tom Morris at Prestwick)
	1901	Death of President McKinley of the USA after being shot on 6th September
15th	1830	Opening of the Liverpool and Manchester railway and death of Liverpool MP William Huskisson (the first man in Britain to be killed by a train)
	1916	First use of tanks in battle

	1940	The climax of the Battle of Britain, 185 German planes shot down in one day
	1975	The start of the Civil War in Beirut
16th	1861	First Post Office Savings Banks opened in Britain
	1968	Introduction of two-tier postal system in Britain (1st Class 5d., 2nd Class 4d.)
17th	1931	First demonstration of long playing records
	1944	Arnhem landings
	1980	Assassination of ex-president Somoza of Nicaragua
18th	1879	Blackpool illuminations switched on for the first time
	1961	Death of Dag Hammarskjoeld, Secretary General of the UN, in an air crash in Northern Rhodesia
	1981	France abolished the use of the guillotine
19th	1356	Battle of Poitiers
	1783	First manned balloon flight by the Montgolfier Brothers
	1893	New Zealand became the first country to grant women the vote
	1955	Military coup in Argentina, Juan Peron overthrown
	1960	First parking tickets were issued in London
20th	1967	QEII launched
	1984	Forty people killed when a truck filled with explosives crashed into the US Embassy in Beirut
21st	1745	Battle of Prestonpans
22nd	1934	Gresford Colliery disaster – 262 miners killed
	1955	Commercial television in Britain for the first time. First ITV transmission
	1980	Founding of the Solidarity movement in Gdansk, Poland
23rd	1940	George Cross instituted
	1973	Peron re-elected President of Argentina

24th	1776	Britain's oldest classic horse race, the St Leger, run for the first time
	1980	Start of the Iran-Iraq War
25th	1818	First blood transfusion using human blood performed at Guys Hospital, London
	1897	First motor bus service in Britain, opened in Bradford
	1957	Race riots at Little Rock, Arkansas, USA
26th	1580	Circumnavigation of the globe completed by Sir Francis Drake
	1934	The launch of the Queen Mary
27th	1825	Stockton–Darlington Railway opened
	1938	Launch of the Queen Elizabeth
28th	1970	Death of President Nasser of Egypt
	1978	Death of Pope John Paul I
29th	1399	Abdication of Richard II
	1952	Death of John Cobb on Loch Ness while attempting a world water speed record
	1983	Lady Mary Donaldson elected first woman Lord Mayor of London
30th	1938	Prime Minister Neville Chamberlain returned from Germany, making his famous "Peace in our time" speech
	1955	Death of James Dean in motor crash

October

1st	1918	Arab forces led by T. E. Lawrence captured Damascus from the Turks
	1938	German troops marched into the Sudetenland
	1985	Street riots in Toxteth, Liverpool
2nd	1187	Capture of Jerusalem by Moslem forces led by Saladin
	1901	Launch of Holland 1 (the Royal Navy's first submarine)
	1935	Invasion of Abyssinia by Italian forces
3rd	1929	The Kingdom of Serbs, Croats and Slovenes was renamed Yugoslavia

	1952	Britain's first atomic bomb exploded at the Monte Bello Islands, North of Australia
4th	1883	Founding of the Boys Brigade by Sir William Smith
	1957	Launch of Sputnik 1 satellite
	1959	Luna III photographed the dark side of the moon
5th	1930	Crash of the airship R101 near Paris, 48 people killed
	1936	Start of the Jarrow hunger march
	1952	The end of tea rationing in Britain
6th	1973	Start of Arab-Israeli war when Egypt and Syria attacked Israel
	1981	Assassination of Egyptian President Anwar Sadat
7th	1571	Battle of Lepanto
	1985	Palastinian terrorists seized the Italian liner Achille Lauro
8th	1871	Fire destroyed much of Chicago
	1952	Harrow rail disaster, 112 people killed
	1965	Opening of Britain's tallest building (the Post Office Tower)
	1967	First use of the breathalyser in Britain
9th	1914	Start of the Battle of Ypres
	1967	Che Guevara shot dead in Bolivia
10th	1899	Start of the Boer War
	1903	Women's Social and Political Union formed by Mrs Emmeline Pankhurst
	1973	American Vice-president Spiro Agnew resigned because of a tax scandal
11th	1957	Jodrell Bank radio telescope became operational
	1982	Raising of the Mary Rose in Portsmouth harbour
12th	1901	The Executive Mansion in Washington was officially renamed The White House

	1915	Execution of Nurse Edith Cavell by a German firing squad in Brussels
	1984	The Grand Hotel in Brighton was badly damaged by an IRA bomb during the week of the Conservative party conference
13th	54 AD	Roman emperor Claudius poisoned
	1988	Results of dating tests on the shroud of Turin proved that it is medieval in origin
14th	1066	Battle of Hastings
	1913	Mining disaster at Sengenhydd, South Wales. Over 400 miners killed
	1939	The battleship Royal Oak torpedoed and sunk in Scapa Flow
	1947	Sound barrier broken for the first time by Chuck Yeager in California
	1969	The 50p coin came into circulation in the UK
15th	1917	Execution of Dutch spy Mata Hari in Paris
	1945	Execution of Pierre Lavall, head of the Vichy government in France
	1946	Suicide of Herman Goering in Nuremberg Prison
	1962	Founding of Amnesty International in London
	1964	Nikita Khrushchev deposed while on holiday on the Black Sea coast
	1987	Britain's worst storms since records began
16th	1793	Execution of Marie Antoinette
	1834	Fire swept through the Palace of Westminster
	1859	Raid on the Harpers Ferry arsenal, Virginia by John Brown
	1902	First Borstal institution opened in Borstal, Kent
	1964	China exploded her first nuclear bomb Return of the first Labour Government for 13 years at the General Election
	1978	Karol Wojtyla, Archbishop of Cracow, elected Pope
17th	1651	Battle of Worcester

	1777	British forces surrendered to the American colonists at Saratoga
	1956	Opening of Britain's first nuclear power station at Calder Hall
18th	1887	USA purchased Alaska from Russia
	1922	Founding of the British Broadcasting Company (forerunner of the British Broadcasting Corporation)
	1963	Resignation of the Prime Minister Harold Macmillan
	1977	Hijacked German airliner stormed by German anti-terrorist troops at Mogadishu airport
19th	1216	Death of King John
	1987	Black Monday. Billions of pounds wiped off the value of shares
20th	1935	Mao Tse-tung's communist army completed their long march at Yenan
	1968	Marriage of Jackie Kennedy, widow of the late President John Kennedy, to Aristotle Onassis
	1973	Official opening of the Sydney Opera House
21st	1805	Battle of Trafalgar. Death of Horatio Nelson
	1958	Women peers took their seats in the House of Lords for the first time
	1966	Aberfan disaster, 116 children and 28 adults killed
22nd	1797	First parachute jump made by Andre-Jacques Garnerin from a hot-air balloon in Paris
	1931	Al Capone sentenced to 11 years' imprisonment for tax evasion
	1962	The Cuban missile crisis. USA imposed a naval blockade against Cuba
		William Vassall jailed for 18 years for passing naval secrets to the Soviet Union.
23rd	42 BC	Suicide of Brutus
	1642	Battle of Edgehill
	1956	Start of Hungarian revolt against Soviet rule
	1972	Launch of the Access credit card in Britain

	1987	Jockey Lester Piggott jailed for three years for tax evasion
24th	1537	Death of Queen Jane Seymour, third wife of Henry VIII, shortly after giving birth to Edward VI
	1908	Mrs Emmeline Pankhurst and her daughter Christabel sentenced to imprisonment for inciting riot
	1924	Publication of the Zinoviev letter, purporting to be from high Soviet sources inciting insurrection in Britain
	1929	Black Thursday – the Wall Street Crash
25th	1415	Battle of Agincourt
	1854	Charge of the Light Brigade at Balaclava
	1961	First edition of Private Eye magazine published
26th	899	Death of Alfred the Great
	1881	Gunfight at the OK Corral, Tombstone, Arizona
	1986	Jeffrey Archer resigned as deputy chairman of the Conservative Party after allegations of his involvement with a prostitute
27th	1951	Conservative win in the general election. Churchill Prime Minister again at the age of 77
28th	1636	Founding of Harvard University
	1962	Khrushchev announced that the USSR would withdraw all its missiles from Cuba, thus ending the Cuban missile crisis
29th	1618	Execution of Sir Walter Raleigh
	1863	Founding of the Red Cross
	1982	Lindy Chamberlain convicted of the murder of her nine-week old child in Australia (the Dingo Baby Case)
30th	1905	Aspirin went on sale in Britain for the first time

	1938	Widespread panic in the USA when Orson Welles's adaptation of War of the Worlds was broadcast
	1942	Beginning of the Battle of El Alamein
31st	1951	Introduction of zebra crossings in Britain
	1984	Assassination of Mrs Indira Gandhi, Prime Minister of India

November

1st	1755	Much of Lisbon destroyed by an earthquake. Tens of thousands killed
	1956	First Premium Bonds went on sale
2nd	1917	Publication of the Balfour declaration, promising Britain's support for the establishment of a Jewish state
	1959	Official opening of the first stretch of the M1 motorway
3rd	1957	Soviet Union launched a dog (Laika) into space in Sputnik 2
4th	1918	Death of the poet Wilfred Owen on the Western Front
	1946	Founding of UNESCO
	1979	Storming of the US Embassy in Tehran by Iranian students. Staff and guards held hostage
5th	1605	Discovery of the Gunpowder Plot
	1854	The Battle of Inkerman
	1909	First Woolworth store in Britain opened in Liverpool
	1927	Britain's first automatic traffic lights installed in Wolverhampton
6th	1924	Conservative victory in general election. Baldwin Prime Minister, Churchill Chancellor of the Exchequer
7th	1885	Completion of the Canadian Pacific Railway
	1974	Murder of Sandra Rivett, nanny in the household of Lord Lucan

8th	1923	The Beer Hall Putsch. Attempt by Hitler and his followers to seize power in Munich
	1932	Election of F. D. Roosevelt as President of the USA
	1987	Bomb planted by the IRA exploded at a Remembrance Day service in Enniskillen. Eleven people killed
9th	1859	Flogging abolished in the British Army
	1960	John F. Kennedy won the American Presidential election
	1970	Death of Charles de Gaulle
10th	1982	Death of Leonid Brezhnev
	1989	Work began on the demolition of the Berlin Wall
11th	1918	Signing of the armistice. End of the World War I
	1921	First "Poppy Day"
	1965	Unilateral declaration of independence by Ian Smith's Rhodesian government
12th	1035	Death of King Canute, English king and early deck chair pioneer
13th	1907	First helicopter flight, by Paul Cornu, near Lisieux in Normandy
	1947	Resignation of Chancellor of the Exchequer, Hugh Dalton, after his admission that he had leaked Budget secrets
14th	1922	First regular radio broadcast (a news bulletin)
	1948	Birth of HRH the Prince of Wales
	1952	First publication of music charts in Britain (in the New Musical Express)
	1963	Eruption of the Surtsey volcano near Iceland
	1969	Transmission of first colour TV programmes by BBCl and ITV
	1973	Marriage of Princess Anne and Captain Mark Phillips
15th	1899	Morning Post correspondent, Winston Churchill, captured by the Boers in South Africa

	1969	Screening of first TV advertisement in colour in Britain (Birds Eye Peas)
	1983	Mass protests as the first Cruise Missiles arrived at Greenham Common
16th	1869	Opening of the Suez Canal
17th	1558	Death of Mary I
	1800	First Congress of the USA
	1959	Duty-free goods on sale at British airports for the first time (Prestwick and Renfrew)
18th	1626	Consecration of St Peters in Rome
	1928	Showing of the first sound cartoon film (Steamboat Willie starring Mickey Mouse)
	1983	Mrs Janet Walton of Liverpool gave birth to sextuplets
	1987	Kings Cross Underground disaster. A fire started on an escalator resulting in the death of 30 people
19th	1863	Abraham Lincoln delivered his 'Gettysburg Address'
20th	1906	Founding of the Rolls Royce Company
	1945	Beginning of the Nuremberg war crimes trials
	1947	Marriage of HRH Princess Elizabeth and Lt. Philip Mountbatten
	1979	Russian spy Anthony Blunt stripped of his knighthood
21st	1831	Faraday delivered his lecture to the Royal Society on his experiments
22nd	1497	Vasco da Gama rounded the Cape of Good Hope
	1774	Suicide of Clive of India
	1946	The first ballpoint pens went on sale
	1963	Assassination of President John F. Kennedy in Dallas
23rd	1499	Execution of Perkin Warbeck (pretender to the English throne)
	1852	The first pillar box came into use
	1910	Execution of Dr Crippin at Holloway

24th	1859	Publication of Darwin's Origin of Species
	1963	Murder of Lee Harvey Oswald by Jack Ruby in Dallas
	1952	The opening of Agatha Christie's play The Mousetrap at the Ambassadors Theatre, London
25th	1953	Hungary became the first overseas country to win a soccer international on English soil when they beat England 6-3 at Wembley
26th	1942	Siege of Stalingrad lifted by Russian forces
27th	1914	Britain's first two police women began work in Grantham, Lincolnshire
	1942	Scuttling of the French fleet at Toulon
	1967	President de Gaulle vetoed Britain's application to join the EEC
	1975	Murder of Ross McWhirter by an IRA terrorist
28th	1660	Founding of the Royal Society
	1905	Founding of Sinn Fein by Arthur Griffith
29th	1530	Death of Cardinal Wolsey
	1929	Admiral Richard Byrd became the first man to fly over the South Pole
30th	1840	The remains of Napoleon Bonaparte were returned to Paris from St Helena
	1936	Crystal Palace destroyed by fire

December

1st	1942	Publication of the Beveridge Report
2nd	1697	Wren's new St Paul's Cathedral opened
	1804	Napoleon crowned Emperor of France
	1805	Battle of Austerlitz
	1901	Launch of the safety razor by King C. Gillette
	1942	World's first nuclear chain reaction (at the University of Chicago)

3rd	1967	First human heart transplantation at the Groote Schuur Hospital, Capetown by Dr Christiaan Barnard. The recipient was Louls Washkansky and the donor was Denise Darvall
4th	1791	Britain's oldest Sunday newspaper, The Observer, was published for the first time
	1961	The birth control pill became available on the National Health
5th	1872	The Marie Celeste found unmanned and drifting near the Azores
	1904	The Russian fleet was destroyed by the Japanese at Port Arthur
	1933	Prohibition came to an end in the USA
	1958	Opening of Britain's first motorway (the Preston Bypass) Inauguration of STD system in Britain by the Post Office
6th	1877	First recording of a human voice by Edison
	1921	Creation of the Irish Free State (and partition of Ireland)
	1975	Beginning of the Balcombe Street siege (it ended on 12th December without bloodshed)
7th	1732	Opening of Covent Garden Opera House (then called the Theatre Royal)
	1916	Lloyd George became Prime Minister (of Britain's coalition government)
	1941	Japanese attack on US fleet in Pearl Harbor
8th	1980	John Lennon shot dead by Mark Chapman outside the Dakota building in New York
9th	1868	Gladstone became Prime Minister for the first time
	1960	First screening of Coronation Street
10th	1768	Founding of the Royal Academy
	1901	Nobel prizes were awarded for the first time
	1984	Leak of poisonous gas at Union Carbide factory, Bhopal, India. Over 2,000 killed

11th	1894	The first ever Motor Show opened in Paris
	1936	Abdication of King Edward VIII
	1952	Derek Bentley and Christopher Craig found guilty of the murder of PC Sidney Miles. Craig who pulled the trigger was too young to hang but Bentley was executed a month later
12th	1988	Clapham Junction rail disaster, 35 people killed and over 100 injured
13th	1779	The first Smithfield Show
	1878	Britain's first street lighting was turned on at the Holborn Viaduct in London
	1939	Battle of the River Plate
14th	1799	Death of George Washington
	1861	Death of Prince Albert
	1911	Roald Amundsen reached the South Pole
	1918	Women vote for the first time in a British general election. Countess Markievicz became the first woman to be elected to the House of Commons (although she never took her seat)
15th	1916	End of the Battle of Verdun 700,000 dead
16th	1773	The Boston Tea Party, signalling the beginning of the American War of Independence
	1944	Beginning of the Ardennes offensive Band leader Glenn Miller presumed dead when his aircraft went missing over the English Channel
17th	1903	First aeroplane flight (by the Wright Brothers in North Carolina)
	1939	Scuttling of the German battleship Graf Spee in the River Plate
18th	1865	Ratification of the thirteenth amendment to the US constitution (abolishing slavery)
	1912	Discovery of the (later discredited): "Piltdown man" skull
19th	1984	Britain and China signed the agreement which will return Hong Kong to China in 1997

20th	1915	Evacuation of allied forces from their positions at Gallipoli
	1989	Overthrow of Panamanian general Manuel Noriega by invading American forces
21st	1620	Landing of the Pilgrim Fathers at Plymouth Rock, Massachusetts
	1913	Publication of the world's first crossword puzzle in The New York World
	1988	The Lockerbie disaster. Nearly 300 people were killed when a terrorist bomb destroyed a jumbo jet over the Scottish town of Lockerbie
22nd	1965	70 mph speed limit introduced in Britain
23rd	1948	Execution of Japanese Prime Minister Hideki Tojo for war crimes
24th	1914	The first bomb to be dropped by plane on British soil fell on Dover
	1979	Invasion of Afghanistan by Soviet troops
25th	1066	Coronation of William the Conqueror
	1932	First royal Christmas broadcast by reigning monarch
	1941	Hong Kong fell to Japanese forces
	1972	Massive earthquake devastated the Nicaraguan capital Managua
	1989	Assassination of Romanian dictator, Nicolae Ceausescu and his wife
26th	1898	Discovery of radium by Pierre and Marie Curie
	1908	Jack Johnson became the first black world heavyweight champion by beating Tommy Burns in Australia
	1943	Sinking of the German battleship Scharnhorst
27th	1879	Tay railway bridge disaster. The bridge collapsed under the weight of a train, 90 people were killed
29th	1170	Murder of Thomas Becket in Canterbury Cathedral

	1930	Radio Luxembourg began broadcasts
	1952	Discovery of a coelacanth off the coast of South Africa (the fish was believed to have been extinct for several millions of years)
30th	1916	Murder of the Russian mystic Rasputin
31st	1695	Introduction of the window tax
	1960	The farthing ceased to be legal tender at midnight

The Calendar – Days to remember

Some of these are well worth committing to memory as they do occur with
regularity.

Month	Date	
Month	*Date*	
January	6th	Epiphany
February	2nd	Candlemas
	14th	St Valentine's Day
March	1st	St David's Day
	9th	Commonwealth Day
	17th	St Patrick's Day
	25th	Lady Day
April	21st	Birthday of Her Majesty the Queen
	23rd	St George's Day
May	8th	V.E. Day (1945)
June	6th	D-Day (1944)
July	15th	St Swithin's Day
August	1st	Lammas Day
	15th	Feast of the Assumption
September	15th	Battle of Britain Day
	29th	Michaelmas
October	31st	Hallowe'en
November	1st	All Saints Day
	2nd	All Souls Day
	30th	St Andrew's Day

Advent Sunday is the nearest Sunday to St Andrew's Day, so
obviously it could be in either November or December. In the USA,
Thanksgiving Day is celebrated on the fourth Thursday in November
(so obviously it is a movable feast).

December	28th	Holy Innocents Day or Childermas

Canadian Provinces

For some reason the capital cities of Canadian provinces are not as popular with quiz setters as American state capitals. This is rather surprising as Canada is part of the British Commonwealth. However, they do crop up regularly in quizzes. Here they are:

Province	Capital City
Alberta	Edmonton
British Columbia	Victoria
Manitoba	Winnipeg
New Brunswick	Fredericton
Newfoundland	St John's
Nova Scotia	Halifax
Ontario	Toronto
Prince Edward Island	Charlottetown
Quebec	Quebec
Saskatchewan	Regina
North West Territories	Yellowknife
Yukon Territory	Whitehorse

Canals

An occasional subject for quiz questions but the following canals and their details are well worth remembering.

Fossdyke   The earliest canal built in Britain. Built by the Romans circa AD 65 and joined Lincoln to the River Trent at Torksey.

Kiel   Opened in 1895 and links the North Sea to the Baltic Sea. It is 61 miles long.

Manchester Ship   Opened in 1894 and links Manchester to the river Mersey at Eastham.
                        It is almost 40 miles long.

Panama   Opened in August 1914 and is almost 51 miles long linking Colon on the Caribbean Sea, it is cut in a north-west/south-easterly direction to Panama on the Pacific.

Suez   Opened on 16 November 1869, it is 100.6 miles long and runs from Port Said to Suez.

Volga–Baltic   1,800 miles. It is the longest canal in the world and links Astrakhan to St Petersburg.

Volga–Don   Opened in 1952 and is slightly over 62 miles long. It links the Black and Caspian Seas.

Welland   Opened in 1931 and circumvents Niagara Falls by linking Lakes Erie and Ontario.
                        It is 28 miles long.

Capital Cities

This was once one of the most common categories for quizzes but its popularity has waned somewhat over the last few years. It would be easy to list every one of the countries of the world and their capital cities but this is unnecessary. It is assumed that even the weakest of quiz players will know that the capital of France is Paris and that Lisbon is the capital of Portugal. This list, therefore, comprises countries whose capital cities may not be as widely known.

Country	Capital City
Albania	Tirana
Andorra	Andorra la Vella
Angola	Luanda
Antigua	St John's
Armenia	Yerevan
Azerbaijan	Baku
Bahamas	Nassau
Bahrain	Manama
Bangladesh	Dhaka
Barbados	Bridgetown
Belarus	Minsk
Belize	Belmopan
Benin	Porto-Novo
Bhutan	Thimphu
Bolivia	La Paz/Sucre (joint capitals)
Botswana	Gaborone
Brunei	Bandar Seri Begawan
Burkina Faso	Ouagadougou
Burundi	Bujumbura
Cambodia	Phnom-Penh
Cameroon	Yaoundé
Cape Verde	Praia
Central African Rep	Bangui
Chad	N'Djamena
Chile	Santiago
Colombia	Bogotá
Congo	Brazzaville

Country	Capital City
Costa Rica	San José
Croatia	Zagreb
Djibouti	Djibouti
Dominica	Roseau
Dominican Repub	Santo Domingo
Ecuador	Quito
El Salvador	San Salvador
Equatorial Guinea	Malabo
Estonia	Tallinn
Fiji	Suva
Gabon	Libreville
Gambia	Banjul
Georgia	Tbilisi
Ghana	Accra
Grenada	St George's
Guatemala	Guatemala City
Guinea	Conakry
Guinea-Bissau	Bissau
Guyana	Georgetown
Haiti	Port-au-Prince
Honduras	Tegucigalpa
Indonesia	Jakarta
Ivory Coast	Yamoussoukro/Abidjan (joint capitals)
Jamaica	Kingston
Jordan	Amman
Kazakhstan	Alma-Ata
Kenya	Nairobi
Kyrgyzstan	Bishkek
Kiribati	Bairiki (on Tarawa atoll)
Korea, North	Pyongyang
Korea, South	Seoul
Laos	Vientiane
Latvia	Riga
Lesotho	Maseru
Liberia	Monrovia

Country	Capital City
Libya	Tripoli
Liechtenstein	Vaduz
Lithuania	Vilnius
Macedonia	Skopje
Madagascar	Antananarivo
Malawi	Lilongwe
Malaysia	Kuala Lumpur
Maldives	Malé
Mali	Bamako
Malta	Valletta
Mauritania	Nouakchott
Mauritius	Port Louis
Moldova	Chisinau
Mongolia	Ulan Bator
Morocco	Rabat
Mozambique	Maputo
Myanmar (Burma)	Rangoon
Nepal	Kathmandu
Nicaragua	Managua
Niger	Niamey
Nigeria	Abuja (formerly Lagos)
Oman	Muscat
Pakistan	Islamabad
Palau	Koror
Papua New Guinea	Port Moresby
Paraguay	Asunción
Peru	Lima
Philippines	Manila
Qatar	Doha
Rwanda	Kigali
St Christopher & Nevis	Basseterre
St Lucia	Castries
St Vincent	Kingstown
Saudi Arabia	Riyadh
Senegal	Dakar

Country	Capital City
Seychelles	Victoria
Sierra Leone	Freetown
Slovakia	Bratislava
Slovenia	Ljubljana
Solomon Islands	Honiara
Somalia	Mogadishu
Sri Lanka	Colombo/Kotte (joint capitals)
Sudan	Khartoum
Suriname	Paramaribo
Swaziland	Mbabane/Lobamba (joint capitals)
Syria	Damascus
Tajikistan	Dushanbe
Taiwan	Taipei
Tanzania	Dodoma
Togo	Lomé
Tonga	Nuku'alofa
Trinidad & Tobago	Port of Spain
Turkmenistan	Ashkhabad
Tuvalu	Fongafale (on Funafuti)
Uganda	Kampala
Ukraine	Kiev
Uruguay	Montevideo
Uzbekistan	Tashkent
Vanuatu	Port-Vila
Venezuela	Caracas
Vietnam	Hanoi
Western Samoa	Apia
Yemen	Sana'a
Zaire	Kinshasa
Zambia	Lusaka
Zimbabwe	Harare

Parts of a castle

Merlons, mottes and loopholes. It is unlikely that these are matters of life and death any longer, but knowing what they are could make the difference between winning and losing a quiz.

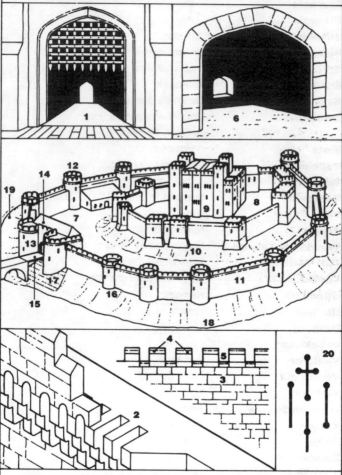

1. Portcullis 2. Machicolation 3. Battlements or crenellation 4. Merlon
5. Crenel or embrasure 6. Casemate 7. Outer ward or bailey 8. Inner ward or bailey 9. Keep or donjon 10. Motte or mound 11. Curtain wall 12.13. Turret 14. Gatehouse 15. Drawbridge 16. Scarp 17. Revetment 18. Ditch or moat 19. Counterscarp 20. Loopholes

Catchphrases

Catchphrases are a bit like signature tunes, everybody used to have one. This list includes those catchphrases which are associated with characters rather than the performor.

Arthur Askey	I thank you
Hilda Baker	She knows you know
Max Bygraves	I've arrived, and to prove it, I'm here
Charlie Chester	I say, what a smasher
Reg Dixon	I've been proper poorly
Charlie Drake	Hello my darlings
Jimmy Edwards	Wake up at the back there
Bruce Forsyth	I'm in charge
Joyce Grenfell	Don't do that, George
Wilfred Pickles	Give him the money Barney
Ken Platt	I won't take me coat off, I'm not stopping
Sandy Powell	Can you hear me Mother
Jack Train	I don't mind if I do
Tommy Trinder	You lucky people
Jack Warner	Mind my bike
Jimmy Wheeler	Ay, ay, that's your lot
Rob Wilton	The day war broke out

Cathedral and church

Perhaps sixty or so years ago when we were a more church-going nation everybody knew the geography of a cathedral and a church but these illustrations should jog the memory.

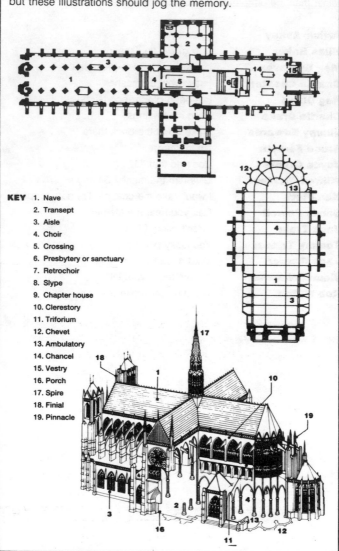

KEY
1. Nave
2. Transept
3. Aisle
4. Choir
5. Crossing
6. Presbytery or sanctuary
7. Retrochoir
8. Slype
9. Chapter house
10. Clerestory
11. Triforium
12. Chevet
13. Ambulatory
14. Chancel
15. Vestry
16. Porch
17. Spire
18. Finial
19. Pinnacle

Chaucer's Canterbury Pilgrims

Always useful to know these, particularly the order in which they come. So here they are:

1   The Knight's Tale
2   The Miller's Tale
3   The Reeve's Tale
4   The Cook's Tale
5   The Man of Law's Tale
6   The Wife of Bath's Tale
7   The Friar's Tale
8   The Summoner's Tale
9   The Clerk's Tale
10 The Merchant's Tale
11 The Squire's Tale
12 The Franklin's Tale
13 The Physician's Tale
14 The Pardoner's Tale
15 The Shipman's Tale
16 The Prioress's Tale
17 Chaucer's Tale of St Thopas
18 Chaucer's Tale of Melibeus
19 The Monk's Tale
20 The Nun's Priest's Tale
21 The Second Nun's Tale
22 The Canon's Yeoman's Tale
23 The Manciple's Tale
24 The Parson's Tale

Chemical Compounds

Old favourites these. Every quiz player should know them. Some of them should be obvious, but to the non-scientific this list will prove useful.

Aspirin	Acetylsalicylic acid
Baking Soda	Sodium hydrogencarbonate
Chalk	Calcium carbonate
Epsom Salts	Magnesium sulphate
Laughing Gas	Nitrous oxide
Marsh Gas	Methane
Plaster of Paris	Calcium sulphate
Salt	Sodium chloride
Vinegar	Ethanoic Acid
Washing Soda	Sodium carbonate

Chemical Elements

Truly scientific questions are rare in pub quizzes, but chemical elements and their symbols occur time and time again. As with most sections in the book this is not a fully comprehensive list, nor is it intended to be – the chemical symbols for carbon, lead, oxygen and sulphur are known to everybody, and certain elements such as terbium never occur in quizzes.

Chemical Element	Symbol	Chemical Element	Symbol
Aluminium	Al	**Magnesium**	Mg
Antimony	Sb	**Manganese**	Mn
Argon	Ar	**Mercury**	Hg
Arsenic	As	**Neon**	Ne
Barium	Ba	**Nickel**	Ni
Bismuth	Bi	**Phosphorus**	P
Boron	B	**Platinum**	Pt
Bromine	Br	**Plutonium**	Pu
Cadmium	Cd	**Potassium**	K
Californium	Cf	**Radium**	Ra
Caesium	Cs	**Radon**	Rn
Chlorine	Cl	**Silver**	Ag
Chromium	Cr	**Sodium**	Na
Cobalt	Co	**Tin**	Sn
Gold	Au	**Tungsten**	W
Helium	He	**Uranium**	U
Lithium	Li		

Chinese Zodiac

The Chinese year changes in January or February and invariably at that time of the year questions like "1995 is the Chinese year of the what?" will crop up. The years are named after animals and there are twelve of them. Here they are alongside the year of the Christian calendar in which the new year begins.

1994	Dog
1995	Pig
1996	Rat
1997	Ox
1998	Tiger
1999	Rabbit
2000	Dragon
2001	Snake
2002	Horse
2003	Sheep
2004	Monkey
2005	Chicken

Cinque Ports

The original five Ports were:

Hastings
Sandwich
Dover
Romney
Hythe

Winchelsea and Rye were added subsequently.
The official residence of the Lord Warden of the Cinque Ports is Walmer Castle.

Cocktails

"Which spirit forms the base for 'xx cocktail'?" This is quite a common quiz question and it is always useful to know the ingredients of popular cocktails. The proportions of the ingredients to each other are never asked in quiz questions so this section confines itself to merely listing the ingredients.

Cocktail	Ingredients
Alexander	Cognac, creme de cacao and cream
Between the Sheets	Brandy, Cointreau, dark rum and lemon juice
Bronx	Gin, French vermouth, Italian vermouth and orange
Bucks Fizz	Champagne and orange juice
John Collins	Gin, lemon juice, spoonful of sugar and soda water
Tom Collins	Gin, lemon juice, castor sugar and soda
Cuba Libra	Dark rum, lime and cola
Daiquiri	Dark rum, lemon juice, lime juice and castor sugar
Gimlet	Gin and lime
Gin Sling	Gin, lemon juice and sugar
Harvey Wallbanger	Vodka, orange juice and Galiano
Highball	Scotch or bourbon, dash of Angostura bitters and ginger ale
Manhattan	Whisky or bourbon, Italian vermouth and a touch of Angostura bitters
Marguerita	Tequila, Cointreau and lemon or lime juice
Monkey Gland	Gin, grenadine and orange
Old Fashioned	Rye whisky, dash of Angostura bitters and a sugar lump
Pina Colada	Dark rum, coconut milk and crushed pineapple
Pink Lady	Egg white and grenadine
Planters Punch	Rum, lime, sugar and a dash of Angostura bitters

Rob Roy	Scotch, French vermouth, Italian vermouth with a dash of Angostura bitters
Rusty Nail	Scotch and Drambuie
Screwdriver	Vodka and fresh orange juice
Sidecar	Brandy, Cointreau and lemon juice
Singapore Sling	Gin, lemon juice, sugar, dash of Angostura bitters
Stinger	Brandy and creme de menthe
White Lady	Gin, Cointreau and lemon juice

Collective Nouns

This subject crops up time after time in quizzes. Although not in general usage, these unusual collective nouns are much favoured by quiz setters. Common collective nouns such as "herd" have not been included in this list.

Badgers	Cete
Bears	Sloth
Budgerigars	Chatter
Choughs	Chattering
Coots	Covert
Cranes	Sedge or a Siege
Crows	Murder
Curlews	Herd
Donkeys	Drove
Ducks (in flight)	Team, Flush or Plump
Eagles	Convocation
Elk	Gang
Ferrets	Fesnyng or Business
Foxes	Skulk or Earth
Frogs	Army or a Colony
Geese (in flight)	Skein
Geese (on the ground)	Gaggle
Goats	Tribe or Trip
Goldfinches	Charm
Goldfish	Troubling
Grouse	Covey
Hares	Down or Husk
Hawks	Cast
Hedgehogs	Array
Herons	Sedge or a Siege
Kangaroos	Troop
Kittens	Kindle
Larks	Exultation
Leopards	Leap
Magpies	Tiding or a Tittering
Mares	Stud

Moles	Labour or a Movement
Monkeys	Troop
Nightingales	Watch
Owls	Parliament
Partridges	Covey
Peacocks	Muster
Penguins	Rookery or a Colony
Pheasants	Nye or Nide or Ostentation
Plover	Wing or a Congregation
Quail	Bevy
Rooks	Building or a Clamour
Seals	Herd or a Pod
Snakes	Den or a Pit
Spiders	Cluster or a Clutter
Starlings	Chattering or a Murmuration
Swans	Herd or a Bevy
Teals	Spring
Thrush	Mutation
Tigers	Ambush
Toads	Knab or a Knot
Turkeys	Dule or a Raffle
Woodcock	Fall or Plump
Woodpeckers	Descent

Comic Characters and Heroes

All of the characters in this section started life in comics or comic strips, although many of them graduated to stardom in films.

Character	Created by	Additional Info
Asterix (The Gaul)	Albert Uderzo and René Goscinny	
Batman	Bob Kane for Detective Comics in 1939	Real Name: Bruce Wayne Home Town: Gotham City
Biggles	Captain W. E. Johns	Full Name: James Bigglesworth
Charlie Brown	Charles M. Schulz	
Andy Capp	Reg Smythe	First appeared in the Daily Mirror in 1957
Captain America	Joe Simon and Jack Kirby	First appeared in 1941 Alter Ego: Steve Rogers
Captain Marvel	C. C. Beck	Appeared in Whiz comics in 1940 Alter Ego: Billy Batson Used the magic word Shazam
Conan, the Barbarian	Robert E. Howard	First appeared in Weird Tales magazine in 1932
Dan Dare	Frank Hampson	First appeared in the Eagle comic in 1950. Arch rival The Mekon
Dennis the Menace (British version)	David Law	First appeared in the Beano comic in 1951. Has a dog named Gnasher
Desperate Dan	Dudley Watkins	First appeared in the Dandy in 1937. Lives in Cactusville

Mike Doonesbury	Gary Trudeau	First appeared in 1968 now a cartoon strip in the Guardian
Flook	Wally Fawkes (Trog)	First appeared in the Daily Mail in 1949
Flash Gordon	Alex Raymond	First appeared in 1934. Arch enemy: Ming the Merciless
Fritz the Cat	Robert Crumb	First appeared in Cavalier magazine in 1968
Garfield	Drawn by cartoonist Jim Davis	
Hagar the Horrible	Dik Browne	Married to Helga
Incredible Hulk	Stan Lea	First appeared in Marvel comics in 1962 Alter Ego: Dr Bruce Banner
Jane	Norman Pett	First appeared in the Daily Mirror in 1932
Krazy Kat	George Herriman	Appeared in 1910. Has a friend, Ignatz Mouse
Li'l Abner	Al Capp	Appeared in 1934 Girlfriend is Daisy Mae Hometown: Dogpatch
Lone Ranger (Included here, even though he was created for a radio series)	George Trendle and Fran Striker	Real name: John Reid
Barry MacKenzie	Barry Humphreys and Nicholas Garland	Cartoon strip first appeared in Private Eye in 1970

Minnie the Minx	Leo Baxendale	First appeared in the Beano in 1953
Oor Wullie	Dudley Watkins	First appeared in the Sunday Post in 1936
Popeye	Elzie Segar	First appeared in Thimble Theater magazine in 1929. Son of: Poopdeck Pappy Home: Island of Sweetwater Name of his ship: The Olive
Roy Race (Roy of the Rovers)	Frank Pepper and Joe Colquohoun	First appeared in Tiger comic in 1954 Player and Manager of Melchester Rovers
Rupert Bear	Mary Toutel	First appeared in the Daily Express in 1920 Artist: Alfred Bestall (who later wrote the narratives for the cartoons) Home town: Nutwood Friends include: Edward Trunk, Bingo the Brainy Pup and Bill Badger
Lord Snooty	Dudley Watkins	First appeared in the Beano in 1938
Spiderman	Stan Lea and Steve Ditko	First appeared in Marvel comics in 1962 **Alter Ego:** Peter Parker (photographer for the Daily Bugle)

Superman	Jerome Seigel and Joe Schuster	First appeared in Action comics in 1938 **Alter Ego:** Clark Kent (a newspaper reporter) Son of: Jor-El and Lara Lor-Van Childhood spent in Smallville Works in the City of Metropolis at the Daily Planet
Tarzan (included here even though he was not originally a cartoon or comic strip character)	Edgar Rice Burroughs	First appeared in All-Story magazine 1912 Real name: John Clayton (Lord Greystoke) Foster mother: Kala (a female ape) Girlfriend (and later, wife) Jane Porter (daughter of Archimedes Q. Porter)
Tin-Tin	Hergé (George Rémi)	First appeared in 1929 Has a dog named Snowy
Dick Tracy	Chester Gould	First appeared in 1931
Wonder Woman		First appeared in All-Star comics in 1941 **Alter Ego:** Diana Prince (a Major in the US Army)
Zorro	Johnston McCulley	Appeared, 1919, in All-Story magazine Real name: Don Diego de la Vega Zorro is the Spanish for fox

Computer Terminology

An attempt by question setters to appear up to date; throw in a question about computers among the old chestnuts and give the quiz a 20th-century look. Unfortunately many of these questions have become silicon chestnuts; I have lost count of the number of times that the acronym ROM has cropped up. However, as the object of this book is to identify such things, here we go.

ALGOL	Algorithmic Oriented Language
BASIC	Beginners' All-Purpose Symbolic Instruction Code
Bit	From Binary digIT. The smallest unit of information. There are 8 bits in a byte
Bootstrap	The process of starting up a computer
COBOL	Common Business Oriented Language
DOS	Disc Operating System
FORTRAN	Formula Translation
GIGO	Garbage in, garbage out
K	kilobyte (1024 bytes)
M	megabyte (1024 kilobytes)
OS	Operating system
Pixel	From picture element – a single dot
RAM	Random access memory
RISC	Reduced instruction – set computer
ROM	Read-only memory
WYSIWYG	What you see is what you get

Continental Extremities

Another of those "silly" type of questions which have no importance whatsoever, but attract question setters. Here they are. In all cases these are *mainland* extremities, offshore islands have not been included.

Africa

Eastern	Cape Hafun
Western	Cape Almadies
Northern	Ras Benn Sekka
Southern	Cape Agulhas

Asia

Eastern	Cape Dezhnev
Western	Cape Baba
Northern	Cape Chelyubinsk
Southern	Cape Piai

Europe

Eastern	As the eastern extremity of Europe is in the centre of a land mass there is no fixed named point
Western	Cape Roca
Northern	Nordkynn
Southern	Point Tarifa

North America

Eastern	A point just south of Battle Harbour, Newfoundland
Western	Cape Prince of Wales
Northern	Tip of the Boothia Peninsula
Southern	The south-western border of Panama

South America

Eastern	Point Coqueiros
Western	Point Parinas
Northern	Point Gallinas
Southern	Cape Forward

Counties – Administrative Headquarters

The location of many Administrative Headquarters are obvious (Norfolk and Norwich, Cheshire and Chester) so these have been excluded from this list. The less obvious locations are favoured by question setters, and here they are.

Berkshire	Reading
Borders	Newton St Boswells
Central Scotland	Stirling
Clwyd	Mold
Cornwall	Truro
Derbyshire	Matlock
Devon	Exeter
Dyfed	Carmarthen
East Sussex	Lewes
Essex	Chelmsford
Grampian	Aberdeen
Gwent	Cwmbran
Gwynedd	Caernarfon
Hampshire	Winchester
Highland	Inverness (Regional Council meets at Dingwall)
Humberside	Beverley
Isle of Wight	Newport
Kent	Maidstone
Lancashire	Preston
Lothian	Edinburgh
Mid Glamorgan	Cardiff (which is in South Glamorgan)
Northumberland	Morpeth
North Yorkshire	Northallerton
Orkney	Kirkwall
Powis	Llandrindod Wells
South Glamorgan	Cardiff
Surrey	Kingston Upon Thames
Tayside	Dundee
West Glamorgan	Swansea
West Sussex	Chichester
West Yorkshire	Wakefield
Western Isles	Stornoway
Wiltshire	Trowbridge

Countries – Previous Names

Many countries have changed their names during the last 50 years, particularly in Africa where many of the new independent states were part of the old European colonial empires. This has long been a favourite hunting ground for question setters. The following is a list of the countries, with their previous names.

Name of Country	Previous Name
Bangladesh	East Pakistan
Belize	British Honduras
Benin	Dahomey (and prior to that part of French West Africa)
Bolivia	Upper Peru
Botswana	Bechuanaland
Burkina Faso	Upper Volta (and prior to that part of French West Africa)
Burundi	Formerly part of Ruanda-Urundi
Cambodia	People's Republic of Kampuchea (1979–1989) Democratic Kampuchea (1976–1979) Khmer Republic (1970–1976) and prior to that Cambodia
Ubangi-Shari	French Equatorial Africa
Congo	Formerly part of French Equatorial Africa (not to be confused with the old Belgian Congo)
Djibouti	French Territory of the Afars and the Issass (1967–1977) Prior to that French Somaliland
Equitorial Guinea	Formed by a merger of two Spanish territories – Rio Muni and Fernando Po
Ethiopia	Abyssinia
Gabon	Formerly part of French Equatorial Africa
Ghana	The Gold Coast (also former British Togoland)

Name of Country	Previous Name
Guinea	French Guinea (part of French West Africa)
Guinea-Bissau	Portuguese Guinea
Guyana	British Guiana
Indonesia	Dutch East Indies
Iran	Persia
Ivory Coast (Cote d'Ivoire)	Formerly part of French West Africa
Jordan	Transjordan
Kiribati	The Gilbert Islands
Lesotho	Basutoland
Malawi	Nyasaland
Mali	French Sudan (part of French West Africa)
Mauritania	Formerly part of French West Africa
Myanmar	Burma
Namibia	South West Africa
Niger	Formerly part of French West Africa
Oman	Muscat and Oman
Panama	Formerly a province of Colombia
Rwanda	Formerly part of Ruanda (Urundi) and prior to that part of German East Africa
Senegal	Formerly part of French West Africa
Sri Lanka	Ceylon
Suriname	Dutch Guiana
Taiwan	Formosa
Tanzania	Formed by the merger of Tanganyika and Zanzibar
Thailand	Siam
Tuvalu	Ellice Islands
Uruguay	Formerly part of Brazil
Vanuatu	New Hebrides
Vietnam	Formerly part of French Indo-China
Yemen (People's Democratic Republic)	Aden

Name of Country	Previous Name
Zaire	Belgian Congo
Zambia	Northern Rhodesia
Zimbabwe	Rhodesia (prior to that, Southern Rhodesia)

Currencies

As with the case of capital cities, all of the world's currencies could be listed here. However, that would be simply a waste of space. It is assumed that everybody knows the currency of the USA is the dollar and that of Germany is the Deutschmark The currencies of many small African countries are never asked in quizzes. This is a list of the countries whose currencies you will most likely to be asked in a quiz.

Country	Currency
Albania	Lek
Algeria	Dinar
Andorra	French and Spanish currencies are legal tender
Argentina	Austral
Austria	Schilling
Bangladesh	Taka
Bolivia	Boliviano (superseded the Peso in 1987)
Brazil	Cruzeiro
Bulgaria	Lev
Cambodia	Riel
Chile	Peso
China	Yuan (also known as the Renminbiao)
Colombia	Peso
Cyprus	Cyprus pound
Czech Republic	Koruna
Denmark	Krone
Ecuador	Sucre
Egypt	Egyptian pound
Finland	Markka (also known as the Finnmark)
Ghana	Cedi

Currency	Country
Greece	Drachma
Guatemala	Quetzal
Haiti	Courde
Hungary	Forint
Iceland	Krona
Indonesia	Rupiah
Iran	Rial
Iraq	Dinar
Israel	Shekel
Jordan	Dinar
Kenya	Shilling
Korea (North)	Won
Korea (South)	Won
Kuwait	Dinar
Laos	Kip
Lebanon	Lebanese pound
Libya	Dinar
Liechtenstein	Swiss franc
Malaysia	Ringgit (also known as the Malaysian dollar)
Mongolia	Tugrik
Morocco	Dirham
Myanmar	Kyat (pronounced chat)
Nicaragua	Cordoba
Nigeria	Naira
Norway	Kroner
Pakistan	Rupee
Panama	Balboa
Paraguay	Guarani
Peru	New sol
Philippines	Peso
Poland	Zloty
Romania	Leu (plural lei)
San Marino	Italian lira
Saudi Arabia	Riyal
Sri Lanka	Rupee
Sudan	Dinar

Country	Currency
Suriname	Suriname Guilder
Sweden	Kronor
Syria	Syrian pound
Thailand	Baht
Tunisia	Dinar
Turkey	Turkish lira
Uganda	Shilling
Venezuela	Bolivar
Vietnam	Dong
Zaire	Zaire
Zambia	Kwacha

If not listed here, a good guide to the currency of a country is as follows:

Hispanic countries
   - the Peso

Commonwealth countries
   - the dollar

Dams

Considering their importance, dams do not crop up in quizzes as often as one would expect. When questions on dams do occur they usually relate to only a handful of structures. Here they are:

Name of Dam	Year of Completion	River
Aswan High Dam	1970	Nile
Grand Coulee	1942	Columbia
Hoover	1936	Colorado
Kariba	1959	Zambezi
Tarbela	1975	Indus

Dickens – Dickensian Characters

Questions on the works of Charles Dickens are concerned almost entirely with the characters in his novels. In many cases these questions relate to minor characters but are asked because of the unusual names they possess, however the same names crop up time and time again. If you know which characters appear in which books you are almost there in answering Dickensian questions correctly. The following is a list of Dickens's novels and the characters therein.

There are literally hundreds of characters but the following should enable you to cope with most Dickensian questions.

Barnaby Rudge	Barnaby's pet raven, Grip
	Sir John Chester
	Edward Chester
	Geoffrey Haredale
	Emma Haredale
	Gabriel Varden
	Dolly Varden
	John and Joe Willett
Bleak House	Richard Carstone
	His cousin, Ada Clare
	John Jarndyce
	Sir Leicester Dedlock
	Lady Dedlock
	Esther Summerson (the illegitimate daughter of Lady Dedlock)
	Captain Hawdon
	Sir Leicester Dedlock's lawyer, Tulkinghorn
	Dr Allan Woodcourt
David Copperfield	Mr Edward Murdstone (Copperfield's stepfather)
	His sister, Miss Jane Murdstone
	Mr Creakle (the headmaster)
	James Steerforth
	Tom Traddles
	Mr Wilkins Micawber
	Betsey Trotwood
	Barkis

Clara and Daniel Peggotty

Uriah Heep

Dora Spenlow (Copperfield's first wife)

Agnes Wickfield (Copperfield's second wife)

A Christmas Carol   Ebenezer Scrooge

The ghost of his ex-partner, Jacob Marley

Bob Cratchit (Scrooge's clerk)

His crippled son, Tiny Tim

Dombey And Son   Mr Dombey, head of the shipping company which bears his name

His son, Paul

His daughter, Florence

Walter Gay (later the husband of Florence)

Edith Granger (Mr Dombey's second wife)

James Carker (Dombey's manager)

Solomon Gills (uncle of Walter Gay)

Captain Cuttle

Susan Nipper

Major Bagstock

Great Expectations   Philip Pirrip (Pip)

Joe Gargery (Pip's brother-in-law and widower of Pip's sister)

Biddy Gargery (Joe's wife)

Miss Havisham

Estella

Bentley Drummle (who marries Estella)

Abel Magwitch (former convict and Pip's benefactor)

Pip's friend, Herbert Pocket

Mr Jaggers, the lawyer

Hard Times   Thomas Gradgrind of Coketown *(believed to be based on Preston)*

His children: Louisa and Tom

Josiah Bounderby (to marry Louisa)

James Harthouse

Stephen Blackpool

Little Dorrit

The book centres around the Debtors Prison of Marshalsea

William Dorrit

His children: Amy (the title character of the book)

             Fanny

             Tip

Arthur Clennam

His swindling mother, Mrs Clennam

Jeremiah Flintwinch

Monsieur Rigaud

Mr and Mrs Merdle

The Meagles family

The Gowan family

Martin Chuzzlewit

Martin Chuzzlewit (the title character)

His grandfather, Martin Chuzzlewit

Mary Graham (whom Martin marries)

Mr Seth Pecksniff

His daughters: Mercy

             Charity

Mark Tapley

Jonas Chuzzlewit (Martin's cousin)

Tom Pinch (Pecksmith's assistant)

His sister, Ruth

Mrs Sarah Gamp (the drunken midwife)

The Mystery Of Edwin Drood

(Dickens's unfinished novel)

Set in Cloisterham and featuring Miss Twinkleton's school there

Edwin Drood

Rosa Bud

John Jasper (Edwin's uncle)

Neville and Helena Landless

Mr Grewgious (Rosa's guardian)

Mr Crisparkle

Mr Tartar

Mr Sapsea

Mr Honeythunder

Nicholas Nickleby	Nicholas
	His sister, Kate
	Their uncle, Ralph Nickleby
	Wackford Squeers (proprietor of Dotheboys Hall)
	Smike (the illegitimate son of Ralph Nickleby)
	The Cheeryble Brothers (Ned and Charles)
	Their nephew, Frank (later to marry Kate)
	Arthur Gride
	Madeline Bray (whom Nicholas marries)
The Old Curiosity Shop	Nell Trent (Little Nell)
	Her brother, Fred
	Their grandfather
	Dick Swiveller (friend of Fred)
	Daniel Quilp
	Sampson Brass
	His sister, Sally
	Kit Nubbles
	Mr and Mrs Garland
	Codlin and Short (the Punch and Judy Men)
Oliver Twist	Oliver
	Mr Bumble, the beadle
	Fagin
	Bill Sikes
	Nancy (Sikes's mistress)
	Jack Dawkins (the Artful Dodger)
	Mr Brownlow
Our Mutual Friend	John Harmon (alias John Rokesmith)
	Bella Wilfer (whom John marries)
	Mr and Mrs Boffin
	Silas Wegg
	Eugene Wrayburn
	Lizzy Hexam
	Bradley Headstone
	The Veneerings

Pickwick Papers	Rogue Riderhood	
	Jenny Wren	
	Samuel Pickwick	⎫ Members of
	Tracy Tupman	⎬ the Pickwick
	Augustus Snodgrass	⎭ Club
	Nathaniel Winkle	
	Sam Weller (Pickwick's servant)	
	Mr Wardle	
	His sister, Emily	
	Alfred Jingle	
	Job Trotter (Jingle's servant)	
	Mrs Bardell	
	Dowler	
	The brother and sister, Arabella and	
	Benjamin Allen	
	(Arabella weds Mr Winkle)	
	Mr Nupkins	
	Bob Sawyer	
A Tale Of Two Cities	Dr Manette	
(London and Paris)	His daughter, Lucie	
	Charles Darnay	
	Sydney Carton	
	Madame Defarge	
	Jerry Cruncher	
	Mr Jarvis Lorry	

Dying Words

Every quiz player has his suspicions about these. They are almost invariably heroic or saintly. For many years George V's dying words were believed to be "How is the empire?" although it was strongly believed that he said something else (see below). It was only in 1992 that the palace actually confirmed what his last words were. Here is a list of the dying words commonly attributable to these famous people.

Person	Dying Words
Prince Albert	"I have such sweet thoughts"
Archimedes	"Wait 'til I have finished my problem"
Francis Bacon	"My name and memory I leave to men's charitable speeches, to foreign nations and the next age"
Thomas Becket	"I am prepared to die for Christ and his Church"
Beethoven	"I shall hear in heaven"
Anne Boleyn	"The executioner is, I believe, very expert, and my neck is very slender"
Robert Burns	"Don't let the awkward squad fire over my grave"
Lord Byron	"I must sleep now"
Julius Caesar	"et tu Brute?"
Nurse Edith Cavell	"Patriotism is not enough. I must have no hatred or bitterness towards anyone"
Charles I	*(Immediately before his execution)* "Remember"
Charles II	"I have been a most unconscionable time dying, but I hope you will excuse it"
Christopher Columbus	"Lord into Thy hands I commend my spirit"
Copernicus	"Now, O Lord, set Thy servant free"
Oliver Cromwell	"My design is to make what haste I can and be gone"
Charles Darwin	"I am not in the least afraid to die"

Person	*Dying Words*
Edward I	"Carry my bones before you on your march, for the rebels will not be able to endure the sight of me alive or dead"
Elizabeth I	"All my possessions for a moment of time"
Thomas Gainsborough	"We are all going to heaven and Van Dyke is of the company"
George V	"Bugger Bognor!"
Hannibal	"Let us now relieve the Romans of their fears by the death of a feeble old man"
Henry VIII	"All is lost! Monks, Monks, Monks"
Joan of Arc	"Jesus, Jesus, Jesus, blessed be God"
Hugh Latimer	"Be of good comfort Mr Ridley and play the man, we shall this day light such a candle by God's grace in England as I trust never shall be put out"
Louix XVI	"Frenchmen I die guiltless of the crimes imputed to me. Pray God my blood falls not on France"
Machiavelli	"I love my country more than my soul"
Mary Tudor	"You will find the word Calais written on my heart"
Michelangelo	"My soul I resign to God, my body to the earth, my worldly goods to my next of kin"
Duke of Monmouth	*(To his executioner)* "There are six guineas for you if you do not hack me as you did my Lord Russell"
St Thomas More	*(on ascending the scaffold)* "See me safe up; for my coming down let me shift for myself"
Horatio, Lord Nelson	"Thank God I have done my duty, kiss me Hardy"
Nero	"What an artist the world is losing in me"

Person	Dying Words
Sir Isaac Newton	"I don't know what I may have seemed to the world. But as to myself I seem to have been only like a boy playing on the seashore and diverting myself in now and then finding a smoother pebble or prettier shell than ordinary, whilst the great ocean of truth lay all undiscovered before me"
Lord Palmerston	"Die, my dear doctor! That's the last thing I shall do"
William Pitt (the younger)	"My country! How I leave my country" *(There is also a belief that his dying words were a request for a veal pie!)*
Edgar Allan Poe	"Lord help my soul"
Sir Walter Raleigh	*(On the scaffold)* "It matters little how the head lies, so the heart be right"
Cecil Rhodes	"So little done so much to do"
Richard III	"Treason, treason"
Sir Walter Scott	"God bless you all, I feel myself again"
Sir Thomas Strafford	"Put not your trust in princes"
Vespasian	"I suppose I am now becoming a god"
Queen Victoria	"Oh that peace may come"
General Wolfe	"What, do they run already? I die happy"
Cardinal Wolsey	"Had I but served my God as diligently as I have served the King he would not have given me over in my grey hairs"
William Wordsworth	"God bless you! Is that you Dora?"

Film Directors and their Films

This is a tricky one. Most decent quiz setters will throw in a current box office hit and ask who directed it; the problem is that today's box office success is tomorrow's forgotten movie. I have therefore confined this section to films which have stood the test of time and are question setters' favourites. Oscar-winning movies have their own section in this publication, and some of the films listed below may have had that honour bestowed upon them. I have omitted the glaringly obvious (Hitchcock and Woody Allen for example).

Robert Aldrich	Whatever Happened to Baby Jane
	The Dirty Dozen
Robert Altman	M*A*S*H
Warren Beatty	Heaven Can Wait
	Reds
Bernardo Bertolucci	Last Tango in Paris
	The Last Emperor
Francis Ford Coppola	The Godfather
	Apocalypse Now
Cecil B. de Mille	The Ten Commandments (twice)
Jonathan Demme	The Silence of the Lambs
Sergei Eisenstein	The Battleship Potemkin
	Alexander Nevsky
Federico Fellini	La Dolce Vita
	Eight and a Half
Victor Fleming	The Wizard of Oz
	Gone With the Wind
John Ford	Stagecoach
	The Grapes of Wrath
	My Darling Clementine
	How the West was Won
William Friedkin	The French Connection
	The Exorcist
D. W. Griffith	The Birth of a Nation
	Intolerance
Howard Hawks	To Have and Have Not
	The Big Sleep

George Roy Hill	Butch Cassidy and the Sundance Kid
	The Sting
John Huston	The Maltese Falcon
	Key Largo
	The Treasure of the Sierra Madre
	The African Queen
Elia Kazan	A Streetcar Named Desire
	On the Waterfront
	East of Eden
Stanley Kubrick	Lolita
	Dr Strangelove
	2001: A Space Odyssey
	A Clockwork Orange
Akira Kurosawa	The Seven Samurai
John Landis	The Blues Brothers
	Trading Places
	Coming to America
David Lean	Brief Encounter
	Bridge over the River Kwai
	Lawrence of Arabia
	Doctor Zhivago
	Ryan's Daughter
	A Passage to India
Barry Levinson	Rain Man
	Good Morning Vietnam
George Lucas	American Graffiti
	Star Wars
Laurence Olivier	The Prince and the Showgirl
	The Entertainer
Roman Polanski	Rosemary's Baby
	Tess
Sydney Pollack	Tootsie
	Out of Africa
Carol Reed	The Third Man
	Oliver
Ken Russell	Women in Love
	The Music Lovers

John Schlesinger	Midnight Cowboy
Martin Scorsese	Taxi Driver
	Raging Bull
	The Mission
	The Color of Money
	The Last Temptation of Christ
Ridley Scott	Alien
Oliver Stone	Platoon
	Wall Street
	Born on the Fourth of July
Jacques Tati	Monsieur Hulot's Holiday
François Truffaut	Jules et Jim
Luchino Visconti	Death in Venice
Robert Wise	The Sound of Music
Robert Zemeckis	Back to the Future
	Who Framed Roger Rabbit
Fred Zinnemann	High Noon
	From Here to Eternity
	A Man for All Seasons

Film Songs – Non Musicals

Some films will forever be associated with certain songs; I suppose the outstanding example is "Casablanca". In many cases the music improves the film, or at least gives it a certain edge. Would "The Graduate" have been as good without Simon and Garfunkel's contribution – I suspect not.

One of the most overused questions at quizes concerns the film "Breakfast at Tiffany's". (Yes!, you know what it is), but in recent years many hit songs have owed some of their popularity to the big screen. None of the films in this section could be described as a musical, they are dealt with separately. This list comprises the songs/films to which question setters have taken a distinct fancy.

As Time Goes By	Obviously "Casablanca" but the Jimmy Durante version was used in "Sleepless in Seattle"
Best That You Can Do (Arthur's Theme)	"Arthur"
Blue Moon/Bad Moon Rising	"An American Werewolf in London"
Everybody's Talkin	"Midnight Cowboy" – Bob Dylan was originally commissioned to write the theme song, but "Lay, Lady, Lay" arrived too late
(Everything I Do) I Do It For You	"Robin Hood, Prince of Thieves"
Eye of the Tiger	"Rocky III"
The Green Fields of Summer	"The Alamo"
A Groovy Kind of Love	"Buster"
I Just Called to Say I Love You	"Woman in Red"
Knockin' on Heaven's Door	Originally in "Pat Garrett and Billy the Kid" but also featured (by Guns N' Roses) in "Days of Thunder" and "Lethal Weapon II"
Up Where We Belong	"An Officer and a Gentleman"
Love, This is My Song	"A Countess from Hong Kong"

Moon River	"Breakfast at Tiffany's"
Nothing's Going to Stop Us Now	"Mannequin"
The Power of Love	"Back to the Future"
Raindrops Keep Falling on My Head	"Butch Cassidy and the Sundance Kid"
Rock Around the Clock	"Blackboard Jungle"
The Shadow of Your Smile	"The Sandpiper"
Somewhere My Love (Lara's Theme)	"Dr Zhivago"
Speak Softly Love	"The Godfather"
Strangers in the Night	"A Man could get Killed"
Take my Breath Away	"Top Gun"
Unchained Melody	"Ghost"
Whatever Will Be Will Be (Que Sera Sera)	"The Man Who Knew Too Much" (*the song later featured in other films*)
Windmills of Your Mind	"The Thomas Crown Affair"

Flags (National)

Quite a popular subject but generally confined to the national flags of European countries. Other nations' flags do occur from time to time, usually if that country is in the news or has a distinctive national flag. The following is a description of the national flags which occur most frequently in quiz questions.

Country	Description
Albania	Red background with black double-headed eagle surmounted by a gold five-pointed star.
Argentina	Horizontal bands of pale blue, white, pale blue.
Australia	Blue ensign with six white stars (one large star and the five stars of the Southern Cross).
Austria	Horizontal bands of red, white, red.
Belgium	Vertical tricolour of black, yellow, red.
Brazil	Green flag with a central yellow lozenge and a blue disc depicting the night sky over Rio de Janeiro.
China	Red flag with gold five pointed star in the upper hoist, surrounded by four smaller gold stars.
Cyprus	White flag with a solid yellow map of the island above two olive branches.
Denmark	White Scandinavian cross on a red background.
Finland	Blue Scandinavian cross on a white background.
Germany	Horizontal tricolour of black, red and yellow.
Greece	Blue and white horizontal stripes with a white cross on a blue background at the upper hoist.
Hungary	Horizontal tricolour of red, white and green.
Iceland	Red Scandinavian cross surrounded by white on a blue background.
India	Horizontal tricolour of orange, white and green with a blue chakra (prayer wheel) in the middle of the central band.
Iran	Horizontal tricolour of green, white and red.
Iraq	Horizontal tricolour of red, white and black with three green stars in the central band.
Ireland	Vertical tricolour of green, white and orange.

Country	Description
Italy	Vertical tricolour of green, white and red.
Japan	White background with single red disc (representing the rising sun) in the centre.
Libya	Plain green rectangle.
Luxembourg	Horizontal tricolour of red, white and blue.
Mexico	Vertical tricolour of green, white and red with a central emblem of an eagle, snake and cactus.
Monaco	Flag halved vertically, top half red and bottom half white.
Nepal	The only national flag in the world which is not rectangular. It comprises two separate triangular pennants.
Netherlands	Horizontal tricolour of red, white and blue.
Poland	Rectangular flag split in half, top half white, bottom half red.
Portugal	Two broad vertical stripes, green and red, with an armillary sphere (an early navigational instrument).
Russia	Horizontal tricolour of white, blue and red.
Saudi Arabia	Green background with white horizontal sword surmounted by the Arabic inscription meaning "There is no God but Allah and Mohammed is the prophet of Allah".
South Africa	Three horizontal bands, red, white and blue, with a triangular section of black, green and yellow towards the hoist, with the apex of the triangle towards the fly.
Spain	Horizontal tricolour of red, yellow, red.
Sweden	Yellow Scandinavian cross on a blue background.
Switzerland	One of only two square flags, white cross on red background.
Syria	Horizontal tricolour of red, white and black with two green stars in the central band.
Turkey	Red background with white crescent moon and white five-pointed star.
Vatican City	The other square flag; halved, yellow and white with the Papal device of a triple tiara and two crossed keys on the white portion.

Football Clubs
Football Grounds

This is one of the most popular sporting subjects in quizzoo. Invariably the question involves a soccer club which has spent most of its history in the lower divisions of the leagues. Consequently you will not find Liverpool, Manchester United or Arsenal here, it is assumed that even inhabitants of Pacific atolls know where these clubs play.

England

Barnet	Underhill
Barnsley	Oakwell
Bournemouth	Dean Court
Brentford	Griffin Park
Brighton	Goldstone Ground
Bristol City	Ashton Gate
Bristol Rovers	Twerton Park, Bath
Bury	Gigg Lane
Cambridge United	Abbey Stadium
Carlisle United	Brunton Park
Chester City	Deva Stadium
Chesterfield	Recreation Ground (sometimes known as Saltergate)
Colchester United	Layer Road
Crewe Alexandra	Gresty Road
Darlington	Feethams
Doncaster Rovers	Belle Vue
Exeter City	St James's Park
Gillingham	Priestfield
Grimsby Town	Blundell Park
Hartlepool United	Victoria Ground
Hereford United	Edgar Street
Huddersfield Town	MacAlpine Stadium
Hull City	Boothferry Park
Leyton Orient	Brisbane Road
Lincoln City	Sincil Bank
Luton Town	Kenilworth Road
Mansfield Town	Field Mill

England

Northampton Town	Sixfields Stadium
Notts County	Meadow Lane (also known as the County Ground)
Oldham Athletic	Boundary Park
Oxford United	Manor Ground
Peterborough United	London Road
Plymouth Argyle	Home Park
Reading	Elm Park
Rochdale	Spotland
Rotherham United	Millmoor
Scarborough	Seamer Road
Scunthorpe United	Glanford Park
Shrewsbury Town	Gay Meadow
Southend United	Roots Hall
Stockport County	Edgeley Park
Swansea City	Vetch Field
Swindon Town	County Ground
Torquay United	Plainmoor
Tranmere Rovers	Prenton Park
Walsall	Bescot Stadium
Wigan Athletic	Springfield Park
Wrexham	The Racecourse Ground
York City	Bootham Crescent

Scotland

Outside of Scotland the grounds of small Scottish Second and Third Division clubs are very rarely asked in quizzes (except in specialist sports quizzes). Apologies to fans of some of the senior Scottish clubs included here, but it is a sad fact that many people in England do not know the name of Dundee United's ground.

Aberdeen	Pittodrie
Dundee	Dens Park
Dundee United	Tannadice
Hearts	Tynecastle

Scotland

Hibernian	Easter Road
Kilmarnock	Rugby Park
Motherwell	Fir Park
Partick Thistle	Firhill Park
St Mirren	Love Street (although more correctly St Mirren Park)

Over the coming years more and more clubs will move from their old grounds into new purpose-built stadia; so beware.

Football Clubs' Nicknames

This is is a strange one. Although most clubs have nicknames many of them are never used even by their most avid fans. It must be many years since anybody shouted "Come on, the Toffees!" at Goodison Park. Once again, this list does not include such obvious nicknames as "the Gunners" or "the Hammers" nor are terms such as "Reds", "Blues" or "United" included.

Name of Club	Nickname
Bolton Wanderers	Trotters
Bournemouth	Cherries
Bradford City	Bantams
Brentford	Bees
Brighton	Seagulls
Bristol City	Robins
Bristol Rovers	Pirates
Cardiff City	Bluebirds
Charlton Athletic	Valiants
Chesterfield	Spireites
Crewe Alexandra	Railwaymen
Crystal Palace	Eagles
Darlington	Quakers
Exeter City	Grecians
Grimsby Town	Mariners
Huddersfield Town	Terriers

Name of Club	Nickname
Hull City	Tigers
Leyton Orient	The O's
Lincoln City	Imps
Luton Town	Hatters
Mansfield Town	Stags
Millwall	Lions
Newcastle United	Magpies
Northampton Town	Cobblers
Norwich City	Canaries
Notts County	Magpies
Peterborough	Posh
Plymouth Argyle	Pilgrims
Preston North End	Lilywhites
Reading	Royals
Rotherham United	Millers
Queens Park Rangers	The Rs
Scunthorpe United	Irons
Torquay United	Gulls
Walsall	Saddlers
Watford	Hornets
West Brom	Baggies
Wimbledon	Dons

Football Clubs' Original Names

Many football clubs started life with a name different to their present one. Many of them originated from church teams or from cricket clubs or works' teams. However, only a limited number are ever asked in general quizzes. Here is a list of the most popular ones.

Club	Previous Name(s)
Birmingham City	Small Heath (originally Small Heath Alliance)
Bolton Wanderers	Christ Church
Bristol Rovers	Black Arabs
Cardiff City	Riverside
Coventry City	Singers FC
Everton	St Domingo
Fulham	Fulham St Andrews
Gillingham	New Brompton
Grimsby Town	Grimsby Pelham
Leicester City	Leicester Fosse
Manchester City	Ardwick
Manchester United	Newton Heath
Newcastle United	Newcastle East End
Oldham Athletic	Pine Villa
Leyton Orient	Clapton Orient
Oxford United	Headington United
Port Vale	Burslem Port Vale
Queens Park Rangers	St Judes
Scunthorpe United	Scunthorpe and Lindsey United
Southampton	St Mary
Stockport County	Heaton Norris
Walsall	Walsall Town Swifts
Watford	West Herts
Wolverhampton Wanderers	St Lukes

Foreign Words and Phrases

Questions on this subject are rarely about what we understand the foreign word or phrase to mean; the words are usually in everyday parlance and most people will be able to provide a reasonable definition of them. However, what is normally asked is an exact (or reasonably accurate) translation of the word or phrase from its original source language. This can cause endless problems for those asking the questions because they will always be in a quandary as to how accurate the translation should be. This can result in unsavoury squabbles. Excluded from this list are such obvious phrases as 'creme de la creme'.

Foreign Word or Phrase	Origin	Translation
Al Fresco	Italian	In the fresh or cool air
Alma Mater	Latin	Bounteous mother
Alter Ego	Latin	Other self
Auto-da-Fé	Portuguese	Act of faith
Avant-Garde	French	Vanguard
Bête Noire	French	Black beast
Blitzkrieg	German	Lightning war
Bona Fides	Latin	Good faith
Bric-a-Brac	French	At random
Carte Blanche	French	White (blank) paper
Cliché	French	Stereotype printing block
Coup de Grâce	French	Blow of mercy
Coup d'État	French	Blow of state
Coupé	French	Cut
Cul de Sac	French	Bottom of the bag
Curriculum Vitae	Latin	Course of Life
Déjà Vu	French	Already seen
De Rigueur	French	Of strictness
Doppelganger	German	Double-goer
Éminence Grise	French	Grey eminence
Ergo	Latin	Therefore or hence
Ersatz	German	Artificial, a substitute, therefore inferior

Foreign Word or Phrase	Origin	Translation
Ex Gratia	Latin	Favour
Ex Officio	Latin	Of offioc
Fait Accompli	French	Accomplished fact
Faux Pas	French	False step
Force Majeure	French	Superior force
Glasnost	Russian	Speaking aloud
Habeas Corpus	Latin	You should have the body
Hara-Kiri	Colloquial Japanese	Belly cutting
Hoi Polloi	Greek	The many
Hors de Combat	French	Out of battle
Iman	Arabic	Leader
In Camera	Latin	In the room (meaning a private room)
Incommunicado	Spanish	Unable to communicate
In Extremis	Latin	At the point of death
In Flagrante Delicto	Latin	Emblazing crime
Infradig	Latin	Below dignity
In Loco Parentis	Latin	In place of a parent
Inter Alia	Latin	Among other things
Je Ne Sais Quoi	French	I don't know what
Jihad	Arabic	Struggle
Judo	Japanese	Gentle way
Ju-Jitsu	Japanese	Gentle science
Karaoke	Japanese	Empty orchestra
Karate	Japanese	Empty hand
Kibbutz	Modern Hebrew	Gathering
Kamikaze	Japanese	Divine wind
Kitsch	German	Rubbish
La Dolce Vita	Italian	Sweet life
Laissez-Faire	French	Let act
Lebensraum	German	Life space or living space

Foreign Word or Phrase	Origin	Translation
Lèse Majesté	Latin	Injured majesty
Lingua Franca	Italian	Frankish tongue
Locum Tenens	Latin	Place holder
Macho	Mexican-Spanish	Male
Mahatma	Sanskrit	Great soul
Maharishi	Sanskrit	Great sage
Mardi Gras	French	Fat Tuesday
Ménage à Trois	French	Household of three
Modus Operandi	Latin	Mode of working
Modus Vivendi	Latin	Mode of living
Née	French	Born
Noblesse Oblige	French	Nobility obliges
Non Sequitur	Latin	Does not follow
Ombudsman	Swedish	Commissioner
Parvenu	French	Arrived
Per Capita	Latin	By heads
Perestroika	Russian	Radical restructuring
Perse	Latin	By or in itself
Pied-a-Terre	French	Foot on the ground
Prima Facie	Latin	At first sight
Primus Inter-Pares	Latin	First among equals
Putsch	Swiss-German	Thrust or blow
Quasi	Latin	As if
Quid Pro Quo	Latin	Something for something
Rabbi	Hebrew	My master
Sang Froid	French	Cold blood
Savoir Faire	French	Know how to do
Sine Die	Latin	Without a day
Shlock	Yiddish	Broken or damaged goods (therefore inferior)
Shmaltz	Yiddish	Melted fat

Foreign Word or Phrase	Origin	Translation
Shmuck	Yiddish	Penis
Shogun	Japanese	Leader of the army
Status Quo	Latin	The state in which
Sub Judice	Latin	Under a judge
Subpoena	Latin	Under penalty
Table d'Hôte	French	Host's table
Tête-à-Tête	French	Head to head
Touché	French	Touched
Tour de Force	French	Turning movement
Ultra Vires	Latin	Beyond strength or beyond powers
Vis-à-Vis	French	Face to face

Fruit – Scientific Names

In these questions you are usually asked to identify a common fruit by its scientific name. I have always thought that this sort of question is a complete irrelevance, after all how often do you ask the greengrocer for 2lb of Malus pumila. Anyway, here they are.

Apple	Malus pumila
Apricot	Prunus armeniaca
Banana	Musa sapientum
Blackcurrant	Ribes nigrum
Cherry	Prunus avium
Date	Phoenix dactylifera
Gooseberry	Ribes grossularia
Grape	Vitis vinifera
Grapefruit	Citrus grandis
Lemon	Citrus limon
Lime	Citrus aurantifolia
Olive	Olea europaea
Orange	Citrus sinensis
Passion Fruit	Passiflora edulis
Peach	Prunus persica
Pear	Pyrus communis
Pineapple	Ananas comosus
Plum	Prunus domestica
Raspberry	Rubus idaeus
Rhubarb	Rheum rhaponticum
Strawberry	Fragaria species
Water Melon	Citrullus laratus

Fruit – Varieties

"Which fruit has varieties named xxxx?" This is not an uncommon question. The following lists are of varieties of fruits which can be grown outdoors in the UK.

Fruit	*Varieties*
Apples	American Mother, Ashmead's Kernel, Beauty of Bath, Charles Ross, Discovery, Epicure,

Fortune, Irish Peach, James Grieve, Lord
Derby, Lord Lambourne, Merton Knave, Mutant
Wonder, Sunset, Suntan, Winston and
Worcester Pearmain.

Blackberries Ashton Cross, Bedford Giant, Fantasia,
Hymalaya Giant, Merton Thornless, Oregon
Thornless.

Blackcurrants Baldwin, Ben Lomond, Ben More, Ben Nevis,
Ben Sarek, Laxton Giant, Malling Jet (be careful
of this one – this is one Malling which is not a
raspberry)

Cherries Early Rivers, May Duke, Merchant, Merton
Bigarreau, Merton Glory, Nabella, Napoleon
Bigarreau, Noir de Guben, Stella, Sunburst,
Van.

Gooseberries Careless, Invictor, Jubilee, Lord Derby, May
Duke, Whimham's Industry.

Pears Concorde, Gorham, Jargonelle, Josephene, De
Malines, Louise Bonne, Merton Pride, Onward,
Packham's Triumph, Thompson, Winter Nelis.

Plums Bullace, Cambridge Gage, Czar, Denniston's
Superb, Early Laxton, Kirke's Blue,
Merryweather, Opal, Oullin's Golden Gage,
Pershore Yellow, Purple Pershore, Early Rivers,
Victoria.

Raspberries Glen Clova, Golden Everest, Heritage, Joy,
anything beginning with the name Malling.

Rhubarb Hawke's Champagne, Prince Albert, Sutton,
Victoria.

Strawberries Alexandria, Aromel, Bounty, Cambridge
Favourite, Cambridge Vigour, Gento, Grandee,
Ostara, Redgauntlet, Tamella, Tantallon,
Troubador.

Geological Time-scale

One of those subjects that hardly anybody understands, but nevertheless crops up in quizzes. Speilberg's "Jurassic Park" awakened quiz setters to the possibilities of this subject. Phraseology is a minefield here, with confusion between eras, ages and periods. This very simplified table should help.

Cenozoic (from the Greek *kainos*, meaning "new")
We are living in the Cenozoic era which started *c.* 65 million years ago.

Mesozoic (from *mesos*, meaning "middle")
From *c.* 65 to 240 million years ago, and containing these geological periods:

	million years ago
Cretaceous	65–135
Jurassic	135–200
Triassic	200–240

Palaeozoic (from *palaeos* meaning "ancient")
From *c.* 240 to 600 million years ago, and containing these geological periods:

	million years ago
Permian	240–280
Carboniferous	280–370
Devonian	370-415
Silurian	415–445
Ordovician	445–515
Cambrian	515–600

Pre-cambrian
From *c.* 600 to 4500 million years ago.

Gilbert and Sullivan Operettas – Subtitles

Another recurring quiz theme, although I have never understood the relevance of Gilbert and Sullivan subtitles. Never mind, here they are.

Opera	*Subtitle*
The Gondoliers	The King of Baratavia
The Grand Duke	The Statutory Duel
Iolanthe	The Peer and the Peri
The Mikado	The Town of Titipu
Patience	Bunthorne's Bride
HMS Pinafore	The Lass That Loved a Sailor
The Pirates Of Penzance	The Slave of Duty
Princess Ida	Castle Adamant
Ruddigore	The Witch's Curse
Thespis	The Gods Grown Old
Utopia Limited	The Flowers of Progress
The Yeomen Of The Guard	The Merryman and His Maid

I have been unable to find subtitles for:
The Sorcerer
or
Trial By Jury

Gods
Greek & Roman
Real old chestnuts these. These have been included in quizzes for years. The following are the major Greek and Roman Gods.

Description of the God	Greek	Roman
King of the Gods	Zeus	Jupiter
Queen of the Gods	Hera	Juno
God of the Sun	Apollo	Apollo
God of War	Ares	Mars
Messenger of the Gods	Hermes	Mercury
God of the Sea	Poseidon	Neptune
God of Fire	Hephaistos	Vulcan
Goddess of Soil and Agriculture	Demeter	Ceres
Goddess of the Moon and Hunting	Artemis	Diana
Goddess of Wisdom	Athene	Minerva
Goddess of Love and Beauty	Aphrodite	Venus
God of Wine	Dionysos	Bacchus
God of the Underworld	Pluton	Pluto
God of the Morning	Eos	Aurora
God of Time	Chronos	Saturn

Greek Muses
A must for all serious quiz players. They occur time and time again. The Nine Muses were the daughters of Zeus and Mnemosyne.

Calliope	Epic poetry
Clio	History
Euterpe	Lyrical poetry and music
Thalia	Comedy
Melpomene	Tragedy
Terpsichore	Song and Dance
Erato	Mime
Polyhymnia	Hymn
Urania	Astronomy

Heraldry – Heraldic Terms

Yet another subject which seems to have no relevance at all to the latter half of the twentieth century but is still favoured by quiz setters. There are literally hundreds of heraldic terms but the following are the most commonly asked.

Colours

Azure	Blue	**Vert**	Green
Gules	Red	**Argent**	Silver
Purpure	Purple	**Or**	Gold
Sable	Black		

Heraldic Terms

Bars	Horizontal band across the middle of a shield
Bend	A diagonal stripe
Chevron	A bent stripe with the point upwards
Couchant	Lying down
Dormant	Sleeping
Fesse	A broad, horizontal strip across the middle of a shield
Gardant	Full-faced
Lodged	Reposing
Martlet	A swallow without feet
Mullet	A star
Pale	Wide vertical stripe in the centre of the shield
Pallet	Narrow vertical stripe
Passant	Walking with the face in profile
Passant gardant	Walking with full face
Pile	A narrow rectangle
Rampant	Rearing, with the face in profile
Rampant gardant	Erect on hind legs with full face showing
Saliant	Springing
Serjant	Seated
Statent	Standing still
Trippant	Running
Volant	Flying

Homes and Houses

One of those odd subjects that takes the fancy of question setters. If a man built an empire, enlightened the scientific world, or created great works of prose, where he lived is completely irrelevant; but not to question setters. This list then is an eclectic mix of castles, stately homes and historic piles that were once inhabited by the great and the good. The families or individuals are those who are most closely associated with the buildings and may not be the present owners. Several stately homes in this list are the property of The National Trust.

Abbotsford House	Sir Walter Scott
Alnwick Castle	The Dukes of Northumberland
Althorp	The Earls Spencer
Alton Towers	Built for the 15th Earl of Shrewsbury
Apsley House	1st Duke of Wellington
Arundel Castle	The Dukes of Norfolk
Shaw's Corner, Ayot St Laurence	G. B. Shaw
Badminton House	The Dukes of Beaufort
Bateman's	Rudyard Kipling
Belvoir Castle	The Dukes of Rutland
Blair Castle	The Dukes of Athol
Blenheim Palace	The Dukes of Marlborough
Buckland Abbey	Sir Francis Drake
Burghley House	The Cecil Family
Carlyle House, Cheyne Walk, London	Thomas Carlyle
Chartwell	Sir Winston Churchill
Chatsworth House	The Dukes of Devonshire
Clarence House	HM The Queen Mother
Cliveden	The Astor Family
Dickens House, Doughty St, London	Charles Dickens
Dove Cottage	William Wordsworth
Floors Castle	The Dukes of Roxburghe
Gads Hill	Charles Dickens
Gatcombe Park	HRH The Princess Anne

Glamis Castle	The Earls of Strathmore and Kinghorne
Goodwood House	The Dukes of Richmond
Gough Square, London	Dr Johnson
Haddon Hall	The Dukes of Rutland
Hatfield House	The Marquesses of Salisbury
Highgrove House	HRH Prince Charles
Inverary Castle	The Dukes of Argyll
Kedleston Hall	The Curzons
Longleat House	The Marquesses of Bath
Newstead Abbey	Lord Byron
Shugborough	The Earls of Lichfield
Sissinghurst Castle	Vita Sackville-West
Sulgrave Manor	Was the home of George Washington's ancestors
Syon House	The Dukes of Northumberland
Wilton House	The Earls of Pembroke
Woburn Abbey	The Dukes of Bedford

Horses

This section is not concerned with "the sport of kings". These are horses from history, folklore, mythology and popular entertainment. This has proved a useful source for question setters for many years. Questions such as "What was the name of Tonto's horse?" or "Who rode the mythical horse Pegasus?" occur quite frequently. This is a list of famous horses and their riders.

Barbary Roan	Richard II
Black Agnes	Mary Queen of Scots
Black Bess	Dick Turpin
Bucephalus	Alexander the Great
Champion	Gene Autry
Copenhagen	Duke of Wellington
Dapple	Sancho Panza
Incitatus	Caligula (Caligula made Incitatus a Consul)
Lamri	King Arthur
Marengo	Napoleon Bonaparte
Pegasus	Bellerophon
Rosinante	Don Quixote
Scout	Tonto
Silver	Lone Ranger
Tony	Tom Mix
Topper	Hopalong Cassidy
Trigger	Roy Rogers
White Surrey	Richard III

Initials

The actual names of people who are best known by initials only (or partly by an initial) has always been a very popular quiz theme. The following is a list of such people much favoured by quiz setters.

W H	(WYSTAN HUGH) Auden
P T	(PHINEAS TAYLOR) Barnum
J M	(JAMES MATTHEW) Barrie
H E	(HERBERT ERNEST) Bates
R D	(RICHARD DODDERRIDGE) Blackmore
G K	(GILBERT KEITH) Chesterton
A J	(ARCHIBALD JOSEPH) Cronin
R F	(RONALD FREDERICK) Deldefield
J P	(JAMES PATRICK) Donleavy
T S	(THOMAS STEARNS) Eliot
W C	(WILLIAM CLAUDE) Fields
E M	(EDWARD MORGAN) Forster
C B	(CHARLES BURGESS) Fry
W S	(WILLIAM SCHWENCK) Gilbert
King C	(CAMP) Gillette
W E	(WILLIAM EWART) Gladstone
W G	(WILLIAM GILBERT) Grace
D W	(DAVID WARK) Griffith
L P	(LESLIE POLES) Hartley
A E	(ALFRED EDWARD) Housman
P D	(PHYLLIS DOROTHY) James
Jerome K	(KLAPKA) Jerome
Captain James T	(TIBERIUS) Kirk
D H	(DAVID HERBERT) Lawrence
T E	(THOMAS EDWARD) Lawrence
C S	(CLIVE STAPLES) Lewis
L S	(LAURENCE STEPHEN) Lowry
A A	(ALAN ALEXANDER) Milne
H H	(HUGH HECTOR) Munro
E	(EDITH) Nesbit
J B	(JOHN BOYNTON) Priestley
V S	(VICTOR SAWDON) Pritchett

J D	(JEROME DAVID) Salinger
J M	(JOHN MILLINGTON) Synge
C P	(CHARLES PERCY) Snow
H M	(HENRY MORTON) Stanley
J R R	(JOHN RONALD REUEL) Tolkien
J M W	(JOSEPH MALLORD WILLIAM) Turner
H G	(HERBERT GEORGE) Wells
P G	(PELHAM GRENVILLE) Wodehouse
W B	(WILLIAM BUTLER) Yeats

Inventions

These are always useful to remember because they have formed part of quiz setters' armoury for years. The great difficulty in assembling this section is knowing what to include and what to leave out. Three criteria have been used for inclusion in this section; it must be an invention which occurs frequently in quiz questions, the inventor(s) must be well documented and the invention must be within the compass of most people's everyday experiences. These criteria have resulted in the exclusion of such beauties as the ophthalmoscope, the tungsten filament and the cream separator.

Medical and scientific developments and innovations are listed in a separate section.

Adding Machine	Some differences of opinion for this invention. Claims have been made for Schickard and Pascal, both in the first half of the 17th Century, but the first commercial machine was certainly the development of William Burroughs in St Louis, USA in 1885.
Aerosol Spray	Goodhue, 1941.
Air Brakes	Westinghouse, 1868.
Ballpoint Pen	First commercially developed by the Biro brothers in 1938.
Barbed Wire	Smith, 1867.
Barometer	Torricelli, 1643.

Battery (Electric)	Volta, 1800.
Bicycle	Macmillan, 1840.
Bicycle Tyres (Pneumatic)	Dunlop, 1888.
Bifocal Lens	Franklin, 1780.
Calculating Machine	Once again some controversy. Sometimes attributed to Pascal (see adding machine) but generally accepted as Babbage in 1823.
Camera	Fox Talbot, 1835.
Camera (Polaroid)	Land, 1948.
Carburettor	Daimler, 1876.
Carpet Sweeper	Bissell, 1876.
Cash Register	Ritty, 1879.
Cement (Portland)	Aspdin, 1824.
Chronometer	Harrison, 1735.
Compact Disc	Philips Co. and the Sony Co., 1978.
Cotton Gin	Whitney, 1793.
Dynamite	Nobel, 1866.
Electric Iron	Seeley, 1882.
Electric Light	There is some dispute once again, between Swan and Edison, but both 1879.
Glider	Cayley, 1853.
Gramophone	Edison, 1878.
Helicopter	First practical craft, Sikorsky, 1939.
Hovercraft	Cockerell, 1955.
Jet Engine	Whittle, 1937.
Kaleidoscope	Brewster, 1817.
Lawn Mower	Hills, 1868.
Lift	Otis, 1852.
Lightning Conductor	Franklin, 1752.
Loudspeaker	Short, 1900.
Machine Gun	First practical model, Gatling, 1861.
Match	Walker, 1826.
Metronome	Malzel, 1816.

Microphone	Some dispute but generally acknowledged as Bell, 1876.
Motor Cycle	Daimler, 1885.
Neon Light	Claude, 1910.
Nylon	Carothers, 1937.
Parachute	Blanchard, 1785.
Parking Meter	Magee, 1935.
Pen (Fountain)	Waterman, 1884.
Pendulum	Galileo, 1581.
Piano	Cristofori, 1709.
Radio Telegraphy	Marconi, 1885.
Razor (Electric)	Schick, 1931.
Razor (Safety)	Gillette, 1895.
Record (Cylinder)	Bell, 1887.
Record (Disc)	Berliner, 1887.
Record (Long playing)	Goldmark, 1948.
Record (Wax Cylinder)	Edison and Midgely, 1888.
Refrigerator	Some dispute, but either Harrison or Twining, both 1850. The first domestic refrigerator was produced in 1913.
Rubber (Vulcanised)	Goodyear, 1839.
Safety Pin	Hunt, 1849.
Sewing Machine	Another disputed attribution, take your pick from any of the following: Thimmonnier, 1829; Saint, 1790; Singer, 1851 or Howe (the most popular choice), 1846.
Spinning Frame	Arkwright, 1769.
Spinning Jenny	Hargreaves, 1764.
Spinning Mule	Crompton, 1779.
Steam Engine (Piston)	Newcomen, 1712.
Steam Turbine	Parsons, 1884.
Steel	Bessemer, 1856.
Steel (Stainless)	Brearley, 1913.

Submarine	Another disputed attribution, perhaps Drebbel in 1624 or Bushnell in 1776 or more probably, for practical purposes, Holland in 1891.
Tank	Swinton, 1914.
Tape Recorder	Poulsen, 1899.
Telephone	Bell, 1876.
Telescope	Lippershey, 1608 (although generally attributed to Galileo in 1609).
Television	Baird, 1926.
Thermometer	Galileo, 1593.
Torpedo	Fulton, 1804.
Type (Movable)	Gutenberg, 1450.
Typewriter	Once again a dispute on attribution. Take your pick from Tarri, 1808 or Soule and Glidden, 1868.
Vacuum Cleaner	Spangler, 1907.
Washing Machine	Hurley Machine Company, 1907.
Zip Fastener	Judson, 1891.

Inventions, Discoveries and Innovations – Scientific & Medical

The first list of inventions dealt with everyday objects. This list confines itself to scientific and medical developments and discoveries. There is obviously an area of overlap between the two lists, all inventions and discoveries have their basis in science, but the first list dealt solely with objects and machinery with which we have some everyday contact. Some elements have been included in this list although they are not strictly discoveries or inventions.

Anaesthetic (Ether)	Long, 1842.
Anaesthetic (Local)	Koller, 1885.
Antiseptic Surgery	Lister, 1867.
Aspirin	Dresser, 1889.
Blood Circulation	Harvey, 1628.
Calcium	Davy, 1808.
Calculus	Newton, 1670.
Chlorine	Davy, 1810.
Chloroform	Guthrie, 1831.
Cocaine	Niermann, 1860.
DDT	Zeidler, 1874.
DNA Structure	Crick, Watson and Wilkins, 1951.
Dynamo	Pixii, 1832.
Hydrogen	Cavendish, 1766.
Insulin	Banting, Best and Macleod, 1922.
Laser	Townes, 1960
LSD	Hoffman, 1943.
Measles Vaccine	Enders and Peebles, 1954.
Microscope	Janssen, 1590
Neutron	Chadwick, 1932.
Nitric Acid	Glauber, 1648.
Nitric Oxide	Priestley, 1772.
Nitrogen	Rutherford, 1772.
Nitroglycerin	Sobrero, 1846.
Oxygen	Priestley, 1774.
Penicillin	Flemming, 1929.
Polio Vaccine	Salk, 1953.

Polio Oral Vaccine	Sabin, 1955.
Potassium	Davy, 1807.
Proton	Rutherford, 1919.
Rabies Vaccine	Pasteur, 1885.
Radar	Taylor and Young, 1922.
Radioactivity	Becquerel, 1896.
Radium	The Curies, 1898.
Rocket Engine	Goddard, 1929.
Slide Rule	Oughtred, 1621.
Smallpox Vaccine	Jenner, 1796.
Sulphuric Acid	Phillips, 1831.
Stethoscope	Laenneck, 1819.
Thermometer (Mercury)	Fahrenheit, 1714.
Transformer	Faraday, 1831.
Transistor	Bardeen, Shockley and Brittain, 1948.
Tuberculin	Coch, 1890.
Typhus Vaccine	Nicolle, 1909.

Jazz Musicians

There is something about jazz virtuosi which attracts questions setters. Perhaps people who set quizzes are by nature jazz enthusiasts, but I doubt it; I suspect that the questions are simply easy to set. They usually come in the form of "With which musical instrument would you associate the jazz musicians 'X', 'Y' and 'Z'?" This little list will be of some use. N.B. Several musicians are or were accomplished performers on more than one instrument.

Musical Instrument	*Musician*
Bass	Jimmy Blanton
	Charles Mingus
	Oscar Pettiford
Clarinet	Barney Bigard
	Benny Carter
	Buddy De Franco
	Johnny Dodds
	Jimmy Dorsey
	Benny Goodman
	Woody Herman
	Jimmie Moone
	Pee Wee Russell
	Artie Shaw
	Zoot Sims
Cornet	Bix Beiderbecke
	Buddy Bolden
	Wild Bill Davison
	Bobby Hackett
	Bunk Johnson
	King Oliver
	Muggsy Spanier
Drums	Art Blakey
	Sidney Catlett
	Cozy Cole
	Lionel Hampton
	Jo Jones
	Gene Krupa
	Buddy Rich

Musical Instrument	*Musician*
	Max Roach
	Chick Webb
Guitar	Charlie Christian
	Eddy Condon
	Milt Jackson
	Wes Montgomery
	Django Reinhardt
Piano	Count Basie
	Duke Ellington
	Bill Evans
	Gil Evans
	Erroll Garner
	Lionel Hampton
	Earl Hines
	Milt Jackson
	Thelonius Monk
	Jelly Roll Morton
	Oscar Peterson
	Bud Powell
	Horace Silver
	Willie 'The Lion' Smith
	Billy Strayhorn
	Art Tatum
	Lennie Tristano
	Joe Turner
	McCoy Tyner
	Fats Waller
	Mary Lou Williams
	Teddy Wilson
	Jimmy Yancey
Saxophone	Cannonball Adderley
	Sidney Bechet
	Harry Carney
	Benny Carter
	Al Cohn
	Ornette Coleman

Musical Instrument	Musician
	John Coltrane
	Paul Desmond
	Jimmy Dorsey
	Dexter Gordon
	Coleman Hawkins
	Woody Herman
	Johnny Hodges
	Gerry Mulligan
	Charlie Parker
	Sonny Rollins
	Zoot Sims
	Sonny Stitt
	Lester Young
Trombone	Vic Dickenson
	Tommy Dorsey
	Jay Higginbotham
	J. J. Johnson
	Glenn Miller
	Turk Murphy
	Kid Ory
	Jack Teagarden
	Kai Winding
Trumpet	Red Allen
	Louis Armstrong
	Bunny Berrigan
	Benny Carter
	Buck Clayton
	Miles Davis
	Roy Eldridge
	Dizzy Gillespie
	Bobby Hackett
	Bunk Johnson
	Thad Jones
	Tommy Ladnier
	Jimmy McPartland
	Fats Navarro

Musical Instrument	Musician
	Shorty Rogers
	Joe Smith
	Cootie Williams
Vibraphone	Lionel Hampton
	Milt Jackson
	Red Norvo
Violin	Stephane Grappelli
	Joe Venuti

Liqueurs

Another "boozy" section, but these questions do crop up regularly. Strictly speaking many of the following are not liqueurs, some are fruit brandies and some are cordials but they are almost invariably referred to as liqueurs.

Source	Liqueur
Almond	Amaretto
Anise	Pastis
	Ouzo
	Mastic
	Raki
	Pernod
	Ricard
Apple	Calvados
Blackcurrant	Cassis
Carroway	Kümmel
Cherry	Kirsch
	Maraschino
Coffee	Kahlua
	Tia Maria
Orange	Curaçao
	Cointreau
	Grand Marnier
	Aurum
Plum	Mirabelle
	Slivovitz
	Aki

Literary/Screen Characters

This is a funny one. Many literary characters "lie dormant" for years, then someone dramatises the story/stories for film or TV and wham!, every quiz setter in the country jumps on them. A good example is the Ellis Peters creation "Brother Cadfael". This 12th-century Benedictine emerged in print during the 1970s and the books were enjoyed by thousands of readers, but he seemed to be unknown to question setters. Then, some of the stories were adapted for TV with Derek Jacobi playing Cadfael, and suddenly he became "flavour of the month" – Who created him? Where are the stories set? etc., etc. This is another example of the power of TV and cinema, and something the devoted quiz player can use to his or her advantage. Just wait for a literary character's TV adaptation, bone up on him, and the question will certainly follow. This list of characters and their creators should prove useful. I have excluded from this list the very obvious – Sherlock Holmes, Miss Marple, and so on.

Inspector Alleyn	Ngaio Marsh
Biggles	W. E. Johns
Sexton Blake	Harry Blyth (Hal Meredith)
Father Brown	G. K. Chesterton
Billy Bunter	Frank Richards
Brother Cadfael	Ellis Peters
Charlie Chan	Earl Derr Biggers
Adam Dalgleish	P. D. James
Dr Doolittle	Hugh Lofting
Dr Finlay	A. J. Cronin
Dracula	Bram Stoker
Bulldog Drummond	Sapper (H. C. McNeile)
Inspector Frost	R. D. Wingfield
Fu Manchu	Sax Rohmer
Worzel Gummidge	Barbara Euphan Todd
Mike Hammer	Mickey Spillane
Matt Helm	Donald Hamilton
Dr Kildare	Max Brand
Lovejoy	Jonathan Gash
Maigret	Georges Simenon
Philip Marlowe	Raymond Chandler

Perry Mason	Erle Stanley Gardner
Inspector Morse	Colin Dexter
Ross Poldark	Winston Graham
Raffles	E. W Hornung
Rambo	David Morrell
Horace Rumpole	John Mortimer
The Saint	Leslie Charteris
John Shaft	Ernest Tidyman
Richard Sharpe	Bernard Cornwell
Jemima Shore	Antonia Fraser
Sam Spade	Dashiell Hammett
Tarzan	Edgar Rice Burroughs
Van der Valk	Nicholas Vreeling
Inspector Wexford	Ruth Rendell
William (Just William)	Richmal Crompton
Lord Peter Wimsey	Dorothy L. Sayers
Wycliff	W. D. Burley

Literary Terms

It is rare in quizzes for anybody to be asked to explain what an oxymoron is, but quite frequently a phrase or sentence is given as an example and the quiz contestant must recognise which literary term describes that particular use of words or style of writing. Here are the most popular ones.

Alliteration
Two or more successive words beginning with the same sound or letter.
Example: Sydney slithered silently southward.

Aphorism
A short statement into which much meaning is compressed.
Example: The King is dead, long live the King.

Bathos
The sudden descent from the sublime to the cor blimey.
Example: His thoughts were in Tahiti, the rest of him was in the lavatory.

Elision
The supression of a letter or syllable in the pronunciation of a word.
Example: I'm, it's.

Euphemism
Deliberate understatement.
Example: Michael Jackson has achieved some success in the world of music.

Hyperbole
Deliberate exaggeration in order to stress the importance of a subject.
Example: Some people think football is a matter of life and death. It is more important than that.

Irony
The expression of the opposite of what is meant, generally used in a derogatory manner.
Example: It may be said of a person whose grasp of mathematics is not particularly good: "He is a real Einstein, is Fred".

Litotes
The expression of an idea by stating a negative of the opposite.
Example: Arnold Schwarzenegger is no weakling.

Meiosis
Usually a colloquial form of litotes.
Example: It may be said of a very rich man: he's got a bob or two.

Metathesis   The transposition of letters or sounds in a word.
Example: Somebody may state that they do not like ornamental food when in fact they do not like Oriental food.

Onomatopoeia   The formation of a word by the imitation of the sound associated with the action or object.
Example: Buzz, Plop, Pop.
It can also mean the evocation of an image by using words which may sound like that image.
Example: Babbling brook.

Oxymoron   The use of two seemingly contradictory terms in words, which used together, make a pointed statement.
Example: Horatio Nelson was only 5 ft. tall. He was a giant in his lifetime.

Palindrome   A word or sentence that reads the same backwards as it does forward.
Example: Rotavator.

Simile   A comparison between two words to illustrate a point.
Example: He was built like a brick out-house.

Local Radio Stations

Local BBC stations usually have very prosaic names (Radio Surrey, Radio Humberside etc) but independent local stations are firm favourites with question setters (even though some of these stations no longer exist), especially when the name of the station gives no clue as to where it is based. The stations listed fall into that category.

Stations	Town/City
Aire FM	Leeds
Beacon Radio	Wolverhampton
BRMB	Birmingham
Central FM	Stirling
Chiltern Radio	Dunstable
Downtown Radio	Newtownards (N. Ireland)
Forth FM	Edinburgh
Fortune Radio	Manchester
Fox FM	Oxford
Hallam FM	Sheffield
Hereward FM	Peterborough
Horizon Radio	Milton Keynes
Invicta Radio	Whitstable
Marcher Gold	Wrexham
Mercia FM	Coventry
Metro FM	Newcastle upon Tyne
Northsound Radio	Aberdeen
Ocean FM	Fareham
Orchard FM	Taunton
Pennine FM	Bradford
Piccadilly Radio	Manchester
The Pulse	Bradford
Radio Borders	Galashiels
Radio Broadland	Norwich
Radio City FM	Liverpool
Radio Mercury	Crawley
Radio Orwell	Ipswich
Radio Tay	Dundee
Radio Wyvern	Worcester

Stations	Town/City
Red Dragon FM	Cardiff
Red Rose Radio	Preston
Saxon Radio	Bury St Edmunds
Severn Sound	Gloucester
Signal Radio	Stoke on Trent
Southern FM	Brighton
TFM Radio	Stockton on Tees
Trent FM	Derby & Nottingham
210 FM	Reading
Viking FM	Hull
West Sound	Ayr

Medical Conditions

Every disease, infection and ailment has its proper medical or scientific name, but the common illnesses such as measles or mumps are the ones favoured by question setters. Once again this is an area where great care should be taken; degrees in medicine are not handed out with the cornflakes, but questions are set from the "Your Own Home Book of Medicine" type of publication. This list will cover most of the words you are likely to be asked.

Disease/Condition	Medical/Scientific Name
Chickenpox	Varicella
Common cold	Coryza
German measles	Rubella
Glandular fever	Infectious mononucleosis
Mumps	Parotitis
Rabies	Hydrophobia
Smallpox	Variola major
Whooping cough	Pertussis

Monarchs

Ever popular, although questions on this subject which predate the Norman Conquest are very rare indeed, so this list of English and British monarchs starts with William the Conqueror. The spouses of monarchs seem to be a popular source of questions so they are included in this list.

Monarch	Reigned	Spouse
House of Normandy		
William I	1066–1087	Matilda
Born 1027		
William II	1087–1100	Died unmarried
Born *c* 1056. Third son of William I and Matilda		
Henry I	1100–1135	1 Matilda (Edith)
Born 1068. Younger brother of William II		2 Adela
House of Blois		
Stephen	1135–1154	Matilda
Born *c* 1098. Nephew of Henry I		
House of Normandy		
Matilda	April–Nov	1 Henry V
Born 1102. Only legitimate daughter of Henry I	1141	(Emperor of Germany)
		2 Geoffrey V
		(Count of Anjou)
House of Plantagenet		
Henry II	1154–1189	Eleanor, divorced wife of
Born 1133. Son of Matilda and Geoffrey V		Louis VII of France
Richard I	1189–1199	Berengaria (daughter of
Born 1157. Son of Henry II and Eleanor		Sancho VI of Navarre)
John	1199–1216	1 Isabel
Born 1167. Brother of Richard I		2 Isabella (daughter of Almir, Count of Angoulême)

Monarch	Reigned	Spouse
Henry III Born 1207. Son of John and Isabella	1216–1272	Eleanor (daughter of Raymond, Count of Provence)
Edward I Born 1239. Son of Henry III and Eleanor	1272–1307	1 Eleanor (daughter of Ferdinand III of Castille) 2 Margaret (daughter of Philip III of France)
Edward II Born 1284. Son of Edward I and Eleanor	1307–1327	Isabella (daughter of Philip IV of France)
Edward III Born 1312. Son of Edward II and Isabella	1327–1377	Philippa (daughter of William I, Count of Holland and Hainault)
Richard II Born 1367. Son of Edward the Black Prince, the eldest son of Edward III	1377–1399	1 Anne (daughter of Emperor Charles IV of Bohemia) 2 Isabelle (daughter of Charles VI of France)
Henry IV Born 1366. Son of John of Gaunt	1399–1413	1 Mary (daughter of Humphrey, Earl of Hereford) 2 Joan (daughter of Charles II of Navarre)
Henry V Born 1387. Son of Henry IV and Mary	1413–1422	Catherine of Valois (Daughter of Charles VI of France)
Henry VI Born 1421. Son of Henry V and Catherine	1422–1461 1470–1471	Margaret (daughter of René, Duke of Anjou)
Edward IV Born 1442. Son of Richard, Duke of York and Lady Cecily Neville	1461–1470 1471–1483	Elizabeth (daughter of Sir Richard Woodville)
Edward V Born 1470. Son of Edward IV and Elizabeth Woodville	April–June 1483	Unmarried

Monarch	Reigned	Spouse
Richard III Born 1452. Brother of Edward IV, uncle of Edward V	1483–1485	Anne (daughter of Richard Neville, Earl of Warwick)

House of Tudor

Monarch	Reigned	Spouse
Henry VII Born 1457. Son of Edmund Tudor, First Earl of Richmond and Margaret Beaufort, Great, great granddaughter of Edward III	1485–1509	Elizabeth (daughter of Edward IV)
Henry VIII Born 1491. Son of Henry VII and Elizabeth	1509–1547	1 Catherine of Aragon (daughter of Ferdinand II of Spain) 2 Anne Boleyn (Marchioness of Pembroke) 3 Jane (daughter of Sir John Seymour) 4 Anne (daughter of John, Duke of Cleves) 5 Catherine (daughter of Lord Edmund Howard) 6 Catherine (daughter of Sir Thomas Parr and widow of: i. Sir Edward Borough; ii. John Neville, Lord Latimer)
Edward VI Born 1537. Son of Henry VIII and Jane Seymour	1547–1553	Unmarried

Monarch	Reigned	Spouse
House of Grey		
Lady Jane Grey Born 1537. Daughter of Henry Grey, Third Marquess of Dorset	Proclaimed Queen 10.7.1553 Deposed 19.7.1553	Lord Guilford Dudley
House of Tudor		
Mary I Born 1516. Daughter of Henry VIII and Catherine of Aragon	1553–1558	Philip II of Spain
Elizabeth I Born 1533. Daughter of Henry VIII and Anne Boleyn	1558–1603	Unmarried
House of Stuart		
James I Born 1566. Son of Mary, Queen of Scots and Henry Stuart, Lord Darnley	1603–1625	Anne (daughter of Frederick II, King of Denmark and Norway)
Charles I Born 1600. Son of James I and Anne	1625–1649	Henrietta Maria (daughter of Henry IV of France)
Charles II Born 1630. Son of Charles I and Henrietta Maria	1660–1685	Catherine (daughter of John, Duke of Braganza)
James II Born 1633. Brother of Charles II	1685–1688	1 Anne (daughter of Edward Hyde) 2 Mary (daughter of Alfonso IV, Duke of Modena)
House of Orange and Stuart		
William III Born 1650. Son of William II, Prince of Orange	1689–1702	William and Mary ruled jointly from 1689–1694

Monarch	Reigned	Spouse
Mary II Born 1662. Daughter of James II and Anne Hyde * Subsequently House of Orange until 1702	1689–1694	
House of Stuart **Anne** Born 1665. Daughter of James II and Anne Hyde	1702–1714	George (son of Frederick III, King of Denmark)
House of Hanover **George I** Born 1660. Son of Ernest Augustus, Elector of Hanover	1714–1727	Sophia Dorothea (daughter of George William, Duke of Lüneberg-Celle)
George II Born 1683. Son of George I and Sophia Dorothea	1727–1760	Wilhelmina Caroline (daughter of John Frederick, Margrave of Brandenburg-Ansbach)
George III Born 1738. Son of Frederick Lewis, Prince of Wales ((Son of George II) and Princess Augusta of Saxe-Gotha)	1760–1820	Charlotte Sophia (daughter of Charles Louis Frederick, Duke of Mecklenburg-Strelitz)
George IV Born 1762. Son of George III and Charlotte	1820–1830	1 Maria FitzHerbert 2 Caroline (daughter of Charles, Duke of Brunswick-Wolfenbüttel)
William IV Born 1765. Brother of George IV and son of George III and Charlotte	1830–1837	Adelaide (daughter of George, Duke of Saxe-Meiningen)
Victoria Born 1819. Daughter of Edward, Duke of Kent, brother of William IV	1837–1901	Albert (son of Ernest I, Duke of Saxe-Coburg Gotha)

Monarch	Reigned	Spouse
House of Saxe-Coburg Gotha/Windsor*		
Edward VII Born 1841. Son of Victoria and Albert	1901–1910	Alexandra (daughter of Christian IX, King of Denmark)
George V Born 1865. Son of Edward VII and Alexandra * By Royal Proclamation the name of the royal house was changed to Windsor on 17 July 1917	1910–1936	Mary (May) (daughter of Francis, Duke of Teck)
House of Windsor		
Edward VIII Born 1894. Son of George V and Mary	20 Jan– 11 Dec 1936	Bessie Wallis Warfield Simpson (divorced wife of: i. Earl Winfield Spencer; ii. Ernest Simpson)
George VI Born 1895. Son of George V and Mary, and brother of Edward VIII	1936–1952	Lady Elizabeth Bowes-Lyon (daughter of the Earl of Strathmore and Kinghorne)
Elizabeth II Born 1926. Daughter of George VI and Elizabeth	From 6.2.52	Philip (son of Prince Andrew and Princess Alice of Greece)

Monopoly

Always a standby for quiz setters; if stuck for a question just take out the Monopoly Board and ask how much Coventry Street is worth. Well here are all of the spaces on a Monopoly Board, along with their values where appropriate. They are listed in the order in which they occur on the board.

Old Kent Road	£60
Community Chest	
Whitechapel Road	£60
Income Tax	(Pay £200)
Kings Cross Station	£200
The Angel Islington	£100
Chance	
Euston Road	£100
Pentonville Road	£120
Jail	
Pall Mall	£140
Electric Company	£150
Whitehall	£140
Northumberland Avenue	£160
Marylebone Station	£200
Bow Street	£180
Community Chest	
Marlborough Street	£180
Vine Street	£200
Free Parking	
Strand	£220
Chance	
Fleet Street	£220
Trafalgar Square	£240
Fenchurch Street Station	£200
Leicester Square	£260
Coventry Street	£260
Waterworks	£150
Piccadilly	£280
Go To Jail	
Regent Street	£300

Oxford Street	£300
Community Chest	
Bond Street	£320
Liverpool Street Station	£200
Chance	
Park Lane	£350
Supertax	(Pay £100)
Mayfair	£400

Motor Cars – Country of Manufacture

We probably all know that Renaults are made in France and Fiats are made in Italy and Ford manufactures in about a hundred different countries, but this list of manufacturers past and present will prove useful.

Some of these motor manufacturers produce cars in more than one country but the countries listed below are those in which they originally started production.

Manufacturer	*Country*
Acura	Japan
Bugatti	France
DAF	Netherlands
Denzel	Austria
Holden	Australia
Hyundai	Korea
Monteverdi	Switzerland
Proton	Malaysia
Sbarro	Switzerland
Skoda	Czech Republic
Wartburg	Former East Germany
Zastava	Yugoslavia

Motor Cars – Makers and Models

Since the first motor car was made over 100 years ago thousands upon thousands of different models have been manufactured, but questions on this subject usually relate to one of the following:

1 Models of motor car manufactured by British motor manufacturers in the 30s, 40s, 50s and 60s.
2 Models with distinctive names which have been manufactured by foreign car manufacturers.
3 Recently introduced models with which the general public is not yet familiar.

I have not included such obvious models as the Escort, the Cavalier, the Granada, etc. These lists should help you answer the "Which manufacturer made or makes model 'X'?" type of question. Once again it must be stressed that the list is not intended to be fully comprehensive; these models are the ones you are most likely to be asked about.

A word of caution. Some model names are common to more than one manufacturer. Excluded from this list are models which were known simply by the cubic capacity of their engines, eg 3.5, 2 litre etc.

British Cars

Manufacturer	*Model*
AC	Ace Roadster
	Bristol
	Cobra
	Greyhound
Alvis	Firebird
	Graber
Armstrong Siddeley	Sapphire
Aston Martin	Anything beginning with the letters DB
	Lagonda
	Vantage
	Virage
	Volante

Manufacturer	*Model*
Austin	Initially all Austins were denoted by a number (7, 8, 10, 12 etc) but the following are model names associated with Austin
	Atlantic
	Cambridge
	Goodwood
	Gypsy
	Hertford
	Mayfair
	Princess
	Ruby
	Westminster
Austin-Healey	Sprite
Bond	Bug
	Equipe
Bristol	Nos. 400
	401
	407
Chrysler	Alpine
	Avenger
Daimler	Majestic
	Consort
Ford	Anglia
	Consul
	Corsair
	Prefect
	Zephyr
	Zodiac
Hillman	Avenger
	Hunter
	Husky
	Imp
	Minx
	Segrave
	Wizard

Manufacturer	Model
Humber	Hawk
	Imperial
	Pullman
	Sceptre
	Snipe
Jensen	Healey
	Interceptor
Jowett	Curlew
	Javelin
	Jupiter
Lagonda	Le Mans
	Rapide
	Rapier
Lotus	Eclat
	Elan
	Elite
	Esprit
	Europa
	Le Mans
	Sprint
MG	Costello
	Judson
	Magna
	Magnette
	Midget
Morgan	Plus 4
	Plus 8
	SS
Morris	Cowley
	Isis
	Oxford
Reliant	Kitten
	Rebel
	Robin
	Scimitar
	Sabre

Manufacturer	Model
Riley	Elf
	Falcon
	Kestrel
	Pathfinder
	Sprite
Rover	Almost all Rovers were given numeric names, such as the 75, the 60, the 90 etc. or the model was designated by its engine capacity (2000, 3500 etc)
Singer	Chamois
	Gazelle
	Roadster
	Vogue
Standard	Avon
	Ensign
	Penant
	Vanguard
	Many standard models used numbers as their designation (eg Flying 10, Flying 20, 12 Saloon etc)
Sunbeam	Alpine
	Imp
	Rapier
	Stiletto
	Talbot
	Tiger
Talbot	Horizon
	Samba
	Solara
	Tagora
Triumph	Dolomite
	Herald
	Spitfire
	Stag
	Toledo
	Vitesse

Manufacturer	Model
TVR	Tasmine
	Tuscan
	Vixen
Vanden Plas	Princess
Vauxhall	Cadet
	Cresta
	Firenza
	Magnum
	Velox
	Ventura
	Victor
	Viscount
	Wyvern
Wolseley	Hornet
	Viper

Foreign Models

Manufacturer	Model
Alfa Romeo	Berlina
	Giulia
	Giulietta
	Spider
Audi	Avant
	Anything followed by the word 'Quattro'
BMW	Almost all BMWs are designated by numbers, eg 320i, 535 etc
Buick	Century
	Riviera
	Skyhawk
	Skylark
	Wildcat
Cadillac	Aurora
	Calais
	Cimarron
	Seville

Manufacturer	*Model*
Chevrolet	Camaro
	Corvette
	Corvair
	Bell Air
	Impala
Citroen	Ami
	Safari
	Pallas
	Visa
DAF	44
	55
	66
Daihatsu	Domino
	Charade
	Charmant
	Applause
Datsun	Cherry
	Laurel
	Maxima
	Scarab
	Stanza
	Sunny
Dodge	Charger
	Colt
	Coronet
	Dart
	Daytona
	Lancer
Ferrari	Daytona
	Dino
	Mondial
	Testa Rossa

Manufacturer	*Model*
Fiat	Fiat models were traditionally designated by numbers (124, 132, 125 etc) but recently models have been given names, here are some of them:
	Brava
	Croma
	Panda
	Strada
	Regata
	Tempra
	Tipo
	Uno
Honda	Civic
	Accord
	Legend
	Prelude
	Integra
Hyundai	Excell
	Lantra
	Pony
	Sonata
	Stellar
Isuzu	Impulse
Lada	Riva
	Samara
Lamborghini	Countach
	Diablo
	Jalpa
Lancia	Beta
	Dedra
	Delta
	Flavia
	Fulvia
	Gamma
	Prisma
	Thema

Manufacturer	*Model*
Lincoln	Continental
Maserati	Biturbo
	Khamsin
	Shamal
Mazda	MX-3
	MX-5
	MX-6
	MX-7
	RX-7
Mercedes Benz	Almost all Mercedes models are designated by numbers (eg 300, 230, 380, 190 etc)
Mercury	Bobcat
	Capri
	Cougar
	Lynx
Mitsubishi	Colt Galant
	Colt Lancer
	Colt Sigma
	Colt Shogun
	Eclipse
	Mirage
	Tredia
Nissan	Bluebird
	Cherry
	Laurel
	Maxima
	Micra
	Primera
	Pulsar
	Stanza
	Sunny
NSU	Prinz
	Spider

Manufacturer	Model
Opel	Ascona
	Kadette
	Manta
	Rekord
Peugeot	Almost every Peugeot model is designated by a number, eg 405, 205, 505 etc
Plymouth	Barracuda
	Fury
	Laser
	Roadrunner
	Valiant
Pontiac	Bonneville
	Fiero
	Firebird
	Phoenix
Porsche	Carrera
	Cabriolet
Proton	Aeroback
Renault	As with many continental producers most of Renault's models were simply given numbers (15, 16, 17 etc). Here are some of the names:
	Caravelle
	Chamade
	Dauphine
	Espace
	Fuego
Saab	Almost all models are designated by numbers, invariably starting with a 9
Seat	Ibiza
	Malaga
Simca	Once again, most models were given numeric titles
Skoda	Estelle
	Rapide

Manufacturer	Model
Subaru	Legacy
	Justy
	XT
Suzuki	Alto
	Swift
	Vitara
Toyota	Camry
	Carina
	Celica
	Corolla
	Corona
	Cressida
	MR2
	Paseo
	Previa
	Starlet
	Supra
	Tercel
Volkswagen	Corrado
	Dasher
	Golf
	Jetta
	Passat
	Polo
	Rabbit
	Santana
	Scirocco
Volvo	Once again another manufacturer who uses numbers to designate models. It is well worth remembering that most of these numbers contain the No. 4 somewhere
Wartburg	Knight
Yugo	Sana

Mountains

Questions about the highest peaks in various countries still occur with some regularity. What is interesting is that the same countries crop up time and time again. Australia is a good example (perhaps because of the unusual name of that country's highest peak). Here is a list of frequently referred to mountains.

Country	Mountain	Height (ft)
Antarctica	Vinson Massif	16,863
Argentina	Aconcagua	22,834
	The highest mountain outside of Asia, first climbed in January 1987. Also highest extinct volcano in the world.	
Australia	Kosciusko	7,316
	It is in New South Wales.	
Austria	Grossglockner	12,462
	First climbed in 1800.	
Canada	Mount Logan	19,850
	First climbed in 1925.	
France	Mont Blanc	15,771
	First climbed in 1786.	
Georgia	Elbrus	18,480
	The highest mountain in Europe.	
Germany	Zugspitze	9,721
	First climbed in 1820.	
Greece	Mount Olympus	9,550
India	Nanda Devi	25,645
	First climbed in 1936.	
Ireland	Carrantuohill	3,414
Italy	Mont Blanc	15,616
Japan	Mount Fuji	12,388
Nepal	Mount Everest	29,028
	First climbed on 29 May 1953.	
New Zealand	Mount Cook	12,349
Pakistan	K2 (Mt. Godwin Austen)	28,250
	First climbed in 1954.	

Country	Mountain	Height (ft)
Spain	**Mount Teide**	12,190
	(On the Canary Islands.)	
Switzerland	**Monte Rosa**	15,203
	First climbed in 1855.	
Tajikistan	**Mount Communism**	24,590
	This was the highest peak in the old Soviet Union.	
Tanzania	**Mount Kilimanjaro**	19,340
	The highest mountain in Africa.	
Turkey	**Mount Ararat**	17,011
United States	**Mount McKinley**	20,320
	The highest point in North America.	

The highest volcano in the world is Cotopaxi in Ecuador at 19,344 ft.

MPs – Constituencies

Questions relating to this subject come in one of two forms; "For which constituency is Mrs X the MP?" or "Who is the well-known member of parliament for constituency Y?" There are 651 MPs but generally only those who hold high office in their party or are recognised as parliamentary "characters" or "personalities" are ever referred to. I am aware of several dangers in compiling this section, some honourable members may pass on to that great debating chamber in the sky, others may resign their seats to take up other appointments, and some previously anonymous members may rise to prominence for one reason or another.

MP	Party	Constituency
Diane Abbott	Labour	Hackney North and Stoke Newington
Paddy Ashdown	Liberal Democrat	Yeovil
Margaret Beckett	Labour	Derby South
Alan Beith	Liberal Democrat	Berwick upon Tweed
Tony Benn	Labour	Chesterfield
Tony Blair	Labour	Sedgefield

MP	Party	Constituency
David Blunkett	Labour	Sheffield Brightside
Paul Boateng	Labour	Brent South
Betty Boothroyd	Speaker	West Bromwich West
Virginia Bottomley	Conservative	Surrey South West
Gyles Brandreth	Conservative	Chester
Peter Brooke	Conservative	City of London and Westminster
Gordon Brown	Labour	Dunfermline East
Menzies Campbell	Liberal Democrat	Fife North East
Dale Campbell-Savours	Labour	Workington
Winston Churchill	Conservative	Davyhulme
Kenneth Clarke	Conservative	Rushcliffe
Sebastian Coe	Conservative	Falmouth and Camborne
Robin Cook	Labour	Livingston
Julian Critchley	Conservative	Aldershot
Dr Jack Cunningham	Labour	Copeland
Edwina Currie	Conservative	Derbyshire South
Tam Dalyell	Labour	Linlithgow
Donald Dewar	Labour	Glasgow Garscadden
Sir Norman Fowler	Conservative	Sutton Coldfield
Sir Marcus Fox	Conservative	Shipley
Tristan Garel-Jones	Conservative	Watford
Bernie Grant	Labour	Tottenham
Harriet Harman	Labour	Peckham
Sir Edward Heath	Conservative	Old Bexley and Sidcup
Michael Heseltine	Conservative	Henley
Michael Howard	Conservative	Folkestone and Hythe
Douglas Hurd	Conservative	Whitney
Glenda Jackson	Labour	Hampstead and Highgate
Tom King	Conservative	Bridgewater
Neil Kinnock	Labour	Islwyn
Norman Lamont	Conservative	Kingston upon Thames
Peter Lilley	Conservative	St Albans

MP	Party	Constituency
Ken Livingstone	Labour	Brent East
John MacGregor	Conservative	Norfolk South
John Major	Conservative	Huntingdon
Sir Patrick Mayhew	Conservative	Tunbridge Wells
Michael Meacher	Labour	Oldham West
David Mellor	Conservative	Putney
The Rev. Ian Paisley	Democratic Unionist Party	Antrim North
John Patten	Conservative	Oxford W. and Abingdon
Michael Portillo	Conservative	Enfield, Southgate
John Prescott	Labour	Kingston upon Hull, East
Malcolm Rifkind	Conservative	Edinburgh, Pentlands
George Robertson	Labour	Hamilton
Angela Rumbold	Conservative	Mitcham and Morden
Gillian Shepherd	Conservative	Norfolk South West
Clare Short	Labour	Birmingham, Ladywood
Dennis Skinner	Labour	Bolsover
Sir David Steel	Liberal Democrat	Tweeddale, Ettrick and Lauderdale
Jack Straw	Labour	Blackburn
Sir Teddy Taylor	Conservative	Southend East
William Waldegrave	Conservative	Bristol West
Nicholas Winterton	Conservative	Macclesfield

Musicals

"From which musical does song xxxx or xxxx come?" or "Which musical featured the songs xxxx and xxxx?" are very common quiz questions. What is strange is that question setters tend be to stuck in some sort of time warp; about 75% of all questions relate to musicals which were made in the 1940s and 1950s. The following list will prove very useful. N.B. Some songs are in more than one musical.

An American In Paris	I Got Rhythm
	S'wonderful
	Love Is Here To Stay
	Nice Work If You Can Get It
Annie Get Your Gun	You Can't Get A Man With A Gun
	My Defences Are Down
	There's No Business Like Show Business
	Doin' What Comes Naturally
	Anything You Can Do
Brigadoon	The Heather On The Hill
	Almost Like Being In Love
Cabaret	Money, Money
	Mein Herr
Calamity Jane	Secret Love
	The Deadwood Stage
	The Black Hills Of Dakota
	Just Blew In From The Windy City
Call Me Madam	You're Just In Love
	The Hostess with the Mostest
Camelot	If Ever I Would Leave You
	How To Handle A Woman
Can Can	C'est Magnifique
	Its Alright With Me
	Let's Do It
	Just One Of Those Things
	You Do Something To Me
Carousel	When I Marry Mr Snow
	If I Loved You
	When The Children Are Asleep
	You'll Never Walk Alone

Easter Parade	Stepping Out With My Baby
	A Couple Of Swells
Fiddler On The Roof	Matchmaker, Matchmaker
	If I Were A Rich Man
	Sunrise, Sunset
Flower Drum Song	I Enjoy Being A Girl
Funny Girl	Don't Rain On My Parade
	People
Gentlemen Prefer Blondes	Diamonds Are A Girl's Best Friend
Gigi	The Night They Invented Champagne
	I'm Glad I'm Not Young Any More
	I Remember It Well
	Thank Heaven For Little Girls
Guys And Dolls	Luck Be A Lady
	A Bushell And A Peck
	A Woman In Love
	Sit Down You're Rockin' The Boat
Gypsy	Some People
	Everything's Coming Up Roses
Half A Sixpence	Flash Bang, Wallop!
High Society	Now You Has Jazz
	Who Wants To Be A Millionaire
	True Love
	Samantha
	Well, Did You Evah
Holiday Inn	White Christmas
	Happy Holiday
	Easter Parade
The Joker Is Wild	All The Way
	Swinging On A Star
	June In January

The King And I	I Whistle A Happy Tune
	Hello Young Lovers
	March Of The Siamese Children
	Getting To Know You
	We Kiss In A Shadow
	Something Wonderful
	Shall We Dance
Kismet	Baubles, Bangles And Beads
	Stranger in Paradise
	This Is My Beloved
Kiss Me Kate	Too Darn Hot
	From This Moment On
	Wunderbar
	Always True To You Darling In My Fashion
	Brush Up Your Shakespeare
A Little Night Music	Send In The Clowns
Mary Poppins	Supercalifrag:listicexpialidocious
	Chim Chim Cheree
	A Spoonful Of Sugar
Me And My Gal	Oh! Johnny, Oh!
	Oh! You Beautiful Doll
	When You Wore A Tulip
	After You've Gone
	How Ya Gonna Keep 'Em Down On The Farm
Meet Me In St Louis	The Trolley Song
	Have Yourself A Merry Little Christmas
The Music Man	Seventy-Six Trombones
	'Til There Was You
My Fair Lady	I Could Have Danced All Night
	Wouldn't It Be Luverly
	The Street Where You Live
	Get Me To The Church On Time
	I've Grown Accustomed To Her Face
No, No Nanette	Tea For Two
	I Want To Be Happy

Oklahoma	Oh What A Beautiful Morning
	Surrey With A Fringe On Top
	I Can't Say No
	People Will Say We're In Love
	All Or Nothing
Oliver	Consider Yourself
	Food, Glorious Food
	I'd Do Anything
Paint Your Wagon	Wanderin' Star
	They Call The Wind Maria
	There's A Coach Comin' In
	I Talk To The Trees
The Pajama Game	Hernando's Hideaway
	Hey There
Pal Joey	Bewitched, Bothered And Bewildered
	I Could Write A Book
	My Funny Valentine
	The Lady Is A Tramp
Pinnochio	When You Wish Upon A Star
(Although not a	Give A Little Whistle
musical in the true	
sense of the word,	
questions are asked	
about these songs)	
Porgy And Bess	Summertime
	I Got Plenty O'Nuttin
	It Ain't Necessarily So
Rhapsody In Blue	Fascinating Rhythm
	Summertime
	The Man I Love
	Oh Lady Be Good
	Love Walked In
	Someone To Watch Over Me
	'Swonderful
	I Got Rhythm
	Embraceable You

Robin And The	My Kind Of Town
Seven Hoods	Style
Seven Brides For	Sobbin' Women
Seven Brothers	Bless Yore Beautiful Hide
	Spring, Spring, Spring
Showboat	Ol' Man River
	Make Believe
	Can't Help Lovin' Dat Man
Singin' In The Rain	All I Do Is Dream of You
	Good Morning!
	You Are My Lucky Star
	You Were Meant For Me
Snow White And	Some Day My Prince Will Come
The Seven Dwarfs	Whistle While You Work
(See the note for	Heigh-Ho!
"Pinnochio")	
Song Of The South	Zip-a-Dee-Doo-Dah
The Sound Of Music	Sixteen Going On Seventeen
	Climb Every Mountain
	My Favourite Things
South Pacific	Happy Talk
	A Cock-eyed Optimist
	Some Enchanted Evening
	There Is Nothing Like A Dame
	I'm Gonna Wash That Man Right Outa My Hair
	I'm In Love With A Wonderful Guy
	Younger Than Springtime
	This Nearly Was Mine
A Star Is Born	The Man That Got Away
(1954 Judy Garland	Born In A Trunk
Version)	I'll Get By
Sweet Charity	Hey Big Spender!
	Rhythm Of Life
	I'm a Brass Band
	If They Could See Me Now

West Side Story	Something's Coming
	America
	Tonight
	I Feel Pretty
White Christmas	Count Your Blessings Instead Of Sheep
	Heatwave
Words And Music	The Lady Is A Tramp
	Thou Swell
	This Can't Be Love
	With A Song In My Heart
	Manhattan
	Blue Moon
	Mountain Greenery
Yankee Doodle Dandy	Give My Regards To Broadway

Musical Terms

Probably anybody with a working knowledge of Italian would be able to translate the musical terms into their English meanings; however, most people do not have a grasp of that beautiful language so here is a list of the most frequently asked musical terms (except those which are easily translated such as *accelerando*) and their English meanings.

Adagio	A slow movement
Allegretto	Quite fast
Allegro	Fast, but not too fast (little quicker than *allegretto*)
Andante	Walking pace
Barcarolle	A song sung by Venetian gondoliers
Buffo	Comic, amusing
Calando	Becoming quieter and slower
Da Capo	Repeat the opening section
Deciso	Firmly
Diminuendo	Gradually becoming softer
Doloroso	Mournfully
Giocoso	With fun
Largo	Slowly
Maestoso	With majesty
Molto	Very much
Obbligato	A vital instrumental part of a piece
Pizzicato	The plucking of string instruments
Presto	Very fast
Rallentando	Slowing down
Ritornello	A recurring passage in a piece of music
Rondo	A recurring passage in a piece of music
Sostenuto	Sustained
Vibrato	The fluctuation in the pitch of a voice or an instrument
Vivace	Lively

Musicians and Their Music

Well-known operas and symphonies are covered in other sections but many musical questions involve music which is neither symphonic nor operatic. This list should prove useful.

Thomas Arne	Rule Britannia
Johann Sebastian Bach	The St John Passion
	The St Matthew Passion
	The Brandenburg Concertos
	The Well-Tempered Clavier
	The Art of Fugue
Alexander Borodin	In the Steppes of Central Asia
Johannes Brahms	German Requiem
	Hungarian Dances
Bejamin Britten	War Requiem (Written for the Consecration of Coventry Cathedral)
	Young Person's guide to the Orchestra
John Cage	4' – 33" (4½ minutes of silence)
Frederic Chopin	Funeral March
Jeremiah Clarke	Trumpet Voluntary (More properly "The Prince of Denmark's March")
Eric Coates	The Dambuster's March
Aaron Copland	Music for the ballets "Appalachian Spring" and "Billy the Kid"
Claude Debussy	Nocturnes
	La Mer
Frederick Delius	Florida Suite
	Brigg Fair
	Sea Drift
Antonin Dvořák	Slavonic Dances
	Moravian Duets
Edward Elgar	The Dream of Gerontius
	Enigma Variations
	Pomp and Circumstance March
George Gershwin	Rhapsody in Blue
Percy Grainger	Country Gardens
	Handel in the Strand
Edvard Grieg	Peer Gynt

George Frideric Handel	Water Music Suite
	Messiah
	Judas Maccabaeus
	Zadok the Priest
	Music for the Royal Fireworks
	St John Passion
	The Resurrection
Joseph Haydn	The Creation
	The Seasons
	Quartets
Gustav Holst	The Planets
Gustav Mahler	The Song of the Earth
Felix Mendelssohn	The Hebrides Overture
Modest Mussorgsky	Night on the Bare Mountain
	Pictures at an Exhibition
Jacques Offenbach	The Tales of Hoffman
Carl Orff	Carmina Burana
Sergei Prokofiev	Peter and the Wolf
	Romeo and Juliet (ballet)
	Cinderella (ballet)
Sergei Rachmaninov	Rhapsody on a Theme by Paganini
Maurice Ravel	Spanish Rhapsody
	Bolero
Nikolai Rimsky-Korsakov	Spanish Caprice
	Scheherazade
Camille Saint-Saëns	Danse Macabre
	Carnival of the Animals
Franz Schubert	Trout Quintet
Jean Sibelius	Finlandia
Johann Straus (Senior)	Radetzky March
Johann Strauss (Junior)	The Blue Danube Waltz
	Tales From the Vienna Woods
Richard Strauss	Also Sprach Zarathustra
Igor Stravinsky	The Firebird (ballet)
	The Rite of Spring (ballet)

Piotr Ilyich Tchaikovsky	Romeo and Juliet
	Sleeping Beauty (ballet)
	The Nutcracker (ballet)
	Swan Lake (ballet)
Ralph Vaughan Williams	The Lark Ascending
	Fantasia on a Theme by Thomas Tallis
Antonio Vivaldi	The Four Seasons
William Walton	Belshazzar's Feast
	Crown Imperial
	Orb and Sceptre

Nobel Prizes – Literature

Nobel prize questions are often reserved for well known people who have won prizes. This usually means that questions relate to Literature or Peace.

Questions on Nobel literature laureates are usually confined to those who wrote in the English language (I have yet to be asked a question on Francois Mauriac who won the prize in 1952). The following is a list of Nobel Literature Prizewinners whose works were in English (or mostly in English).

1907	Rudyard Kipling
1923	W. B. Yeats
1925	George Bernard Shaw
1930	Sinclair Lewis
1932	John Galsworthy
1936	Eugene O'Neill
1938	Pearl Buck
1948	T. S. Eliot
1949	William Faulkner
1950	Bertrand Russell
1953	Sir Winston Churchill
1954	Ernest Hemingway
1962	John Steinbeck
1969	Samuel Beckett
1973	Patrick White
1976	Saul Bellow
1978	Isaac Bashevis Singer
1983	William Golding
1987	Joseph Brodsky
1991	Nadine Gordimer
1993	Toni Morrison

Nobel Prizes – Peace

A very common source of questions because many of the Peace laureates were internationally known figures, many were not. The following is a list of well-known Nobel Peace laureates. Exclusion from this list does not infer that the award was not merited nor the achievements of other laureates were less deserving but questions are very rarely asked on laureates such as Viscount Cecil, Rene Cassin or Cordell Hull.

1906 Theodore Roosevelt

1919 Woodrow Wilson

1925 Sir Austen Chamberlain

Charles Gates Dawes (Mr Dawes is included because to my knowledge he is the only Nobel Peace laureate to have written a No. 1 hit single, "Its All in the Game" by Tommy Edwards)

1952 Albert Schweitzer

1961 Dag Hammarskjöld (the only posthumous award of a Nobel Prize)

1962 Linus Pauling (who won the Nobel Prize for Chemistry in 1954)

1964 Martin Luther King

1971 Willie Brandt

1973 Henry Kissinger

Le Duc Tho (declined the award)

1975 Andrei Sakharov

1976 Mairead Corrigan

Betty Williams

1978 Menachem Begin

Anwar al-Sadat

1979 Mother Teresa

1983 Lech Walesa

1984 Desmond Tutu

1990 Mikhail Gorbachov

1993 F. W. de Klerk

Nelson Mandela

Olympic Games Venues

Always useful to know, particularly the Games that were cancelled due to war.

Summer Olympic Games

1896	Athens
1900	Paris
1904	St Louis
1908	London
1912	Stockholm
1916	Scheduled for Berlin but cancelled due to World War I
1920	Antwerp
1924	Paris (the first city to host the Olympic Games twice)
1928	Amsterdam
1932	Los Angeles
1936	Berlin
1940	Scheduled for Tokyo, and later Helsinki but cancelled due to World War II
1944	Scheduled for London but cancelled due to World War II
1948	London
1952	Helsinki
1956	Melbourne (the equestrian events were staged in Stockholm)
1960	Rome
1964	Tokyo
1968	Mexico City
1972	Munich
1976	Montreal
1980	Moscow
1984	Los Angeles
1988	Seoul
1992	Barcelona
1996	Atlanta
2000	Sydney

Winter Olympic Games

1924	Chamonix
1928	St Moritz
1932	Lake Placid
1936	Garmisch-Partenkirchen
1948	St Moritz (the first resort to stage the games twice)
1952	Oslo (the only capital city to host the winter Olympics)
1956	Cortina
1960	Squaw Valley
1964	Innsbruck
1968	Grenoble
1972	Sapporo
1976	Innsbruck
1980	Lake Placid
1984	Sarajevo
1988	Calgary
1992	Albertville
1994	Lillehammer
1998	Nagano

Opera

Always a popular category, although I wonder how many quiz players have ever been to the opera. In recent years the scope of opera questions has broadened, not in the style of questions but in the composers covered by the question. Ten years ago almost all operas mentioned in quizzes were written by either Germans or Italians, this is not the case any longer. Apart from one or two notable exceptions the questions are invariably about the composer of an opera. The following is a list of the operas which most frequently surface in quizzes, along with their composers.

Title of Opera	Composer	
Aida	Verdi	Commissioned for the new Cairo Opera House and in celebration of the opening of the Suez Canal in 1869. However, It was not performed until 1871.
Barber of Seville	Rossini	First performed in St Petersburg in 1782.
The Bartered Bride	Smetana	First performed in Prague in 1866 *(an old quiz favourite this one)*.
La Bohème	Puccini	First performance was conducted by Toscanini in Turin in 1896.
Boris Godunov	Mussorgski	Initially rejected by the St Petersburg Opera in 1870.
Carmen	Bizet	First performed in Paris in 1875 (the opera originally included spoken dialogue).
Cavalleria Rusticana	Mascagni	First performed in Rome in 1890.
Dido and Aeneas	Purcell	First performed in London in 1689.

Title of Opera	Composer	
Don Carlos	Verdi	First performed in Paris in 1867.
Don Giovanni	Mozart	The full title of the opera is "Don Giovanni (The Rake Punished)" or "Don Juan", first performed in Prague in 1787.
Eugene Onegin	Tchaikovsky	First performed at the Bolshoi in 1881.
Götterdämmerung (Twilight of the Gods)	Wagner	First performed at Bayreuth in 1876 (the fourth and last part of Wagner's Ring Cycle).
Falstaff	Verdi	First performed in Milan in 1893 (Verdi's last opera).
Faust	Gounod	First performed in Paris in 1859 (not to be confused with the "Faust Overture" by Wagner or the "Faust Symphony" by Liszt.
Fidelio	Beethoven	First performed in Vienna in 1805 (Beethoven's only opera).
Die Fledermaus	Johann Strauss	First performed in Vienna in 1874.
The Flying Dutchman	Wagner	First performed in Dresden in 1843.
From the House of the Dead	Janacek	First performed at Brno in 1930, two years after the composer's death.
The Girl of the Golden West	Puccini	First performed in New York in 1910 (set in California at the time of the Gold Rush).

Title of Opera	*Composer*	
Gloriana	Britten	First performed in London in 1953 (commissioned by Covent Garden for the Coronation of Queen Elizabeth II).
The Golden Cockerel	Rimsky-Korsakov	First performed in Moscow in 1909, after the composer's death. (It was Rimsky-Korsakov's last opera and was banned during his lifetime).
Hansel and Gretel	Humperdinck	First performed at Weimar in 1893 (probably only occurs in quizzes because of the composer's name).
Lady Macbeth of Mzensk	Shostakovich	First performed in Moscow in 1934 (the title of the opera was later changed to "Katerina Ismailova".
Lohengrin	Wagner	First performed at Weimar in 1850, and conducted by Liszt.
Lucia di Lammermoor	Donizetti	First performed in Naples in 1835.
Madame Butterfly	Puccini	First performed in Milan in 1904 (unusual in that the United States National Anthem forms part of the opera).
The Magic Flute	Mozart	First performed in Vienna in 1791, two months before the composer's death.

Title of Opera	*Composer*	
The Marriage of Figaro	Mozart	First performed in Vienna in 1786.
A Masked Ball	Verdi	First performed in 1859.
Die Meistersinger von Nürnberg (The Master Singers Of Nuremberg)	Wagner	First performed in Munich in 1868.
Moses and Aaron	Schoenberg	First performed on German radio in 1954, three years after the composer's death, but not staged until 1957 in Zurich *(unusual that the work took over 20 years to compose and is still unfinished. Schoenberg completed the first two acts in 1932 but did not begin the third act until 1951, shortly before his death).*
Nabucco	Verdi	First performed in Milan in 1842 (Verdi's first major success).
Otello	Verdi	The title of several operas but the two best known are by Verdi – first performed in Milan in 1887; and Rossini, first performed in Naples in 1816.
Otello	Rossini	
I Pagliacci (The Clowns)	Leoncavallo	First performed in Milan in 1892 (conducted by Toscanini).

Title of Opera	Composer	
Parsifal	Wagner	First performed at Bayreuth in 1882 (Wagner's last opera).
Peter Grimes	Britten	First performed in London in 1945 (Britten's first published opera).
Prince Igor	Borodin	The work was unfinished at the time of the composer's death in 1887. It was completed by Rimsky-Korsakov and Glazunov. First performed at St Petersburg in 1890.
The Queen of Spades	Tchaikovsky	First performed at St Petersburg in 1890 (the libretto was written by his brother Modest).
The Rake's Progress	Stravinsky	First performed in Venice in 1951 (the libretto was written by W. H. Auden).
The Rape of Lucretia	Britten	First performed at Glyndebourne in 1946.
Das Rheingold	Wagner	First performed in Munich in 1869 (the first part of the Ring Cycle).
Rigoletto	Verdi	First performed in Venice in 1851.
Romeo and Juliet	Gounod	First performed in Paris in 1867 (not to be confused with the symphony by Berlioz, the orchestral piece of Tchaikovsky, nor the ballet by Prokofiev).
Der Rosenkavalier (The Knight Of The Rose)	Richard Strauss	First performed in Dresden in 1911.

Title of Opera	Composer	
Salome	Richard Strauss	First performed in Dresden in 1905 (although it is doubtful that Salome took off all seven veils at that performance).
Siegfried	Wagner	First performed at Bayreuth in 1876. (The third part of the Ring Cycle).
The Silken Ladder	Rossini	First performed in Venice in 1812.
Simon Boccanegra	Verdi	First performed in Venice in 1857.
The Snow Maiden	Rimsky-Korsakov	First performed in St Petersburg in 1882.
The Tales of Hoffmann	Offenbach	First performed in Paris in 1881 (four months after the death of the composer).
Tannhäuser (Tannhäuser Und Der Säangerkrieg Auf Wartburg)	Wagner	First performed in Dresden in 1845.
The Pearl-Fishers	Bizet	First performed in Paris in 1863.
The Thieving Magpie	Rossini	First performed in Milan in 1817 (for obvious reasons it is useful to know the Italian title which is "La Gazza Ladra".
The Threepenny Opera	Weill	First performed in Berlin in 1928 (the librettist was Bertolt Brecht).
Tosca	Puccini	First performed in Rome in 1900.

Title of Opera	Composer	
La Traviata (The Woman Who Was Led Astray)	Verdi	First performed in Venice in 1853.
Tristan and Isolde	Wagner	First performed in Munich in 1865.
Troilus and Cressida	Walton	First performed in London in 1954.
The Trojans	Berlioz	First performed in Karlsruhe in 1890.
Il Trovatore (The Troubador)	Verdi	First performed in Rome in 1853.
Turandot	Puccini	At least eight operas have been written with this title but the most famous is by Puccini. The composer left the work unfinished and it was first performed in Milan in 1926 after Alfano had completed the work *(its claim to fame is that it contains the well known pop song Nessun dorma).*
The Valkyrie (Die Walküre)	Wagner	First performed in Munich in 1870 (the second part of the Ring Cycle).
A Village Romeo and Juliet	Delius	First performed in Berlin in 1907.
William Tell	Rossini	First performed in Paris in 1829. (Rossini's last opera.)
Xerxes	Handel	First performed in London in 1738.

Oscars (Academy Awards)

Usually questions on this subject relate to the most recent awards and occasionally to the less well publicised Oscars (best sound track, best animation etc) but questions such as "Who won an Oscar for film x?" or "For which film did Miss 'Y' win an Oscar?" are still very common. Occasionally these are wrapped up in the "spot the year" type of question, you know the sort of thing "In which year did Spurs win the Cup and Sophia Loren win an Oscar?". Anyway here they are and they are well worth remembering. The years given are the years in which the Oscars were awarded.

Actor	Actress	Director	Film
1929			
Emil Jannings (The Way Of All Flesh)	Janet Gaynor (Seventh Heaven)	Frank Borzage (Seventh Heaven) Lewis Milestone (Two Arabian Knights)	Wings
1930			
Warner Baxter (In Old Arizona)	Mary Pickford (Coquette)	Frank Lloyd (The Divine Lady)	Broadway Melody
1931			
George Arliss (Disraeli)	Norma Shearer (The Divorcee)	Lewis Milestone (All Quiet On The Western Front)	All Quiet On The Western Front
1932			
Lionel Barrymore (Free Soul)	Marie Dressler (Min and Bill)	Norman Taurog (Skippy)	Cimarron
1933			
Fredric March (Dr Jekyll & Mr Hyde) Wallace Beery (The Champ)	Helen Hayes (Sin Of Madelon Claudet)	Frank Borzage (Bad Girl)	Grand Hotel

Actor	Actress	Director	Film
1934			
Charles Laughton (Private Life Of Henry VIII)	Katharine Hepburn (Morning Glory)	Frank Lloyd (Cavalcade)	Cavalcade
1935			
Clark Gable (It Happened One Night)	Claudette Colbert (It Happened One Night)	Frank Capra (It Happened One Night)	It Happened One Night
1936			
Victor McLaglen (The Informer)	Bette Davis (Dangerous)	John Ford (The Informer)	Mutiny On The Bounty
1937			
Paul Muni (The Story Of Louis Pasteur)	Luise Rainer (The Great Ziegfeld)	Frank Capra (Mr Deeds Goes To Town)	The Great Ziegfeld
1938			
Spencer Tracy (Captains Courageous)	Luise Rainer (The Good Earth)	Leo McCarey (The Awful Truth)	The Life Of Emile Zola
1939			
Spencer Tracy (Boys Town)	Bette Davis (Jezebel)	Frank Capra (You Can't Take It With You)	You Can't Take It With You
1940			
Robert Donat (Goodbye, Mr Chips)	Vivien Leigh (Gone With The Wind)	Victor Fleming (Gone With The Wind)	Gone With The Wind
1941			
James Stewart (The Philadelphia Story)	Ginger Rogers (Kitty Foyle)	John Ford (The Grapes Of Wrath)	Rebecca

Actor	Actress	Director	Film
1942			
Gary Cooper (Sergeant York)	Joan Fontaine (Suspicion)	John Ford (How Green Was My Valley)	How Green Was My Valley
1943			
James Cagney (Yankee Doodle Dandy)	Greer Garson (Mrs Miniver)	William Wyler (Mrs Miniver)	Mrs Miniver
1944			
Paul Lukas (Watch On The Rhine)	Jennifer Jones (The Song Of Bernadette)	Michael Curtiz (Casablanca)	Casablanca
1945			
Bing Crosby (Going My Way)	Ingrid Bergman (Gaslight)	Leo McCarey (Going My Way)	Going My Way
1946			
Ray Milland (The Lost Weekend)	Joan Crawford (Mildred Pierce)	Billy Wilder (The Lost Weekend)	The Lost Weekend
1947			
Fredric March (The Best Years Of Our Lives)	Olivia de Havilland (To Each His Own)	William Wyler (The Best Years Of Our Lives)	The Best Years Of Our Lives
1948			
Ronald Colman (A Double Life)	Loretta Young (The Farmer's Daughter)	Elia Kazan (Gentleman's Agreement)	Gentleman's Agreement
1949			
Laurence Olivier (Hamlet)	Jane Wyman (Johnny Belinda)	John Huston (The Treasure Of The Sierra Madre)	Hamlet
1950			
Broderick Crawford (All The King's Men)	Olivia de Havilland (The Heiress)	Joseph L. Mankiewicz (A Letter To Three Wives)	All The King's Men

Actor	Actress	Director	Film
1951			
José Ferrer (Cyrano de Bergerac)	Judy Holliday (Born Yesterday)	Joseph L. Mankiewicz (All About Eve)	All About Eve
1952			
Humphrey Bogart (The African Queen)	Vivien Leigh (A Streetcar Named Desire)	George Stevens (A Place In The Sun)	An American In Paris
1953			
Gary Cooper (High Noon)	Shirley Booth (Come Back, Little Sheba)	John Ford (The Quiet Man)	The Greatest Show On Earth
1954			
William Holden (Stalag 17)	Audrey Hepburn (Roman Holiday)	Fred Zinnemann (From Here To Eternity)	From Here To Eternity
1955			
Marlon Brando (On The Waterfront)	Grace Kelly (The Country Girl)	Elia Kazan (On The Waterfront)	On The Waterfront
1956			
Ernest Borgnine (Marty)	Anna Magnani (The Rose Tattoo)	Delbert Mann (Marty)	Marty
1957			
Yul Brynner (The King And I)	Ingrid Bergman (Anastasia)	George Stevens (Giant)	Around The World In Eighty Days
1958			
Alec Guinness (The Bridge On The River Kwai)	Joanne Woodward (The Three Faces Of Eve)	David Lean (The Bridge On The River Kwai)	The Bridge On The River Kwai

Actor	Actress	Director	Film
1959			
David Niven (Separate Tables)	Susan Hayward (I Want To Live)	Vincento Minnelli (Gigi)	Gigi
1960			
Charlton Heston (Ben-Hur)	Simone Signoret (Room At The Top)	William Wyler (Ben-Hur)	Ben-Hur
1961			
Burt Lancaster (Elmer Gantry)	Elizabeth Taylor (Butterfield 8)	Billy Wilder (The Apartment)	The Apartment
1962			
Maximilian Schell (Judgment at Nuremberg)	Sophia Loren (Two Women)	Jerome Robbins Robert Wise (West Side Story)	West Side Story
1963			
Gregory Peck (To Kill A Mockingbird)	Anne Bancroft (The Miracle Worker)	David Lean (Lawrence Of Arabia)	Lawrence Of Arabia
1964			
Sidney Poitier (Lilies of the Field)	Patricia Neal (Hud)	Tony Richardson (Tom Jones)	Tom Jones
1965			
Rex Harrison (My Fair Lady)	Julie Andrews (Mary Poppins)	George Cukor (My Fair Lady)	My Fair Lady
1966			
Lee Marvin (Cat Ballou)	Julie Christie (Darling)	Robert Wise (The Sound Of Music)	The Sound Of Music
1967			
Paul Scofield (A Man For All Seasons)	Elizabeth Taylor (Who's Afraid Of Virginia Woolf?)	Fred Zinnemann (A Man For All Seasons)	A Man For All Seasons

Actor	Actress	Director	Film
1968			
Rod Steiger (In The Heat Of the Night)	Katharine Hepburn (Guess Who's Coming To Dinner)	Mike Nichols (The Graduate)	In The Heat Of The Night
1969			
Cliff Robertson (Charly)	Katharine Hepburn (The Lion In Winter) Barbra Streisand (Funny Girl)	Sir Carol Reed (Oliver!)	Oliver!
1970			
John Wayne (True Grit)	Maggie Smith (The Prime Of Miss Jean Brodie)	John Schlesinger (Midnight Cowboy)	Midnight Cowboy
1971			
George C. Scott (Refused Oscar) (Patton)	Glenda Jackson (Women In Love)	Franklin Schaffner (Patton)	Patton
1972			
Gene Hackman (The French Connection)	Jane Fonda (Klute)	William Friedkin (The French Connection)	The French Connection
1973			
Marlon Brando (Refused Oscar) (The Godfather)	Liza Minnelli (Cabaret)	Bob Fosse (Cabaret)	The Godfather
1974			
Jack Lemmon (Save The Tiger)	Glenda Jackson (A Touch Of Class)	George Roy Hill (The Sting)	The Sting

Actor	Actress	Director	Film
1975			
Art Carney (Harry And Tonto)	Ellen Burstyn (Alice Doesn't Live Here Any More)	Francis Ford Coppola (The Godfather Part II)	The Godfather Part II
1976			
Jack Nicholson (One Flew Over The Cuckoo's Nest)	Louise Fletcher (One Flew Over The Cuckoo's Nest)	Milos Forman (One Flew Over The Cuckoo's Nest)	One Flew Over The Cuckoo's Nest
1977			
Peter Finch (Posthumous Award) (Network)	Faye Dunaway (Network)	John G. Avildsen (Rocky)	Rocky
1978			
Richard Dreyfuss (The Goodbye Girl)	Diane Keaton (Annie Hall)	Woody Allen (Annie Hall)	Annie Hall
1979			
John Voight (Coming Home)	Jane Fonda (Coming Home)	Michael Cimino (The Deer Hunter)	The Deer Hunter
1980			
Dustin Hoffman (Kramer vs Kramer)	Sally Field (Norma Rae)	Robert Benton (Kramer vs Kramer)	Kramer vs Kramer
1981			
Robert de Niro (Raging Bull)	Sissy Spacek (Coal Miner's Daughter)	Robert Redford (Ordinary People)	Ordinary People
1982			
Henry Fonda (On Golden Pond)	Katharine Hepburn (On Golden Pond)	Warren Beatty (Reds)	Chariots Of Fire

Actor	Actress	Director	Film
1983			
Ben Kingsley (Gandhi)	Meryl Streep (Sophie's Choice)	Richard Attenborough (Gandhi)	Gandhi
1984			
Robert Duvall (Tender Mercies)	Shirley MacLaine (Terms Of Endearment)	James L. Brooks (Terms Of Endearment)	Terms Of Endearment
1985			
F. Murray Abraham (Amadeus)	Sally Field (Places In The Heart)	Milos Forman (Amadeus)	Amadeus
1986			
William Hurt (Kiss Of The Spider Woman)	Geraldine Page (The Trip To Bountiful)	Sidney Pollack (Out Of Africa)	Out Of Africa
1987			
Paul Newman (The Color Of Money)	Marlee Matlin (Children Of A Lesser God)	Oliver Stone (Platoon)	Platoon
1988			
Michael Douglas (Wall Street)	Cher (Moonstruck)	Bernardo Bertolucci (The Last Emperor)	The Last Emperor
1989			
Dustin Hoffman (Rain Man)	Jodie Foster (The Accused)	Barry Levinson (Rain Man)	Rain Man
1990			
Daniel Day Lewis (My Left Foot)	Jessica Tandy (Driving Miss Daisy)	Oliver Stone (Born On The Fourth Of July)	Driving Miss Daisy
1991			
Jeremy Irons (Reversal Of Fortune)	Kathy Bates (Misery)	Kevin Costner (Dances With Wolves)	Dances With Wolves

Actor	Actress	Director	Film
1992			
Anthony Hopkins (The Silence Of The Lambs)	Jodie Foster (The Silence Of The Lambs)	Jonathan Demme (The Silence Of The Lambs)	The Silence Of The Lambs
1993			
Al Pacino (Scent Of A Woman)	Emma Thompson (Howard's End)	Clint Eastwood (Unforgiven)	Unforgiven
1994			
Tom Hanks (Philadelphia)	Holly Hunter (The Piano)	Steven Spielberg (Schindler's List)	Schindler's List
1995			
Tom Hanks (Forrest Gump)	Jessica Lange (Blue Sky)	Robert Zemeckis (Forrest Gump)	Forrest Gump

Painters and Paintings

Although occasionally questions relate to the schools to which various artists belonged, by far the most common sort of question is the "Who painted picture 'X' type?" This is a list of the most frequently occurring artists along with their most frequently occurring works.

Artist	Painting(s)
Hieronymus Bosch	The Garden Of Earthly Delights
	The Temptation Of St Anthony
	Christ Crowned With Thorns
Alessandro Botticelli	The Birth Of Venus
	Mystic Nativity
	The Adoration Of The Magi
	Primavera
	Minerva And The Centaur
Ford Madox Brown	The Last Of England

Artist	Painting(s)
Pieter Bruegel	Hunters In The Snow
(The Elder)	The Peasant Dance
	The Peasant Wedding
	The Blind Leading The Blind
	The Adoration Of The Kings
	The Triumph Of Death
	The Skaters
Giovanni Canaletto	(Many Venetian Scenes)
	A Regatta On The Grand Canal
	Ascension Day At Venice
	The Stonemason's Yard
Michelangelo Caravaggio	Sick Bacchus
	Boy With A Fruit Basket
	Music Party
	Lute Player
	The Beheading Of Saint John The Baptist
	The Martyrdom Of Saint Matthew
	The Supper At Emmaus
	The Death Of The Virgin
	David with Goliath's Head
Paul Cézanne	Bathers
	Mont Sainte-Victoire
	Le Jardinier
Marc Chagall	Bathing Women
	Calvary
	I And The Village
	The Musician
	Apples And Oranges
John Constable	The Hay Wain
	The Country Lane
	View On The Stour
	The White Horse
Antonio Correggio	Christ Taking Leave Of His Mother
	The Agony In The Garden
	Assumption Of The Virgin

Artist	*Painting(s)*
Salvador Dali	The Persistence Of Memory
	The Crucifixion
	The Transformation Of The
	Narcissus
Leonardo da Vinci	Mona Lisa
	Last Supper
	Madonna Of The Rocks
	Adoration Of The Kings
	Madonna And Child With St Anne
	And The Infant St John
	Leda And The Swan
Jacques Louis David	The Oath Of The Horatii
	The Death Of Socrates
	The Death Of Marat
	The Rape Of The Sabines
Edgar Degas	Dancer At The Barre
(Any paintings which sound	
as if they may be of ballet	
dancers, guess at Degas)	
Eugène Delacroix	The Massacre Of Chios
	Algerian Women
	The Death Of Sardanapalus
	Dante And Virgil Crossing The Styx
	Liberty Guiding The People
Anthony van Dyck	(Court Painter To Charles I and
	assistant To Rubens)
	Many portraits of Charles I
	Carrying Of The Cross
	The Deposition
Jan van Eyck	The Adoration Of The Lamb
	The Arnolfini Marriage
	Man In A Red Turban
Thomas Gainsborough	Blue Boy
	The Watering Place
	The Honourable Mrs Graham
	Mr And Mrs Andrews
	Peasant Girl Gathering Sticks

Artist	Painting(s)
Paul Gauguin	Where Do We Come From? What Are We? Where Are We Going?
	The Vision After The Sermon
	Still Life With Three Puppies
	Tahitian Women
Giotto di Bondone	The Legend Of St Francis
	Life And Passion Of Christ
	Lamentation
	The Madonna Enthroned
Vincent van Gogh	Starry Night
	The Potato Eaters
	Night Cafe
	The Sunflowers
	Cornfields With Flight Of Birds
	Self Portrait With Bandaged Ear
	Road With The Cypresses
	Old Peasant
	Les Souliers
Francisco Goya	The Naked Maja
	The Clothed Maja
	The Disasters Of War
	The Shooting Of The Third of May
El Greco	The Burial Of Count Orgaz
	A View Of Toledo
	The Saviour Of The World
	The Disrobing Of Christ
Nicholas Hilliard	The Young Man Among Roses
	Queen Elizabeth I
	Sir Walter Raleigh
David Hockney	Mr And Mrs Clark And Percy
	A Bigger Splash
	Dancer
William Hogarth	The Rake's Progress
	Marriage à la Mode
	The Harlot's Progress

Artist	Painting(s)
Hans Holbein (The Younger)	Henry VIII
	The Ambassadors
	Anne Of Cleves
	Bonifacius Amerbach
	Christ In The Tomb
	(Woodcuts) The Dance Of Death
William Holman Hunt	The Light Of The World
	The Scapegoat
	The Awakening Conscience
	The Hireling Shepherd
Augustus John	The Smiling Woman
	Portrait Of A Lady In Black
Sir Edwin Landseer	The Monarch Of The Glen
	Shoeing
	The Old Shepherd's Chief Mourner
	Fighting Gods In The Wind
Georges de La Tour	St Sebastian Attended By The Holy Women
	St Jerome Reading
	The Denial Of St Peter
	The Newborn Child
Roy Lichtenstein	Whaam!
	As I Opened Fire
René Magritte	The Menaced Assassin
	Loving Perspective
	Presence Of Mind
	The Key Of Dreams
Edouard Manet	Déjeuner Sur l'Herbe
	The Bar At The Follies Bergères
	Olympia
	The Balcony
	Ball At The Opera
Henri Matisse	L'Escargot
	Notre Dame
	Odalisque

Artist	*Painting(s)*
Michelangelo	The Ceiling Of The Sistine Chapel
	The Last Judgement
	The Conversion Of St Paul
	The Crucifixion Of St Peter
Sir John Everett Millais	Bubbles
	Order Of Release
	Gladstone
	The Blind Girl
Jean-François Millet	The Angelus
	The Gleaners
	The Death Of The Pig
	The Man With The Hoe
Claude Monet	Impression: Sunrise
	(Lots of studies of) Rouen Cathedral
	Water Lilies
	Hay Stacks
Edvard Munch	The Shriek (sometimes known as
	The Scream)
	The Kiss
	Self Portrait Between the Clock And
	The Bed
Pablo Picasso	Guernica
	Les Demoiselles d'Avignon
	The Three Dancers
	Pigeon With Baby Peas
	Three Musicians
	Two Seated Women
	The Charnel-House
Jackson Pollock	Autumn Rhythm
	Guardians Of The Secret
	Wyoming
Nicolas Poussin	The Worship Of The Golden Calf
	Inspiration Of The Poet
	The Martyrdom Of St Erasmus
	The Dance Of Time
	The Seven Sacraments

Artist	Painting(s)
Raphael	Coronation Of The Virgin
	Marriage Of The Virgin
	The Sistine Madonna
	The Panshanger Madonna
	The Ansidei Madonna
	Transfiguration
Rembrandt	(Dozens of self-portraits)
	The Night Watch
	The Anatomy Lesson Of Doctor Tulp
	Aristotle Contemplating The Bust Of Homer
	The Mill
	The Conspiracy Of Claudius
	The Blinding Of Samson
Pierre Auguste Renoir	Luncheon Of The Boating Party
	The Swing
	The Bathers
	Woman In Blue
	Woman Reading
Sir Joshua Reynolds	Mrs Siddons As The Tragic Muse
	Master Henry Hoare
	Miss Bowles With Her Dog
	The Three Graces
Dante Gabriel Rossetti	The Girlhood Of The Virgin Mary
	Found
	Beata Beatrix
	Arthur's Tomb
Henri Rousseau	The Dream
	Wall
	The Snake Charmer
	The Sleeping Gypsy
Sir Peter Paul Rubens	Adoration Of The Magi
	Battle Of The Amazons
	Garden Of Love
	Elevation Of The Cross
	Descent From The Cross

Artist	*Painting(s)*
Georges Seurat	Sunday Afternoon On The Grande Jatte
	Bathers At Asniéres
	Le Cirque
Walter Sickert	Ennui
	Many studies of London theatres
	Many nudes In grubby rooms
Sir Stanley Spencer	The Resurrection: Cookham
	The Resurrection: Port Glasgow
	The Visitation; Christ Carrying The Cross
George Stubbs	(Many studies of horses)
	The Anatomy Of The Horse
	Gimcrack On Newmarket Heath
	The Grosvenor Hunt
	Hambletonian, Rubbing Down
	Horse Frightened By A Lion
Graham Sutherland	Portraits of: Somerset Maugham
	Lord Beaverbrook
	Winston Churchill (later destroyed by Lady Churchill)
	Crucifixion
	Christ In Glory (Coventry Cathedral)
Tintoretto	St Mark Rescuing A Slave
	Paradise
	Last Supper
	Miracle Of The Slave
	St George And The Dragon
	The Golden Calf
Titian	The Assumption
	Man With A Glove
	Bacchus And Ariadne
	The Tribute Money
	Crowning With Thorns
	The Pesaro Madonna

Artist	Painting(s)
Henri Toulouse-Lautrec	At The Moulin Rouge
	The Jockey
	The Modiste
J. M. W. Turner	Rain, Steam And Speed
	The Fighting Téméraire
	The Grand Canal, Venice
	Shipwreck
	Juliet And Her Nurse
	Fishermen At Sea
	Moonlight At Millbank
Diego Velázquez	The Rokeby Venus
	The Waterseller Of Seville
	The Immaculate Conception
	Pope Innocent X
	Las Meniñas
	The Crucufixion
	Surrender Of Breda
Jan Vermeer	Woman With A Water Jug
	A Woman At The Virginals
	Christ In The Hands Of Martha
	Diana And Her Companions
	The Lacemaker
	View Of Delft
	The Painter's Studio
Andy Warhol	Campbell's Soup Cans
	Marilyn
	Electric Chair
James Whistler	Arrangement In Grey And Black – The Artist's Mother
	(One of several Arrangements)
	The Falling Rocket (which resulted in a law suit against Ruskin)

Painting – Schools of Painting

You don't have to be able to recognise a style or technique to answer these commonly set questions; just remember the schools of painting and the artists belonging to them and you should be OK.

Abstract Expressionism School founded in New York in the 1940s. Leading figures include: Kandinsky, Gorky, Pollock.

Action Painting
(*a favourite with setters*) The phrase was coined by Harold Rosenberg in 1952. Jackson Pollock is the only name you have to remember.

Art Nouveau The name is taken from a Parisian gallery opened in 1895 by Siegfried Bing. Exponents include Beardsley, Gilbert and Troop.

Arts and Crafts Movement From the Arts and Crafts Exhibition of 1888. Ruskin, Pugin and Morris are the names to remember.

Baroque Flourished in the late 16th and 17th centuries. Leading figures include: Bernini, Rubens and Caravaggio.

Bauhaus From the German Bau = Building + Haus = House. Founded in 1919. Leading figures include: Gropius, Kandinsky and Klee.

Camden Town Group Painters included Bevan, Gilman, Gore and Sickert.

Cubism Movement founded about 1907. Leading figures include: Picasso and Braque.

Dadaism
(*a real favourite with setters*) Founded in Zurich in 1915, Dada means "hobby-horse". Exponents include: Arp, Duchamp and Man Ray.

Expressionism Exponents include: van Gogh, Ensor and Munch.

Fauvism From the French "Fauve" meaning "wild beast". Matisse is generally regarded as the founder of Fauvism.

Futurism
Originally a literary movement founded by the poet Marinetti. Exponents include: Boccioni, Balla and Severini.

Impressionism
The movement took its name from the Monet painting, "Impression, Sunrise". Exponents include: Manet, Cézanne, Monet, Pissarro, Renoir and Sisley.

Pop Art
The phrase was coined by the art critic, Lawrence Alloway. Leading figures include: Johns, Warhol, Lichtenstein, Rauschenberg.

Post Impressionism
The expression was first used at an exhibition at the Grafton Galleries in 1910, staged by Roger Fry. Exponents include: Cézanne, Gauguin, van Gogh and Seurat (who developed the neo-impressionism technique of "pointillism").

Surrealism
Exponents include: Breton, de Chirico, Masson, Miro, Dali and Magritte.

Symbolism
Originally a literary movement, but Moreau, Redon and Munch are usually described as Symbolists.

Patron Saints

This is another strange section. There is only one reason why anybody would want to know the patron saint of bricklayers, because they may ask it in a quiz sometime. It would be interesting to know how many brickies actually seek guidance from St Stephen when they are building your conservatory or kitchen extension (not many I suspect). Almost every trade or profession has its own patron saint but the following are the most frequently asked.

There are some contradictions in reference sources in this subject so occasionally two patron saints are listed.

Accountants, Bankers, Book-Keepers	St Matthew
Actors	St Vitus and St Genesius
Architects	St Thomas
Artists	St Luke
Athletes	St Sebastian
Bakers	St Elizabeth and St Nicholas
Blacksmiths	St Dunstan
Brewers	St Augustine, St Luke and St Nicholas
Bricklayers	St Stephen
Builders	St Vincent Ferrer
Carpenters	St Joseph
Cooks	St Lawrence
Dentists	St Apollonia
Engineers	St Ferdinand
Farmers	St George
Grocers	St Michael
Housewives	St Anne
Hunters	St Hubert
Lawyers	St Ivo, St Genesius and St Thomas More
Librarians	St Jerome
Miners	St Barbara
Motorists	St Christopher
Musicians	St Cecilia
Physicians	St Luke

Poets	St David and St Cecilia
Printers	St John and St Augustine
Sailors	St Christopher and St Cuthbert
Shoemakers	St Crispin
Soldiers	St George, St Sebastian, St Joan of Arc
Tax Collectors	St Matthew
Teachers	St Gregory, St Catherine
Television	St Clare *(frequently asked, but it does seem strange doesn't it?)*
Travellers	St Christopher

Patron Saints of Countries

Belgium	St Joseph
France	St Denis
Germany	St Boniface
Greece	St Nicholas and St Andrew
Hungary	St Stephen
Italy	St Francis of Assissi
Poland	St Stanislaus
Russia	St Andrew and St Nicholas
Spain	St James
Sweden	St Bridget and St Eric

Phobias

Phobias crop up in quizzes all of the time and some which are listed in authoritative reference books do seem a little silly (Hyalinopygophobia is a phobia relating to glass bottoms!!) This is a list of frequently asked phobias:

Name of Phobia	Definition
Achluophobia	Fear of darkness or the night
Acrophobia	Fear of heights
Ailurophobia	Fear of cats
Altophobia	Fear of heights
Androphobia	Fear of men
Anthophobia	Fear of flowers
Apiphobia	Fear of bees
Arachnophobia	Fear of spiders
Astraphobia	Fear of lightning
Bathophobia	Fear of depth
Batrachophobia	Fear of reptiles
Belonophobia	Fear of needles
Bibliophobia	Fear of books
Brontophobia	Fear of thunder
Carnophobia	Fear of meat
Claustrophobia	Fear of enclosed spaces
Coitophobia	Fear of sexual intercourse
Cynophobia	Fear of dogs
Demophobia	Fear of crowds
Dendrophobia	Fear of trees
Dipsophobia	Fear of drinking
Dromophobia	Fear of crossing streets
Eisoptrophobia	Fear of mirrors
Entomophobia	Fear of insects
Ergasiophobia	Fear of surgery
Ergophobia	Fear of work
Erotophobia	Fear of sex
Gatophobia	Fear of cats
Genophobia	Fear of sex
Gymnophobia	Fear of being naked

Name of Phobia	*Definition*
Gynophobia	Fear of women
Haematophobia	Fear of blood
Heliophobia	Fear of the sun
Helminthophobia	Fear of worms
Hippophobia	Fear of horses
Hydrophobia	Fear of water
Hypnophobia	Fear of sleep
Ichthyophobia	Fear of fish
Linonophobia	Fear of string
Monophobia	Fear of being alone
Musophobia	Fear of mice
Mysophobia	Fear of dirt
Necrophobia	Fear of death or corpses
Nephophobia	Fear of clouds
Nosophobia	Fear of disease
Nyctophobia	Fear of darkness or the night
Ochlophobia	Fear of crowds
Odynophobia	Fear of pain
Oneirophobia	Fear of dreams
Ophidiophobia	Fear of snakes
Pathophobia	Fear of disease
Phagophobia	Fear of eating
Phasmophobia	Fear of ghosts
Photophobia	Fear of strong light
Pogonophobia	Fear of beards
Potamophobia	Fear of rivers
Potophobia	Fear of alcoholic drink
Pyrophobia	Fear of fire
Sciophobia	Fear of shadows
Spermophobia	Fear of germs
Spheksophobia	Fear of wasps
Taphophobia	Fear of being buried alive or graves
Terdekaphobia	*(A favourite one)* Fear of the number 13
Thanatophobia	Fear of death
Theophobia	Fear of God
Xenophobia	Fear of foreigners

Place Names – Origins

The sources of some place names are obvious (loch, castle, church), however some are well worth remembering as they do occur sometimes. This section is divided into two parts, the first part being prefixes, the second being suffixes.

Ben	Mountain Peak, eg BEN NEVIS
(In place names in Ireland and Scotland)	
Caer	A fortified place, eg CAERNARFON,
(Welsh place names)	CAERPHILLY
Chipping	Marketplace, eg CHIPPING CAMPDEN, CHIPPING NORTON
Dun	
(In England)	Hill, eg DUNMOW
(In Ireland & Scotland)	Fort eg DUNBAR, DUNFIRMLINE
Glen	Valley or Glen
Inver	River mouth, eg INVERNESS, INVERARAY
Kil	
Generally; in Ireland –	Place of a church
and Scotland –	Place of a wood
Llan	Site of a church, eg LLANDUDNO,
(Usually in Wales)	LLANBERIS, LLANDEG
Mickle	Great or much, eg MICKLEOVER
Pen	Hilltop, eg PENARTH,
(In many Cornish and	PENZANCE
Welsh place names)	
Pont	Bridge, eg PONTYPOOL, PONTEFRACT
Stock	Place (often a religious place), eg STOCKPORT, STOCKTON-on-TEES
Stoke	See "Stock"
Tre	Homestead, village or town
(In Wales and the far southwest of England)	

Borough (Also brogh, burg or bury)	Fortified place. Hundreds of examples.
Bourne	Stream, eg EASTBOURNE, FISHBOURNE, etc
By	Farmstead or village. Thousands of examples
Den	Valley (especially a narrow, wooded one).
Don	Hill. Thousands of examples
Ey	An island or area of dry or higher land surrounded by marsh, eg ROMSEY, HACKNEY
Ham	Homestead or village. There are thousands of examples
Hampton	Home farm or village. Thousands of examples, NORTHAMPTON, SOUTHAMPTON, LITTLEHAMPTON
Head	Headland or hill, eg BIRKENHEAD, GATESHEAD
Hurst	Hillock or wooded hill
Ing	Usually preceded by the name of the person or people who lived there, eg SPALDING, READING, HASTINGS
Ley (also Leigh and Le)	Woodland glade or clearing (see earlier 'ey' entry)
Shot (also Shott)	Angle of land or piece of protruding land, eg ALDERSHOT
Stow (also Stowe)	A place of assembly or holy place, eg CHEPSTOW, FELIXSTOWE
Ton	Farm or village
Tree (also Try)	This can mean not only tree but a post, cross or crucifix. There are thousands of examples
Worth	An enclosure or homestead, eg TAMWORTH, WANDSWORTH

Planets and Their Satellites

This has been a popular subject for many years. Originally the questions were phrased as "Which planet has moons or satellites called xxxx?" but now they are invariably wrapped up with phrases such as "Which planet's satellites are named after Shakespearian characters?" or "Where will you find a mythological ferryman close to a Walt Disney dog?" etc. The closest satellite to each of the planets is listed first and the most remote last. Anyway, here they are.

Mars	Phobos
	Deimos
Jupiter	Metis
	Adrastea
	Amalthea
	Thebe
	Io
	Europa
	Ganymede*
	Callisto
	Leda
	Himalia
	Lysithea
	Elara
	Ananke
	Carme
	Pasiphae
	Sinope
	* *With a diameter of 3,270 miles, this is the largest satellite in our solar system*
Saturn	Atlas
	Prometheus
	Pandora
	Epinetheus
	Janus
	Mimas
	Enceladus
	Tethys

	Telesto
	Calyps
	Dion
	Helene
	Rhea
	Titan
	Hyperion
	Iapetus
	Phoebe
Uranus	Cordelia
	Ophelia
	Bianca
	Cressida
	Desdemona
	Juliet
	Portia
	Rosalind
	Belinda
	Puck
	Miranda
	Ariel
	Umbriel
	Titania
	Oberon
Neptune	Triton
	Neried
Pluto	Charon

Playwrights and Their Plays

It is rare for quiz setters to ask detailed questions about plays (except old chestnuts involving the likes of Mrs Malaprop). You will be able to answer most theatrical questions by learning the most frequently asked plays and their writers. Here they are (playwright and the plays which attract question setters).

Edward Albee	Who's Afraid of Virginia Woolf?
Aristophanes	The Clouds
	The Wasps
	The Birds
	The Frogs
Alan Ayckbourn	The Norman Conquests
J. M. Barrie	The Admirable Crichton
	Peter Pan
	Quality Street
	What Every Woman Knows
Samuel Beckett	Waiting For Godot
	End-game
Brendan Behan	Borstal Boy
	The Hostage
	The Quare Fellow
Alan Bennett	Forty Years On
	Getting On
	Habeas Corpus
	An Englishman Abroad
Bertolt Brecht	Mother Courage
	The Threepenny Opera
	The Caucasian Chalk Circle
Anton Chekhov	The Seagull
	Uncle Vanya
	Three Sisters
	The Cherry Orchard
William Congreve	The Way of the World
Noel Coward	The Vortex
	Hay Fever
	Private Lives
	Blithe Spirit

John Dryden	Marriage à-la-Mode
	All for Love
T. S. Eliot	Murder in the Cathedral
	The Family Reunion
	The Cocktail Party
	The Confidential Clerk
	The Elder Statesman
Christopher Fry	The Lady's not for Burning
John Gay	The Beggar's Opera
Oliver Goldsmith	She Stoops to Conquer
	The Good-Natur'd Man
Thomas Hardy	The Dynasts
Henrik Ibsen	Peer Gynt
	A Doll's House
	Ghosts
	Hedda Gabler
	The Master Builder
	An Enemy of the People
Ben Jonson	Every Man in his Humour
	The Alchemist
	Bartholomew Fair
Christopher Marlowe	Tamburlaine
	The Jew of Malta
	Edward II
	Dr Faustus
Arthur Miller	All My Sons
	Death of a Salesman
	The Crucible
	A View from the Bridge
	After the Fall
Molière	Le Malade Imaginaire
John Mortimer	The Dock Brief
	A Voyage Round my Father
Peter Nichols	A Day in the Death of Joe Egg
	The National Health

Sean O'Casey	The Shadow of a Gunman
	Juno and the Paycock
	The Plough and the Stars
	The Silver Tassie
Eugene O'Neill	Mourning Becomes Electra
	Ah! Wilderness
	Days without End
	The Iceman Cometh
	Long Day's Journey into Night
Joe Orton	Entertaining Mr Sloane
	Loot
John Osborne	Look Back in Anger
	The Entertainer
	Luther
	Inadmissible Evidence
	A Patriot for Me
Arthur Wing Pinero	Lady Bountiful
	The Second Mrs Tanqueray
	Trelawny of the "Wells"
Harold Pinter	The Room
	The Birthday Party
	The Caretaker
Dennis Potter	Vote, Vote, Vote for Nigel Barton
	Stand Up, Nigel Barton
	Blue Remembered Hills
	Brimstone and Treacle
	The Singing Detective
J. B. Priestley	Dangerous Corner
	An Inspector Calls
	When we are Married
Terence Rattigan	French without Tears
	The Winslow Boy
	The Browning Version
	The Deep Blue Sea
	Separate Tables
	Ross
	Cause Célèbre

Peter Shaffer	The Royal Hunt of the Sun
	Equus
	Amadeus
George Bernard Shaw	Widowers' Houses
	Arms and the Man
	Caesar and Cleopatra
	Mrs Warren's Profession
	John Bull's other Island
	Man and Superman
	Major Barbara
	The Doctor's Dilemma
	Pygmalion
	Heartbreak House
	Back to Methuselah
Richard Brinsley Sheridan	The Rivals
	The School for Scandal
	The Critic
R. C Sheriff	Journey's End
Neil Simon	Barefoot in the Park
	The Sunshine Boys
	Biloxi Blues
	The Odd Couple
Sophocles	Oedipus the King
Tom Stoppard	Rosencrantz and Guildenstern are Dead
	Every Good Boy Deserves Favour
	Dirty Linen
	The Real Thing
	Professional Foul
J. M. Synge	The Playboy of the Western World
Ben Travers	A Cuckoo in the Nest
	Rookery Nook
Ivan Turgenev	A Month in the Country
John Vanbrugh	The Relapse
	The Provok'd Wife
	The Provok'd Husband
	The Confederacy

Arnold Wesker	Chicken Soup with Barley
	Roots
	I'm Talking About Jerusalem
	Chips with Everything
Oscar Wilde	Lady Windermere's Fan
	A Woman of No Importance
	An Ideal Husband
	The Importance of Being Earnest
	Salomé
Thornton Wilder	Our Town
	The Merchant of Yonkers
Tennessee Williams	The Glass Menagerie
	A Streetcar Named Desire
	The Rose Tattoo
	Cat on a Hot Tin Roof
	Suddenly Last Summer
	Sweet Bird of Youth
	The Night of the Iguana
William Wycherley	The Country Wife
	The Plain-Dealer

Poets and Poems

People who set poetry questions for quizzes seem to have an obsession with the nineteenth century. I don't think that I have ever heard a question on the works of Ted Hughes or Philip Larkin in a pub quiz; however, the poems of Keats, Wordsworth and Byron proliferate. The following is a list of poems which crop up time and time again.

Poet	Poems
Matthew Arnold	Dover Beach
	The Scholar Gypsy
W. H. Auden	In Memory Of W. B. Yeats
Hilaire Belloc	Matilda Who Told Lies, And Was Burned To Death
John Betjeman	Death Of King George V
	Parliament Hill Fields
	The Cottage Hospital
	Death In Leamington
	Slough
	A Subaltern's Love-song
Laurence Binyon	For The Fallen
William Blake	The Tiger
	Jerusalem
Rupert Brooke	The Old Vicarage At Grantchester
	The Soldier
Robert Browning	Home Thoughts From Abroad
	The Pied Piper Of Hamelin
	My Last Duchess
Robert Burns	Tam O'Shanter
	A Red, Red, Rose
	To A Mouse
	Holy Willie's Prayer
Lord Byron	Childe Harold's Pilgrimage
	Don Juan
	Prometheus
G. K. Chesterton	The Rolling English Road
	The Donkey
	Lepanto

Poet	*Poems*
Samuel Taylor Coleridge	Kubla Khan
	The Rime Of The Ancient Mariner
	Christabel
	Frost At Midnight
	Dejection: An Ode
T. S. Eliot	The Lovesong Of J. Alfred Prufrock
	The Waste Land
	Little Gidding
Oliver Goldsmith	The Deserted Village
	(Sweet Auburn)
Thomas Gray	Elegy Written In A Country
	Churchyard
	Ode On The Death Of A Favourite
	Cat Drowned In A Tub Of Gold
	Fishes
	Ode On A Distant Prospect Of Eton
	College
Thomas Hood	I Remember, I Remember
A. E. Housman	A Shropshire Lad
	On Wenlock Edge
Ben Jonson	To Celia
	To The Memory Of My Beloved Mr
	William Shakespeare
John Keats	Endymion
	Ode To A Nightingale
	Ode On A Grecian Urn
	Ode To Psyche
	Ode On Melancholy
	To Autumn
	La Belle Dame Sans Merci
	Hyperion
	The Fall Of Hyperion
	The Eve Of St Agnes
William Langland	Piers Plowman
Edward Lear	The Owl And The Pussycat
Louis MacNeice	The British Museum Reading Room

Poet	Poems
John Masefield	Cargos
	Reynard The Fox
	Sea Fever
	Upon The Downs
John Milton	Hymn On The Morning Of Christ's Nativity
	On His Blindness
	On His Dead Wife
	Paradise Lost
	Paradise Regained
	Samson Agonistes
Wilfred Owen	Anthem For Doomed Youth
	Dulce Et Decorum Est
	Miners
	Strange Meeting
	Spring Offensive
Alexander Pope	The Rape Of The Lock
	The Triumph Of Vice
Siegfried Sassoon	Attack!
	Blighters
	Everyone Sang
	The General
Sir Walter Scott	Lochinvar
Percy Bysshe Shelley	Mourn Not For Adonais
	Ozymandias
	Ode To A Skylark
	Queen Mab
	Prometheus Unbound
Stevie Smith	Not Waving But Drowning
Edmund Spenser	The Faerie Queen
Alfred, Lord Tennyson	The Charge Of The Light Brigade
	Mort d'Arthur
	Idylls Of The King
	Song Of The Lotus Eaters
	The Lady Of Shalott
	Ulysses

Poet	*Poems*
Dylan Thomas	A Refusal To Mourn The Death, By Fire, Of A Child In London
	Fern Hill
	The Hand That Signed the Paper
	Do Not Go Gentle Into That Good Night
Oscar Wilde	The Ballad Of Reading Gaol
William Wordsworth	Daffodils
	Lines Composed A Few Miles Above Tintern Abbey
	Lucy
	The Solitary Reaper
	Upon Westminster Bridge September 3 1802
W. B. Yeats	Byzantium
	Easter 1916
	The Lake Isle Of Innisfree
	Lapis Lazuli
	Sailing To Byzantium

Politicians – Political Leaders

Questions, can arise in a variety of ways: "Of which country was Mr X the president?" or "Who was the dictator overthrown in country Y in 1982?". This list provides some essential facts which will enable you to cope with most of the questions which you are likely to be asked.

Albania	Enver Hoxha – Communist dictator 1944–1985.
Argentina	Leopoldo Galtieri – President and head of the military junta which initiated the invasion of the Falklands in 1982. Replaced by Reynaldo Bignone.
Australia	Gough Whitlam – Labour prime minister dismissed from office by Governor General Sir John Kerr in November 1975.
Austria	Engelbert Dollfus – Chancellor, murdered by Nazi supporters in 1934. Kurt Waldheim – Elected president in 1986, despite accusations that he was involved in war-time Nazi atrocities.
Bangladesh	Ziaur Rahman – President from 1977 until his assassination in 1981.
Cambodia	Prince Norodom Sihanouk – Head of state, and several times prime minister until 1968 – the Khymer Republic was established in 1970. Pol Pot – Infamous prime minister of the Khymer Republic between 1976 and 1979.
Chile	Salvador Allende – Communist president, elected to office in September 1970. Assassinated in 1973 in a coup which brought a military dictatorship, led by General Augusto Pinochet, to power.

China   It is important to get the terminology of political
                            office correct with Communist states. This
                            may help.
                            Mao Tse-tung – President of the People's
                            Republic of China from 1949 to 1959.
                            Chairman of the Communist party from 1935
                            to 1976.

Cuba   Fulgencio Batista – President from 1952 to
                            1959, when he was overthrown by a popular
                            revolutionary movement led by Fidel Castro
                            – Prime Minister and First Secretary from
                            1959 to 1976, when he became President.

Cyprus   Archbishop Makarios – First President of an
                            independent Cyprus, 1960–1977.

The Czech Republic   Alexander Dubcek – First Secretary of Czech
(formerly   Communist Party, 1968–1969. Ousted from
Czechoslovakia)   power after the Soviet invasion of 1968.
                            Vaclav Havel – Playwright and leader of the
                            Civic Forum movement. Elected president in
                            1989 after the fall of the Communist regime.

Egypt   Mohammed Neguib – First President of the
                            Republic of Egypt (1952–1954). Overthrown
                            in military coup by Gamel Abdel Nasser
                            (1954–1970). Died in office. Succeeded by
                            Mohammed Anwar Sadat (1970–1981) who
                            was assassinated by members of his own
                            armed forces. Succeeded by Mohammed
                            Hosni Mubarak.

Haiti   Francois Duvalier (Papa Doc) – President
                            1957–1971
                            Jean-Claude Duvalier (Baby Doc) – President
                            1971–1986
                            Jean-Bertrand Aristide – Elected President in
                            1991. Overthrown in a military coup led by
                            Raoul Cedras. Reinstated in 1994 with US
                            assistance.

Hungary

Imre Nagy – Reforming Prime Minister whose liberal policies resulted in the Soviet invasion of 1956.

Janos Kadar – Installed as Premier by the USSR after the 1956 invasion.

India

Succession appears to be a favourite aspect of India's politics. The following list of prime ministers will be useful.

Jawaharlal Nehru	1947–1964
Lal Bahadur Shastri	1964–1966
Indira Gandhi	1966–1977
Morarji Desai	1977–1979
Charan Singh	1979–1980
Indira Gandhi (assassinated)	1980–1984
Rajiv Gandhi (assassinated June 1991)	1984–1989
V. P. Singh	1989–1990
Chandra Shekhar	1990–1991
P. V. Narasimha Rao	1991–

Iran

Important to remember that Ayatollah *Khomeini* was succeeded by Ali *Khamenei* in 1989.

Ireland

Mary Robinson (Labour) became Ireland's first woman president when she succeeded Patrick Hillery in 1990. The dates of the most recent prime ministers may prove useful.

Jack Lynch	1977–1979
Charles Haughey	1979–1981 (and Mar–Dec 1982)
Garrett Fitzgerald	1981–1987
Charles Haughey	1987–1992
Albert Reynolds	1992–1994
John Bruton	1994–

France

The Presidency of France is pretty stable and the last few presidents are well known. However, it changes its prime ministers more frequently. Here are a few worth committing to memory.

Philippe Pétain – Leader of the wartime Vichy Government.

Charles de Gaulle – Prime Minister 1944–1946 and again from 1958–1959 (when he was also President).

Georges Pompidou – Prime Minister from 1962–1968. President from 1969–1974.

Edith Cresson – France's first woman prime minister from 1991–1992 – she believed that all Englishmen were repressed homosexuals.

Germany

Lots of different titles here (and diffferent countries until 1990), but these few should help.

East Germany (DDR)

Chairman of the State Council

Walter Ulbricht	1960–1973
Erich Honecker	1976–1989

West Germany (FDR)

Chancellor

Konrad Adenauer	1949–1963
Ludwig Erhard	1963–1966
Kurt Kiesinger	1966–1969
Willy Brandt	1969–1974
Helmut Schmidt	1974–1982
Helmut Kohl	1982–

Ghana

Kwame Nkrumah – First President of Ghana from 1960–1966.

Jerry Rawlings – Chairman of the Armed Revolutionary Council, 1979 and then again in 1981.

Grenada

Maurice Bishop – Prime Minister 1979 to 1983 when he was executed and his government

overthrown by the Revolutionary Military
Council, leading to the invasion of the island
by US forces in October of that year.

Italy
Aldo Moro, twice prime minister (1963–1968,
1974–1976), kidnapped and murdered by
Red Brigade terrorists in 1978.

Kenya
Jomo Kenyatta, Kenya's first President
(1964–1978) succeeded by Daniel arap Moi.

Liberia
William Tubman – President from 1944 to his
death in 1971. Succeeded by William Tolbert,
who was assassinated in a 1980 coup led
by Samuel Doe. Doe was Chairman of the
People's Redemption Council until 1986
when he was proclaimed President. He was
killed during the civil war of 1990.

Libya
Since 1969 Muammar al-Gaddafi has held the
title "Leader of the Revolution". Gaddafi led
the coup which deposed King Idris.

Malawi
The "Life Presidency" of Hastings Banda
proved not to be so.

Malta
Dom Mintoff – Prime Minister 1955–1962,
1971–1984.

Nicaragua
The country was a dictatorship under the
control of the Somoza family from the 1930s
until 1980.

Pakistan
Zulfiqar Ali Bhutto was executed in 1979 after
a military coup led by General Zia ul Haq.
Zia was killed in a plane crash in 1988.
Bhutto's daughter, Benazir, was elected
prime minister in November of that year. She
was dismissed from office in 1990.

Panama
General Noriega was declared head of
government by the National Assembly in
1989 but invading US troops deposed him.
He was found guilty of drugs offences in a
US court in 1992.

Paraguay
Was a military dictatorship under Alfredo Stroessner from 1954 to 1989.

Philippines
Ferdinand Marcos was elected President in 1965. Benigno Aquino the opposition leader was murdered by the military guard as he returned to the country in 1983. His widow Corazon Aquino formed the People's Power Movement and overthrew Marcos in 1986. Marcos died in exile in 1989. Fidel Ramos was elected President in 1992.

Poland
Wojciech Jaruzelski was the effective head of government from 1985 to 1990 (becoming President in 1989). Solidarity was legalised in 1989 and in 1990 Lech Walesa was elected President. In 1992 Hannah Suchocka became Poland's first woman Prime Minister.

Portugal
Antonio Salazar headed the military dictatorship from 1932 until 1968, when he was succeeded by Marcelo Caetano. Caetano was overthrown by a military coup in 1974, led by Antonio Spinola, who in turn was replaced by Francisco Gomes later that year. In 1976 Socialist, Mario Soares formed a minority government which governed for two years. He became Portuguese President in 1986.

Romania
Nicolae Ceausescu's totalitarian Communist regime was overthrown at Christmas 1989.

South Africa
In 1964 Nelson Mandela, Walter Sisulu and other ANC leaders were sentenced to life imprisonment. In 1966 Hendrik Verwoerd was assassinated and was succeeded as Premier by B. J. Vorster. In 1977 Pan African Congress activist Steve Biko was murdered while in police custody. Vorster resigned in 1978 and was replaced by P. W. Botha, who resigned in 1989 and was replaced by F. W.

de Klerk. In 1990 de Klerk lifted the ban on the ANC and Mandela was released from imprisonment. The exiled Oliver Tambo returned to South Africa. In 1994 Mandela was elected State President with de Klerk as Vice President.

Sweden
Olof Palme, Swedish Prime Minister, was shot dead in a Stockholm street in 1986.

Syria
Hafez Al Assad became president in 1971.

Uganda
King Mutesa II was overthrown in 1966 in a coup led by Milton Obote. In 1971 Idi Amin seized power. He was overthrown in 1978 and Yusef Lule became President. He was replaced by Godfrey Binaisa. In 1980 Binaisa was overthrown by the army. Elections were held and Obote was returned to power. Obote was ousted in 1985.

USSR
Despite the break-up of the Soviet Union, questions on its politics and politicians are still popular. The problem with Soviet politics is understanding the titles and what they mean, this is not easy. The following may illustrate the point. From 1953 to 1964 Nikita Khrushchev was the most powerful man in the USSR, but he wasn't the President. Leonid Brezhnev was the de facto head of state from 1964 until his death in 1982, but he was president from 1977 to 1982. Got it? There were three important offices in Soviet politics up to the break up of the union; President, Chairman of the Council; and the most powerful, General Secretary. The General Secretary was the head of government, and could have also occupied either of the other offices during his tenure. When newsreaders announced that the president of the USA was to meet the Soviet

leader they were always referring to the General Secretary; he may also have been the President or the Chairman of the Council, but not necessarily.

The two lists that follow may help.

General Secretary

Joseph Stalin	1922–1953
Georgiy Malenkov	1953
Nikita Khrushchev	1953–1964
Leonid Brezhnev	1964–1982
Yuri Andropov	1982–1984
Konstantin Chernenko	1984–1985
Mikhail Gorbachov	1985–1991

President

Leonid Brezhnev	1960–1964
Anastas Mikoyan	1964–1965
Nikolai Podgorny	1965–1977
Leonid Brezhnev	1977–1982
Vassili Kuznetsov	1982–1983
Yuri Andropov	1983–1984
Konstantin Chernenko	1984–1985
Andrei Gromyko	1985–1988
Mikhail Gorbachov	1988–1991

Zambia   Kenneth Kaunda became President and Prime Minister on Zambia's independence in 1964

Zimbabwe   On independence Canaan Banana (an easy one to remember) was appointed President, with Robert Mugabe, Prime Minister. Mugabe assumed both offices in 1987.

Pop Groups – Origins of their Names

This type of question has become increasingly more popular since groups and bands stopped using titles like 'The Four Pennies', 'Gerry and the Pacemakers' etc. Some of them are quite interesting.

Art Of Noise	From an Italian futurist manifesto
Aswad	From the arabic word Aswad, meaning black
Bachman–Turner Overdrive	From two founder members of the group, Bachman and Turner, and the name of a trucking magazine, Overdrive
Bad Company	From a 1972 Jeff Bridges film
Bauhaus	From the German art movement
Bay City Rollers	By sticking a pin in a map of the USA and finding Bay City
Bee Gees	From the initials of their founder, Barry Gibb
Buffalo Springfield	After a make of steamroller
Clannad	From the Gaelic word 'clannad,' meaning family
Alice Cooper	Name given by a Ouija board
Creedence Clearwater Revival	The creedence bit comes from the name of a friend of the group and clearwater from a beer commercial
Deacon Blue	From the title of a Steely Dan number
Depeche Mode	Taken from a phrase in a French fashion magazine meaning 'fast fashion'
Dexy's Midnight Runners	Derives the name from Dexedrine
Dr Feelgood	From a number by Piano Red
Doors	From an Aldous Huxley quote "All the other chemical doors in the wall are labelled 'dope'"
Duran Duran	Character in the science fiction film Barbarella
Eurythmics	Name of a technique used to teach children dance and mime appreciation

Everything But The Girl	From a secondhand furniture store in Hull
Faith No More	From the name of a greyhound
Fine Young Cannibals	From a 1960 Natalie Wood/Robert Wagner film All The Fine Young Cannibals
Mindbenders	From a Dirk Bogarde film of that name
Frankie Goes To Hollywood	From a newspaper headline about Frank Sinatra making a film
Heaven 17	From a group in the book A Clockwork Orange
Human League	From a computer game
Jethro Tull	From the British agriculturalist
Judas Priest	From the Bob Dylan number Ballad of Frankie Lee and Judas Priest
Led Zeppelin	From a phrase often used by Who drummer, Keith Moon "Going down like a lead zeppelin"
Level 42	From the Douglas Adams book A Hitch-Hiker's Guide to the Galaxy in which 42 is the answer to just about everything (this is sometimes disputed)
Mott The Hoople	After a book by Willard Manus
The Pogues	Abbreviated from their original name Pogue Mo Chrone which means "kiss my arse" in Gaelic.
Procol Harum	From the Latin "procol" meaning "far from these things"
Reo Speedwaggon	After a make of fire engine
Searchers	From a John Wayne film of that name
Sex Pistols	After the Malcolm McLaren shop "Sex"
Steely Dan	From a William Burroughs novel
Steppenwolf	From the Herman Hesse novel
Supertramp	From the W. H. Davies book The Autobiography Of A Supertramp
Teardrop Explodes	After a caption in a comic
10cc	The average ejaculation of sperm

Thompson Twins	After a pair of characters in Herge's Adventures of Tin Tin
Three Dog Night	After an Australian aboriginal expression (If it was very cold you slept against three dogs rather than one or two)
Toto	From the dog in the Wizard of Oz
UB40	From the number of an unemployment benefit form
Velvet Underground	From the title of a pornographic publication
Wet Wet Wet	Lyrics from a Scritti Politti number

....

Prime Ministers – of Great Britain

Whilst it is now rare to be asked "Who was prime minister in the year xx?" questions on prime ministers do crop up with some regularity. They may be wrapped up in phrases such as "Who was prime minister when 'this' or 'that' happened?" or "Who succeeded whom as prime minister?" So prime ministers and their terms of office are very useful to know. Only prime ministers who actually formed a government are listed here, one or two men were appointed to the office but were unable to form a government. (Although it could be argued that several of them did not form a proper government!)

Name of Prime Minister	Political Party	Term of Office
Sir Robert Walpole (created the first Earl of Orford on his retirement from office)	Whig	1721–1742
Earl of Wilmington	Whig	1742–1743
Henry Pelham	Whig	1743–1754
Duke of Newcastle	Whig	1754–1756
Duke of Devonshire	Whig	1756–1757
Duke of Newcastle	Whig	1757–1762
Earl of Bute	Tory	1762–1763
George Grenville	Whig	1763–1765

Name of Prime Minister	Political Party	Term of Office
Marquis of Rockingham	Whig	1765–1766
Duke of Grafton	Whig	1766–1770
Lord North	Tory	1770–1782
Marquis of Rockingham	Whig	1782–1782
Earl of Shelbourne	Whig	1782–1783
Duke of Portland	Coalition	1783–1783
William Pitt	Tory	1783–1801
(known as "Pitt the Younger", Britain's youngest prime minister)		
Henry Addington	Tory	1801–1804
William Pitt	Tory	1804–1806
Lord Grenville	Whig	1806–1807
Duke of Portland	Tory	1807–1809
Spencer Perceval	Tory	1809–1812
(the only British prime minister to have been assassinated)		
Earl of Liverpool	Tory	1812–1827
George Canning	Tory	1827–1827
Viscount Goderich	Tory	1827–1828
Duke of Wellington	Tory	1828–1830
Earl Grey	Whig	1830–1834
Viscount Melbourne	Whig	1834–1834
Sir Robert Peel	Conservative	1834–1835
Viscount Melbourne	Whig	1835–1841
Sir Robert Peel	Conservative	1841–1846
Lord John Russell	Liberal	1846–1852
Earl of Derby	Conservative	1852
Lord Aberdeen	Peelite	1852–1855
Viscount Palmerston	Liberal	1855–1858
Earl of Derby	Conservative	1858–1859
Viscount Palmerston	Liberal	1859–1865
Lord John Russell	Liberal	1865–1866
Earl of Derby	Conservative	1866–1868
Benjamin Disraeli	Conservative	1868–1868
(became the first and last Earl of Beaconsfield)		

Name of Prime Minister	*Political Party*	*Term of Office*
William Ewart Gladstone	Liberal	1868–1874
Benjamin Disraeli	Conservative	1874–1880
William Ewart Gladstone	Liberal	1880–1885
Marquis of Salisbury	Conservative	1885–1886
William Ewart Gladstone	Liberal	1886–1886
Marquis of Salisbury	Conservative	1886–1892
William Ewart Gladstone (Britain's oldest prime minister)	Liberal	1892–1894
Earl of Rosebery	Liberal	1894–1895
Marquis of Salisbury	Conservative	1895–1902
Arthur Balfour	Conservative	1902–1905
Sir Henry Campbell-Bannerman (the only prime minister to die in 10 Downing Street – although he had relinquished office at the time)	Liberal	1905–1908
Henry Herbert Asquith (became the first Earl of Oxford and Asquith, and last prime minister of a Liberal Government)	Liberal / Coalition	1908–1915 / 1915–1916
David Lloyd George (created the first Earl of Dwyfor shortly before his death in 1945)	Coalition	1916–1922
Andrew Bonar Law (the only British prime minister to be born overseas – in Canada)	Conservative	1922–1923
Stanley Baldwin (became the first Earl of Bewdley when he was elevated to the peerage)	Conservative	1923–1924
James Ramsay Macdonald (Labour's first prime minister and the only British prime minister who was genuinely a bastard)	Labour	1924
Stanley Baldwin	Conservative	1924–1929
James Ramsay Macdonald	Labour / National	1929–1931 / 1931–1935

Name of Prime Minister	Political Party	Term of Office
Stanley Baldwin	National	1935–1937
Neville Chamberlain	National	1937–1940
Winston Churchill	Coalition	1940–1945
Stanley Baldwin	National	1935–1937
Neville Chamberlain	National	1937–1940
Winston Churchill	Coalition	1940–1945
Clement Attlee	Labour	1945–1951
Winston Churchill	Conservative	1951–1955
Sir Anthony Eden (later created the first Earl of Avon)	Conservative	1955–1957
Harold Macmillan (became the first Earl of Stockton on his elevation to the peerage in 1984)	Conservative	1957–1963
Sir Alec Douglas-Home (the first prime minister to have disclaimed his peerage; he was the 14th Earl of Home and later took the tile of Lord Home of the Hirsel when he was created a life peer in 1974)	Conservative	1963–1964
Harold Wilson (created Baron Wilson of Rievaulx 1983)	Labour	1964–1970
Edward Heath	Conservative	1970–1974
Harold Wilson	Labour	1974–1976
James Callaghan (became Baron Callaghan of Cardiff when he was made a life peer)	Labour	1976–1979
Margaret Thatcher (became Baroness Thatcher of Kesteven when made a life peer)	Conservative	1979–1990
John Major	Conservative	1990 onwards

....

Radio Call Signs

Although few people apart from police officers, airline pilots, and the Armed Forces use these, they have always been a popular source of questions. Usually the more forgettable ones are asked or the question is "wrapped up" in phraseology such as "Which make of motor car is a radio call sign?" Sometimes this system is referred to as the "phonetic alphabet" although this is erroneous.

A	Alpha
B	Bravo
C	Charlie
D	Delta
E	Echo
F	Foxtrot
G	Golf
H	Hotel
I	India
J	Juliet
K	Kilo
L	Lima
M	Mike
N	November
O	Oscar
P	Papa
Q	Quebec
R	Romeo
S	Sierra
T	Tango
U	Uniform
V	Victor
W	Whisky
X	X-Ray
Y	Yankie
Z	Zulu

Railway Stations

Some main line railway stations with distinctive names. Some of these stations have ceased to operate but their names still crop up in quiz questions. Common names such as Central or Exchange are not listed.

Bath	Spa
Birmingham	New Street
	Snow Hill
Bradford	Forster Square
Bristol	Temple Meads
	Parkway
Canterbury	East
	West
Cardiff	Queen Street
Carlisle	Citadel
Darlington	Bank Top
Derby	Midland
Dover	Priory
	Marine
Edinburgh	Waverley
	Haymarket
Exeter	St Davids
Folkestone	Harbour
Glasgow	St Enoch
	Buchanan Street
	Queen Street
Hull	Paragon
Leicester	London Road
Liverpool	Lime Street
Norwich	Thorpe
Nuneaton	Trent Valley
Oldham	Mumps
Portsmouth	Harbour
Swansea	High Street
Wolverhampton	High Level
	Low Level
Worcester	Foregate Street
	Shrub Hill

Real Name (Entertainers)

A very popular subject indeed. The great difficulty with this category is that there have been thousands of entertainers who have never used their real names. Therefore two criteria have been used for inclusion in this list, one, the entertainer must be well known, two, the name or pseudonym should be a popular source for quiz questions.

Alan Alda	Alfonso D'abruzzo
Dave Allen	David O'Mahoney
Woody Allen	Allen Konigsberg
Julie Andrews	Julia Wells
Adam Ant	Stuart Goddard
Fred Astaire	Frederick Austerlitz
Charles Atlas	Angelo Siciliano
Lauren Bacall	Betty Joan Perske
Lucille Ball	Lucille Hunt
Anne Bancroft	Anna Maria Italiano
Brigitte Bardot	Camille Javal
John Barry	John Barry Prendergast
Lionel Bart	Lionel Begleiter
Count Basie	William Basie
Lennie Bennett	Michael Berry
Tony Bennett	Anthony Dominic Benevetto
Jack Benny	Benjamin Kubelsky
Irving Berlin	Israel Baline
Sarah Bernhardt	Rosine Bernhard
Big Daddy	Shirley Crabtree
Cilla Black	Priscilla White
Dirk Bogarde	Derek van den Bogaerde
Marc Bolan	Marc Feld
David Bowie	David Jones
Jeremy Brett	Peter Jeremy Huggins
May Britt	Maybritt Wilkens
Charles Bronson	Charles Buchinski
Elkie Brooks	Elaine Bookbinder
Mel Brooks	Melvin Kaminsky
Dora Bryan	Dora Broadbent

George Burns	Nathan Birnbaum
Richard Burton	Richard Jenkins
Max Bygraves	Walter Bygraves
Marti Caine	Lynda Denise Crapper
Michael Caine	Maurice Micklewhite
Jasper Carrott	Robert Davies
Jeff Chandler	Ira Grossell
Ray Charles	Ray Charles Robinson
Cher	Cherilyn La Pierre
Eric Clapton	Eric Clapp
Coco (the Clown)	Nikolai Poliakov
Nat King Cole	Nathaniel Adams Coles
Perry Como	Nick Perido
Sean Connery	Thomas Connery
Alice Cooper	Vince Furnier
Gary Cooper	Frank Cooper
Elvis Costello	Declan McManus
Michael Crawford	Michael Dumble-Smith
Kid Creole	Thomas August Darnell Browder
Bing Crosby	Harry Lillis Crosby
Tony Curtis	Bernard Schwartz
Bobby Darin	Walden Robert Cassotto
Doris Day	Doris Kappelhoff
Kiki Dee	Pauline Matthews
Neil Diamond	Noah Kaminsky
Kirk Douglas	Issur Danielovitch
Bob Dylan	Robert Allan Zimmerman
David Essex	David Cook
Kenny Everett	Maurice Cole
Douglas Fairbanks	Douglas Ullman
(Jnr. and Snr.)	
Adam Faith	Terry Nelhams
Georgie Fame	Clive Powell
Gracie Fields	Grace Stansfield
W. C. Fields	William Claude Dukinfield
Peter Finch	Ian Mitchell

John Ford	Sean O'Feeny
George Formby	George Hoy Booth
Bruce Forsyth	Bruce Johnson
Billy Fury	Ronald Wycherly
Judy Garland	Frances Gumm
James Garner	James Baumgartner
Boy George	George O'Dowd
Gary Glitter	Paul Gadd
Stewart Granger	James Stewart
Larry Grayson	William White
Jean Harlow	Harlean Carpentier
Giant Haystacks	Luke McMasters
Rita Hayworth	Marguerita Cansino
Charlton Heston	Charlton Carter
William Holden	William Beedle
Harry Houdini	Erik Weisz
Engelbert Humperdinck	Arnold Dorsey
Burl Ives	Burl Ivanhoe
Elton John	Reginald Dwight
Tom Jones	Thomas Woodward
Chaka Khan	Yvette Marie Stephens
Boris Karloff	William Pratt
Fred Karno	Fred Westcott
Danny Kaye	David Daniel Kaminsky
Jeremy Kemp	Edmund Walker
Ben E. King	Benjamin Nelson
Denny Laine	Brian Haynes
Frankie Laine	Frank Lo Vecchio
Mario Lanza	Alfredo Cocozza
Eddie Large	Edward McGinnis
Danny La Rue	Daniel Carroll
Stan Laurel	Arthur Stanley Jefferson
Peggy Lee	Norma Egstrom
Jerry Lewis	Joseph Levitch

Syd Little	Cyril Mead
Little Richard	Richard Penniman
Marie Lloyd	Mathilda Wood
Lulu	Marie McLaughlin
Vera Lynn	Vera Welch
Madonna	Madonna Louise Ciccone
Manfred Mann	Michael Lubowitz
Jayne Mansfield	Vera Jayne Palmer
Dean Martin	Dino Crocetti
Marx Brothers	
Chico	Leonard Marx
Groucho	Julius Marx
Gummo	Milton Marx
Harpo	Adolph Marx
Zeppo	Herbert Marx
Meatloaf	Marvin Lee Aday
Freddie Mercury	Fredrick Bulsara
George Michael	Georgios Panayiotou
Guy Mitchell	Al Cernick
Joni Mitchell	Roberta Anderson
Marilyn Monroe	Norma Jean Baker
Yves Montand	Ivo Levy
Ron Moody	Ronald Moodnick
Eric Morecambe	Eric Bartholomew
Van Morrison	George Ivan Morrison
Ivor Novello	David Ivor Davies
Gary Numan	Gary Webb
Maureen O'Hara	Maureen Fitzsimmons
Gilbert O'Sullivan	Raymond O'Sullivan
Jackie Pallo	John Gutteridge
John Peel	John Ravenscroft
Edith Piaf	Edith Gassion
Mary Pickford	Gladys Mary Smith
Iggy Pop	James Osterburg
Prince	Prince Rogers Nelson

P J Proby	James Marcus Smith
Ted Ray	Charles Olden
Lou Reed	Louis Firbank
Cliff Richard	Harold Webb
Edward G. Robinson	Emmanuel Goldenberg
Ginger Rogers	Virginnia McMath
Roy Rogers	Leonard Slye
Johnny Rotten	John Lydon
Sadé	Helen Folasade Adu
Omar Sharif	Michel Shalhoub
Sandie Shaw	Sandra Goodrich
Siouxsie Sioux	Susan Dallion
Alvin Stardust	Bernard Jewry
Ringo Starr	Richard Starkey
Tommy Steele	Thomas Hicks
Cat Stevens	Steven Giorgiou
Ed Stewart	Edward Stewart Mainwaring
Sting	Gordon Sumner
Jacques Tati	Jack Tatischeff
Tina Turner	Annie Mae Bullock
Bonnie Tyler	Gaynor Sullivan
Frankie Vaughan	Frank Abelsohn
Sid Vicious	John Ritchie
Gene Vincent	Eugene Vincent Craddock
Marty Wilde	Reginald Smith
Barbara Windsor	Barbara Deeks
Shelley Winters	Shirley Schrift
Ernie Wise	Ernest Wiseman
Stevie Wonder	Stephen Judkins
Natalie Wood	Natasha Gurdin
Bill Wyman	William Perks

Real Name (The Arts)

This section deals with writers who have used nom de plumes, the real or full names of certain much-asked artists and composers and other sundry individuals associated with the arts who were not known by their real names.

William Atheling	Ezra Pound
Atticus	Originally used by Joseph Addison
Beachcomber	J. C. Morton
Acton Bell	Anne Bronte
Currer Bell	Charlotte Bronte
Ellis Bell	Emily Bronte
Botticelli	Alessandro Filipepi
Boz	Charles Dickens
Canaletto	Giovanni Antonio Canale
Lewis Carroll	Charles Lutwidge Dodgson
Cassandra	William Connor
Leslie Charteris	Leslie Boyer Yin
Colette	Sidonie Gabriel Claudine Colette
Joseph Conrad	Jozef Korzeniowski
Le Corbusier	Charles Edouard Jeannerep
Corno di Bassetto	George Bernard Shaw (used as a pseudonym when he worked as a theatre and music critic)
Correggio	Antonio Allegri
Richmal Crompton	Richmal Lambourn
Daniel Defoe	Daniel Foe
Thomas DeQuincey	Thomas Quincey
George Eliot	Mary Ann Evans
Peter Goldsmith	J. B. Priestley
Richard Gordon	Gordon Ostlere
El Greco	Domenikos Theotokopoulos
O. Henry	William Sydney Porter
James Herriot	James Wight
Jack Higgins	Henry Patterson
Anthony Hope	Anthony Hawkins
Diedrich Knickerbocker	Washington Irving

John Le Carré	David Cornwell
Parson Lot	Charles Kingsley
Hugh MacDiarmid	Christopher Grieve
Alicia Markova	Lillian Marks
Sebastian Melmoth	Oscar Wilde
Merlin	Alfred Lord Tennyson
Michelangelo	Michelangelo di Buonarroti
Moliere	Jean-Baptiste Poquelin
Jacques Offenbach	Jakob Eberst
George Orwell	Eric Arthur Blair
Dorothy Parker	Dorothy Rothschild
Phiz	Hablot Knight Browne
Q	Sir Arthur Quiller-Couch
Ellery Queen	Frederic Dannay and Manfred Lee
Raphael	Raffaello Santi
Uncle Remus	Joel Chandler Harris
Frank Richards	Charles Hamilton
Ralph Robinson	George III (used as a pseudonym in correspondence to gardening periodicals)
Sax Rohmer	Arthur Ward
T. E. Ross	T. E. Lawrence
Saki	Hector Hugh Munro
George Sand	Amandine Lucile Aurore Dudevant
Sapper	H. C. McNeile
T. E. Shaw	T. E. Lawrence
Stendahl	Marie-Henri Beyle
Tom Stoppard	Thomas Straussler
Tintoretto	Jacopo Robusti
Titian	Tiziano Vecellio
Michael Angelo Titmarsh	William Makepeace Thackeray
Mark Twain	Samuel Langhorne Clemens
Voltaire	François Marie Arouet
Artemus Ward	Charles Farrar Browne
Peter Warlock	Philip Heseltine
Mary Westmacott	Agatha Christie

Religions

Questions on religion and religions frequently involve those beliefs which are in a minority in the UK (ie non-Christian). The following brief notes cover those facts which question setters home in on.

Buddhism	Founded by Siddhartha Guatama about 500 BC. Buddha means "the enlightened one". There are two main divisions – Therevada Buddhism and Mahayana Buddhism; and a third minor division – Vajrayana or Tantric Buddhism. The holy texts of Buddhism are collectively known as the Tripitaka and comprise: The Vanaya Pitakas; The Dharma Pitakas; and The Abhidharma Pitakas. The doctrine of Karma; good or evil deeds meeting with appropriate rewards or punishments, is espoused by Buddhists. The Buddha's teachings are described as the four noble truths and by following the eight fold path a believer can break the chain of Karma to reach the enlightened state of nirvana. Two Buddhist festivals worth remembering are: Wesak – the celebration of the birth of the Buddha; and Dhammacakka – celebrates the preaching of the Buddha's first sermon.
Confucianism	Based on the teaching and philosophies of K'ung tsu (Confucius) of about 500 BC. There is no formal clergy or organised worship, but ancestor worship and the symbolism of yin and yang (the passive and active elements of life) are important aspects of the faith.
Hinduism	Originating in Northern India about 4,000 years ago. The three major deities of the Hindu religion are: Brahma – the creator and supreme being; Vishnu – the preserver; and Shiva – the creator and destroyer. Samsara is the cycle of birth and rebirth and Karma is the law which governs this

cycle. The Veda (meaning knowledge) is the most sacred text of Hinduism.

Islam

Founded in what is now Saudi Arabia by the the prophet Mohammed (570–632). The Islamic calendar takes as its starting point the Hegira, the Prophet's flight from Mecca to Medina (in the year 622 of the Christian calendar). New Year's day is the first day of Muharram. The sacred text, the Koran, is divided into 114 suras or chapters. The five pillars of the Islamic faith are

Shahada	The profession of faith in the one God and his prophet, Mohammed
Salat	Daily worship after ritual cleansing
Zakat	The giving of alms to the needy
Saum	Fasting during daylight hours during the month of Ramadan
Hajj	The pilgrimage to Mecca, which should be undertaken at least once in the lifetime of a believer.

Jainism

Founded in India in the 6th century BC by Mahavira, a Jina (a name which means "those who overcome"). Jains practise an extreme form of non-violence (ahimsa) and believe that all life is sacred.

Judaism

The Hebrew bible comprises 24 books. The other sacred text is the Talmud, which is made up of the Mishna, the oral rabinical law; and the Gemara which is legal discussion and commentary. Two important Jewish festivals which are worth remembering are Rosh Hashanah – New Year, and Yom Kippur – the Day of Atonement.

Shintoism

Shinto, meaning "the teaching" or "the way of the gods", was founded in Japan in the 8th century AD. Shintoism was divided into two main sects in the 19th century, Jinja and Kyoha. The sacred texts are Kojiki and Nihon Shoki.

Sikhism   Founded in the 15th century by the Guru, Nanak.
The holy book is the Guru Granth Sahib,
sometimes known as the Adi Granth.

....

Riparian Towns and Cities

We are all familiar with this type of question, you know the sort "On which
river does 'X' or 'Y' stand?" The annoying thing is they never ask you the
ones you know, do they? There are two separate lists in this section, one
for the British Isles and one for the rest of the world. I know this may seem
rather xenophobic, but it is only a reflection of proportions in which these
questions appear.

   I have assumed that everybody's pet cat knows that Paris is on the
Seine, Rome is on the Tiber and London is on the Thames. Also excluded
from these lists are towns and cities whose name gives the game away
(eg Innsbruck is on the Inn and Dartmouth is at the mouth of the Dart).

British Isles

Town	River
Aberdeen	Between the mouths of the Dee and the Don
Bedford	Ouse
Belfast	Lagan
Chester	Dee
Colchester	Colne
Cork	Lee
Derby	Derwent
Dorchester	Frome
Dublin	Liffey
Dumfries	Nith
Durham	Wear
Evesham	Avon
Gillingham	Medway
Grantham	Witham
Guildford	Wey
Harrogate	Nid
Harwich	Stour

Town	River
Hertford	Lea
Huntington	Ouse
Ipswich	Orwell
Kidderminster	Stour
Kilmarnock	Irvine
Kings Lynn	Great Ouse
Leeds	Aire
Leicester	Soar
Limerick	Shannon
Lincoln	Witham
Londonderry	Foyle
Maidstone	Medway
Newbury	Kennet
Northampton	Nene
Norwich	Wensum
Nuneaton	Anker
Peterborough	Nene
Reading	Confluence of Thames and Kennet
Richmond (Yorkshire)	Swale
Rugby	Avon
Salisbury	Confluence of Avon and Wily
Sheffield	Don
Shrewsbury	Severn
Stafford	Sow
Taunton	Tone
Wakefield	Calder
Warwick	Avon
Winchester	Itchen
York	Ouse

Around the World

Town	River
Adelaide	Torrens
Albuquerque	Rio Grande
Amsterdam	Amstel
Augusta	Savannah
Avignon	Rhone
Baghdad	Tigris
Basel	Rhine
Belgrade	Sava
Berlin	Spree
Bonn	Confluence of the Seig and Rhine
Bucharest	Dambovita (tributary of the Danube)
Budapest	Danube
Calcutta	Hooghly
Cincinnati	Ohio
Cologne	Rhine
Dresden	Elbe
Dusseldorf	Rhine
Florence	Arno
Geneva	Rhone
Hamburg	Elbe
Hanoi	Red (Song-Koi)
Heidelberg	Neckar
Ho Chi-Minh City	Saigon (just east of the Mekong Delta)
Indianapolis	White
Leipzig	Confluence of the Pleisse, Elster and Parthe
Lisbon	Tagus
Louisville	Ohio
Lyons	Confluence of the Saone and Rhone
Madrid	Mazanares
Melbourne	Yarra

Town	River
Milan	Olono
Montreal	Confluence of the Ottawa and St Lawrence
Moscow	Moskva
Munich	Isar
Nantes	Loire
Nashville	Cumberland
Oporto	Duoro
Perth	Swan
Philadelphia	Delaware
Phnom-Penh	Mekong
Pisa	Arno
Pittsburgh	Ohio
Prague	Vltava
Quebec	Confluence of St Charles and St Lawrence
Rangoon	Irrawaddy
Rotterdam	Rhine, Maas, Scheldt Delta
St Louis	Mississippi (10 miles from the confluence of the Missouri)
St Petersburg	Neva
Seoul	Han
Shanghai	Hwangpu (15 miles from its confluence with the Yangtze)
Strasbourg	Rhine
Stuttgart	Neckar
Timbuktu	(nine miles north of) Niger
Warsaw	Vistula
Washington DC	Potomac

The Seven Wonders of the World

A firm favourite for "jackpot" type questions. Here they are.

1   The Pyramids of Egypt
2   The Hanging Gardens of Babylon
3   The Tomb of Mausolus of Halicarnassus
4   The Temple of Artemis at Ephesus
5   The Colossus of Rhodes
6   The Statue of Zeus at Olympia
7   The Pharos at Alexandria

Scrabble – Tile Values

A useful one to remember. We have all played the game, but for some of us it was years ago. Probably more easily remembered if the letters are grouped in "value groups".

Blank tile	Worth nothing
One point	A, E, I, L, N, O, R, S, T, U
Two points	D, G
Three points	B, C, M, P
Four points	F, H, V, W, Y
Five points	K (*worth remembering as it is the only five pointer*)
Eight Points	J, X
Ten points	Q, Z

Shakespeare

This section is not intended to be a learned discourse on the works of
the bard. Quiz setters never ask for a critical appraisal of Polonius's role
in Hamlet, nor do they ever ask anybody to quote extensively from the
works of Shakespeare; questions invariably revolve around the characters in the plays, the settings and one or two well-known quotations.

This section merely lists some of the characters in each of the plays,
the setting of the plays and, where appropriate, some well-known
quotations from each of the plays. It is rare that any questions are asked
regarding some of the rarely performed work (such as Pericles, or Titus
Andronicus) but questions arising from Hamlet, Macbeth, Julius Caesar
abound and this is reflected in the length of entry for each of the plays
in the section.

Title of Play	*Quotations*
All's Well That Ends Well	
14th Century France and Italy	Our remedies oft in ourselves lie Which we ascribe to heaven.
Characters:	————
Bertram, Count of Rousillon	Praising what is lost Makes the remembrance dear.
The Dowager Countess of Rousillon	————
The King of France	
Helena	
Parolles	
Diana	
The Duke of Florence	
La Feu	
Lavache	
Antony And Cleopatra	
Alexandria, Rome and several places between in the 1st Century BC	In time we hate that which we often fear.
Characters:	————
Cleopatra	My salad days,
Mark Antony	When I was green in judgment, cold in blood,

Title of Play	Quotations
Pompey	To say as I said then.
Octavia, Antony's wife	
and Caesar's sister	————
Enobarbus	Age cannot wither her, nor custom
Ventidius	stale
Eros	Her infinite variety; other women cloy
Scarus	The appetites they feed,
Demetrius	but she makes hungry
Philo	Where most she satisfies;
Agrippa	
Dolabella	

As You Like It

The Forest of Arden	All the world's a stage,
(probably during the 14th	And all the men and women merely
Century)	players; . . .
Characters:	. . . And one man in his time plays
Fredrick	many parts,
Celia	His act being seven ages.
Rosalind	
Oliver	————
Amiens	Blow, blow, thou winter wind,
Jaques	Thou art not so unkind
Orlando	As man's ingratitude.
Touchstone	————
Sir Oliver Martext	If it be true that good wine needs
Adam	"no bush"
Dennis	'tis true that a good play needs
Phebe	no epilogue.
Audrey	

The Comedy Of Errors

Ephesus (probably 14th	
Century)	
Characters:	
Aegeon	
Aemilia	
Antipholus of Ephesus	

Title of Play	**Quotations**
Antipholus of Syracuse	
Dromio of Ephesus	
Dromio of Syracuse	
Adriana	
Luciana	
Balthazar	

Coriolanus

Basically Rome, about 490 BC	Let me have war, say I; it exceeds peace as far as day does night;
Characters:	
Caius Marcius	————
Coriolanus	
Volumnia	
Virgilia	
Tullus Aufidius	
Titus Lartius	
Cominius	

Cymbeline

Britain and Italy, shortly before the Christian era	
Characters:	
Cymbeline	
Imogen	
Cloten	
Posthumus Leonatus	
Iachimo	
Guiderius	
Arviragus	
Belarius	

Hamlet, Prince of Denmark

Denmark, some time in the Dark Ages	For this relief much thanks; tis bitter cold And I am sick at heart
Characters:	
Hamlet, Prince of Denmark	————
	Frailty, thy name is woman

Title of Play	Quotations
Claudius, King of Denmark, brother of Hamlet's late father and husband of his widow, Gertrude	——————
	A countenance more in sorrow than in anger
Polonius	——————
Ophelia	Neither a borrower, nor a lender be
Laertes	——————
Horatio	But to my mind - though I am native here, And to the manor born . . .
Fortinbras, Prince of Norway	——————
Rosencrantz and Guildenstern	Brevity is the soul of wit
	——————
	Though this be madness, yet there is method in't
	——————
	The lady doth protest too much, methinks
	——————
	I must be cruel only to be kind
	——————
	The play's the thing. Wherein I'll catch the conscience of the King
	——————
	For 'tis sport to have the engineer Hoist with his own petar
	——————
	Be thou as chaste as ice, as pure as snow, thou shalt not escape calumny. Get thee to a nunnery, go; farewell.
	——————
	There is rosemary, that's for remembrance
	——————

Title of Play

Quotations

Imperious Caesar, dead, and
turn'd to clay,
Might stop a hole to keep the
wind away

_____

Now cracks a noble heart. Good-
night, sweet prince,
And flights of angels sing thee
to thy rest

_____

And finally the last one of the play
Go, bid the soldiers shoot

**King Henry IV
Part I**

England, between 1402 and
1413
Characters:
Henry IV, King of England
His sons: Henry, Prince of
Wales and Prince John
of Lancaster
Earl of Westmoreland
Sir Walter Blunt
Edmund Mortimer, Earl
of March
Thomas Percy, Earl
of Worcester
Henry Percy, Earl of
Northumberland
Archibald, Earl of Douglas
Scroop, Archbishop of York
Owen Glendower
Henry Hotspur
Mistress Quickly, Keeper of
the Boar's Head Inn

Instinct is a great matter, I was a
coward on instinct

_____

Now I perceive the devil
understands Welsh

_____

Two stars keep not their motion
in one sphere

Title of Play	Quotations
Sir John Falstaff	
Edward Poynes	
Bardolph	
Peto	
Gadshill	

Henry IV
Part II

England, between 1402 and 1413
Characters:
Many of the characters are as those in Part I but Pistol is introduced into Sir John Falstaff's circle of acquaintances and some characters with names worth remembering appear;
Fang
Snare
Mouldy
Shadow
Wart
Feeble
Bullcalf

Is it not strange that desire should so many years outlive performance.

King Henry V

England & France between 1414 and 1420
Characters:
King Henry V of England
His brothers: The Dukes of Gloucester and Bedford
His uncle the Duke of Exeter, his cousin the Duke of York
Earl of Salisbury

O! For a muse of fire, that would ascend
The brightest heaven of invention
(These are the opening lines of the prologue)

————

Once more into the breach, dear friends, once more;

————

A little touch of Harry in the night

————

Title of Play	Quotations
Earl of Westmoreland	Old men forget; yet all shall be
Earl of Warwick	forgot,
Archbishop of Canterbury	But he'll remember with advantages
Bishop of Ely	What feats he did that day.
Earl of Cambridge	
Lord Scroop	I think the King is but a man, as I am;
Charles VI of France	The violet smells to him as it doth
Lewis, the Dauphin	to me
Duke of Burgundy	
Duke of Orleans	
Duke of Britaine	
Duke of Bourbon	
Constable of France	
Montjoy, the French Herald	
Isabel, Queen of France	
Katherine, daughter of	
Charles and Isabel	
Soldiers in the King's Army:	
Nym, Bardolph,	
Pistol, Williams, Bates	

Henry VI
Parts I, II and III

Set in England and France	*(From Henry VI, Part III)*
between 1422 and 1471	Oh tiger's heart wrapp'd in a
Characters:	woman's hide
The usual list of dukes,	
earls, archbishops and	
knights, but most notably	
in Part I Joan of Arc and	
in Part II Jack Cade, the	
Kentish rebel leader	

Title of Play	**Quotations**
King Henry VIII	

Set in London, Westminster and Kimbolton between 1521 and 1533

Characters:

Various dukes, earls and knights but amongst the dramatis personae are

Thomas Wolsey

Thomas Cranmer, Archbishop of Canterbury

Two of Henry's wives: Katherine of Aragon Anne Boleyn

Had I but serv'd my God with half the zeal
I serv'd my King, he would not in mine age
Have left me naked to mine enemies

————

Men's evil manners live in brass; their virtues
We write in water

————

Julius Caesar

Rome, Sardis and near Philippi between 44 and 42 BC

Characters:

Julius Caesar
Octavius Caesar
Marcus Antonius
Marcus Aemilius Lepidus
Cicero; Publius
Popilius Lena
Marcus Brutus
Cassius; Casca
Trebonius; Ligarius
Decius Brutus
Metellus Cimba
Cinna; Lucilius
Titinius; Messala
Cato; Volumnius
Varro; Clitus
Claudius; Strato
Lucius; Dardanius

Why, man he doth bestride the narrow world
Like a colossus;

————

Let me have men about me who are fat
Sleek-headed men and such as sleep o'nights;
'Yond Cassius has a lean and hungry look
He thinks too much; such men are dangerous

————

Et tu, Brute?
Then fall Caesar

————

Cry "Havoc" and let slip the dogs of war;

————

This was the most unkindest cut of all;

Title of Play	*Quotations*
Pindarus	
Calphurnia	There is a tide in the affairs of men,
Portia	Which, taken at the flood, leads on to
	fortune

King John

England and France between 1199 and 1216

To gild refined gold, to paint the lily

Characters:
King John
Prince Henry, his son
Arthur, Duke of Britaine
Earl of Pembroke
Earl of Essex
Earl of Salisbury
Lord Bigot
Hubert de Burgh
Robert Faulconbridge
Philip the Bastard
James Gurney
Peter of Pomfret
King Philip of France
Lewis, the Dauphin
Lymoges, Duke of
Austria
Cardinal Pandulph
Melun
Chatillon
Queen Eleanor, Widow
of Henry II
Constance
Blanch of Spain
Lady Faulconbridge

King Lear

Britain

. . . I am a man
More sinned against than sinning

Characters:
Lear, King of Britain

Title of Play	Quotations
The King of France	This is the foul fiend flibbertigibbet;
Duke of Burgundy	he begins at curfew, and walks 'til
Duke of Cornwall	the first cock;
Duke of Albany	————
Earl of Kent	. . . Fie, foh and fum,
Earl of Gloucester	I smell the blood of a British man
Edgar, Son of Gloucester	————
Edmund, Bastard son of	*The final lines of the play:*
Gloucester	The oldest hath borne most;
Curan; Oswald	we that are young shall never
and bear these in mind:	see so much nor live so long.
Lear's daughters:	
Goneril	
Regan	
Cordelia	

Love's Labour's Lost

Navarre, probably in the 14th
Century
Characters:
Ferdinand, King of
Navarre
Berowne
Longaville
Dumain
Boyet
Marcade
Sir Nathaniel
Holofernes
Dull (a constable)
Costard (a clown)
Moth
The Princess of France
Rosaline
Maria
Katherine
Jaquenetta

Title of Play	*Quotations*
Macbeth	

Scotland and England
between 1039 and 1057
Characters:
Duncan, King of
Scotland
His sons: Malcolm
and Donalbain
Macbeth
Banquo
Macduff
Lady Macbeth
Lady Macduff
Lennox
Ross
Menteith
Angus
Caithness
Fleance (Banquo's son)

The Thane of Cawdor lives; why
do you dress me
In borrow'd robes

_____

. . . Yet I do fear thy nature;
It is too full of o'milk of human
kindness

_____

Is this a dagger which I see before
me?,
The handle towards my hand? Come,
let me clutch thee:

_____

(of drink) It provokes the desire but
takes away the performance

_____

Duncan is in his grave;
After life's fitful fever he sleeps well;

_____

Double double toil and trouble;
Fire burn and cauldron bubble

_____

Out, damn spot, out, I say

_____

To-morrow, and to-morrow and
to-morrow and to-morrow,
Creeps in this petty pace from day
to day,
To the last syllable of recorded time;
And all our yesterdays have lighted
fools
The way to dusty death

_____

I bear a charmed life, which must
not yield to one of woman born

Title of Play	Quotations

Measure For Measure

Vienna at the end of the 15th Century

We must not make a scarecrow of the law,
Setting it up to fear the birds of prey,

———————

Characters:
Vincentio, the Duke
Angelo, the Deputy
Escalus

Tis one thing to be tempted, Escalus,
Another thing to fall.

———————

Claudio
Lucio
Varrius
Mistress Overdone
Pompey
Abhorson

O! It is excellent
To have a giant's strength, but it is tyranous
To use it like a giant

———————

Barnardine
Isabella
Mariana
Juliet
Francisca
Elbow
Froth

Every true man's apparel fits your thief

The Merchant Of Venice

Venice and Belmont (probably in the 14th Century)

It is a wise father that knows his own child

———————

Characters:
Antonio, a merchant of Venice
Bassanio
Shylock

If you prick us, do we not bleed?,
If you tickle us, do we not laugh?
If you poison us do we not die?,
And if you wrong us, shall we not revenge?

———————

Launcelot Gobbo (Shylock's servant)
Jessica, daughter of Shylock
Portia
Leonardo (Bassanio's servant)

Then it was not for nothing that my nose fell a-bleeding on Black Monday

Title of Play	Quotations
Nerissa (Portia's maid)	
The Prince of Morocco	
The Prince of Arragon	

The Merry Wives of Windsor

Windsor, some time in the middle of the 15th Century	Why, the world's mine oyster Which I with sword will open
Characters:	
Sir John Falstaff	
Mistress Ford	
Mistress Page	
Mistress Anne Page	
Mistress Quickly	
Shallow	
Slender	
Bardolph	
Pistol	
Nym	
Dr Caius	
Robin	
Simple	
Rugby	

A Midsummer Night's Dream

Athens and neighbouring woods during the reign of Theseus	The course of true love never did run smooth
	————
Characters:	Ill met by moonlight, proud Titania
Theseus, Duke of Athens	————
Egeus	I'll put a girdle round the earth In forty minutes
Hermia, daughter of Egeus	
Lysander	
Demetrius	
Quince, a carpenter	

Title of Play	**Quotations**
Snug, a joiner	
Bottom, a weaver	
Flute, a bellows mender	
Snout, a tinker	
Starveling, a tailor	
Hippolyta, Queen of the Amazons	
Oberon, King of the Fairies	
Titania, Queen of the Fairies	
Puck (Robin Goodfellow)	
Peaseblossom ⎫	
Cobweb ⎬ Fairies	
Moth ⎪	
Mustardseed ⎭	

Much Ado About Nothing

Messina	Comparisons are odorous
Characters:	
Don Pedro, Prince of Aragon	
Don John, his bastard brother	
Claudio	
Benedick	
Leonato	
Antonio	
Balthazar	
Friar Francis	
Dogberry (a constable)	
Hero	
Beatrice	
Margaret	
Ursula	
Verges	

Title of Play	Quotations
Borachio	
Conrade	

Othello, The Moor Of Venice

Venice and Cyprus about 1570	But I will wear my heart upon my sleeve
Characters:	For daws to peck at it: I am not what I am
The Duke of Venice	
Brabantio	
Desdemona, daughter of Brabantio and wife of Othello	Who steals my purse steals trash; 'tis something, nothing, 'Twas mine, 'tis his, and has been slave to thousands;
Othello	But he that filches from me my good name
Iago	Robs me of that which not enriches him,
Emelia, wife of Iago	And makes me poor indeed.
Cassio	
Roderigo	......Then, must you speak
Gratiano	Of one that lov'd not wisely but too well;
Lodovico	
Montano	
Bianca	O! beware, my lord, of jealousy; It is the green-ey'd monster which doth mock The meat it feeds on

Pericles, Prince Of Tyre

Antioch, Tyre, Tarsus, Pentapolis, Ephesus, Mitylene	O you gods! Why do you make us love your goodly gifts, And snatch them straight away
Characters:	
Antiochus, King of Antioch	
Pericles, Prince of Tyre	
Helicanus	

Title of Play	**Quotations**
Escanes	
Simonides, King of	
Pentapolis	
Cleon	
Cerimon	
Lysimachus	
Thaliard	
Dionyza	
Thaisa (wife of Pericles)	
Marina (daughter of	
Pericles)	
Lychorida	
Leonine	

King Richard II

England and Wales at the turn of the 14th and 15th Centuries	*Worth remembering that it is John of Gaunt who makes the speech that begins as follows:*
Characters:	————
King Richard II and the usual collection of dukes, earls and knights, *but the following characters are worth remembering* Henry Percy (Hotspur) son of the Earl of Northumberland and the following: Bushy Bagot and Green	This royal throne of kings, this scepter'd isle This earth of majesty, this seat of Mars, . . .

King Richard III

England between 1471 and 1485 Characters: Once again a collection	*(The opening lines)* Now is the winter of our discontent Made glorious summer by this sun of York ————

Title of Play	Quotations
of royal dukes, earls, knights and archbishops *but it is worth remembering that the* Lord Mayor of London *makes an appearance in this play*	A horse! A horse! My kingdom for a horse

Romeo And Juliet

Verona and Mantua early in the 14th Century	What's in a name? That which we call a rose
Characters:	By any other name would smell
Romeo, son of the	as sweet
House of Montague	————
Juliet, daughter of	Good-night, Good-night!
the house of Capulet	Parting is such sweet sorrow
Escalus, Prince of Verona	That I should say good-night 'til
Romeo's friends:	it be morrow
Mercutio and	————
Benvolio	A plague o'both your houses!
Balthasar (Romeo's servant)	
Sampson and Gregory (servants to the House of Capulet)	
Friar Lawrence	
Friar John	
Various members of the Houses of Montague and Capulet	

The Taming Of The Shrew

Padua and Petruchio's house
in the country (probably
during the 14th Century)
Characters:
Baptista Minola of Padua

Title of Play	Quotations
His daughters:	
Katherina (the shrew)	
Bianca (a widow)	
Petruchio (Katherina's suitor)	
Gremio and Hortensio (suitors of Bianca)	
Tranio	
Biondello	
Curtis	
Christopher Sly	
Grumio	
Hortensio	

The Tempest

On board ship and on an island (probably 14th Century)	Full fathom five, thy father lies; Of his bones are coral made: . . . . . . But doth suffer a sea-change into something rich and strange.
Characters:	
Prospero (the rightful Duke of Milan)	————
Antonio (his brother who usurped the dukedom)	Misery acquaints a man with strange bedfellows
Alonso, King of Naples	————
Sebastian (Alonso's brother)	Where the bee sucks, there suck I In a cowslip's bell I lie
Ferdinand (Alonso's son)	————
Miranda (daughter of Prospero)	How many goodly creatures are there here!
Caliban (Prospero's savage and deformed slave)	How beauteous mankind is! O brave new world
Ariel (a spirit controlled by Prospero)	That has such people in't

Title of Play	Quotations

Timon Of Athens

Athens and neighbouring
woods (chronological setting
unknown)
Characters:
Timon of Athens
Lucius
Lucullus
Sempronius
Ventidius
Alcibiades
Apemantus
Flavius
Phrynia
Timandra
Flaminius
Lucilius
Servilius
Caphis
Philotus
Titus
Hortensius
Cupid

Titus Andronicus

Rome and its neighbourhood
(time unknown)
Characters:
Titus Andronicus
Marcus Andronicus
(Titus's brother)
Titus's sons:
Lucius ⎫
Quintus ⎪
Martius ⎬
Mutius ⎭
His daughter: Lavinia

Title of Play	**Quotations**
Marcus Andronicus	
His son Publius	
Saturninus	
His brother, Bassianus	
Tamora (Queen of the	
Goths) and her sons:	
Alarbus	
Demetrius	
Chiron	

Troilus And Cressida

Troy and the Greek camp	How my achievements mock me!
during the Trojan War	
Characters:	
Priam, King of Troy	
His sons:	
Hector	
Troilus	
Paris	
Deiphobus	
Helenus	
Agamemnon (a Greek	
general)	
His brother: Menelaus	
Helen (the wife of	
Menelaus)	
The Greek commanders:	
Achilles	
Ajax	
Ulysses	
Nestor	
Diomedes	
Patroclus	
Calchas (a Trojan priest)	
and his daughter: Cressida	
Andromache (wife of Hector)	
Cassandra (daughter of Priam)	

Title of Play	Quotations

Twelfth Night, or What You Will

Illyria (time unknown)

Characters:
Olivia
Malvolio (steward
to Olivia)
Sir Andrew Aguecheek
Sir Toby Belch (uncle
of Olivia)
Maria (Olivia's maid)
Orsino (Duke of Illyria)
Sebastian
Viola (sister of
Sebastian)
Antonio (friend of
Sebastian)
Valentine
Curio
Fabian ⎱ servants of
Feste ⎰ Olivia

The opening lines:
If music be the food of love, play on;
Give me excess of it, that, surfeiting,
The appetite may sicken, and so die.

———

Dost thou think, because thou art
virtuous, there shall be no more
cakes and ale?

———

Be not afraid of greatness: some
men are born great, some achieve
greatness, and some have greatness
thrust upon them.

———

Why, this is very midsummer
madness

———

*The final lines are worth
remembering:*
A great while ago the world
begun,
With hey, ho, the wind and the
rain,
But that's all one, our play is done,
And we'll strive to please you
every day.

The Two Gentlemen Of Verona

Verona, Milan and the
frontiers of Mantua (time
unknown)
Characters:
Valentine ⎱ the two
Proteus ⎰ gentlemen
of Verona

Who is Silvia? What is she,
That all our swains commend her

———

How use doth breed a habit
in man!

Title of Play	Quotations
Antonio (the father of Proteus)	
Julia (the love of Proteus's life)	
Silvia (the love of Valentine's life)	
The Duke of Milan (Silvia's father)	
Thurio	
Eglamour	
Speed	
Launce	
Panthino	
Lucetta	

The Winter's Tale

Sicilia and Bohemia
(probably in the 14th
Century)
Characters:
Leontes, King of Sicilia
His wife, Hermione
His son, Mamillius
His daughter, Perdita
Polixenes, King of Bohemia
Florizel, his son
Camillo
Antigonus
Cleomenes
Dion
Archidamus
Paulina
Emilia
Autolycus
Mopsa
Dorcas

It is worth bearing in mind that this play contains the stage direction "Exit, pursued by a bear" (an old quiz question)

Lawn as white as driven snow

Shipping Forecast areas

Most of us hear these mentioned every day of our lives, and questions on the subject are popular. you know the sort "Which shipping forecast area is due south of Fastnet?". Here they are:

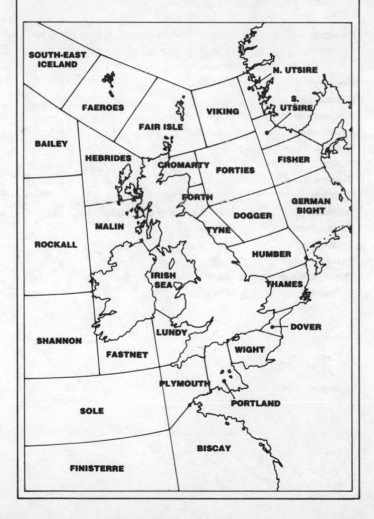

Ships and Sailors

Although great navigators are sometimes associated with a particular
vessel, most of them commanded several ships during their careers;
conversely, some famous vessels were under the command of more
than one great navigator (The Fram, for example, had been used by
Amundsen). The following, however, are the ships which are the subject
of the most frequently asked questions.

Beagle	Commanded by Fitzroy. Darwin made his famous voyage in the ship as scientific officer
Bounty	Bligh
Discovery	Scott
Endeavour	Cook
Endurance	Shackleton
Erebus	Ross
Fram	Nansen
Golden Hind	Drake
Matthew	Cabot
Pelican	Former name of the Golden Hind
Resolution	Cook
Santa Maria	Columbus
Terror	Ross
Theodore Roosevelt	Peary
Vittoria	Magellan

SI Units

Scientific questions are generally as rare as hens' teeth in quizzes, but the old favourites "SI Units" are well worth remembering, although it is doubtful whether many of us actually understand what they are.

Quantity	SI Unit	Symbol
Electrical Capacitance	Farad	F
Electrical Charge	Coulomb	C
Electrical Conductance	Siemens	S
Electrical Current	Ampere	A
Energy or Work	Joule	J
Force	Newton	N
Frequency	Hertz	Hz
Illuminance	Lux	lx
Inductance	Henry	H
Length	Metre	M
Luminous Intensity	Candela	cd
Magnetic Flux	Weber	Wb
Mass	Kilogram	kg
Potential Difference	Volt	V
Power	Watt	W
Pressure	Pascal	Pa
Radiation Exposure	Roentgen	r
Radioactivity	Becquerel	Bq
Resistance	Ohm	Ω
Sound Intensity	Decibel	dB
Temperature	Degree Celsius	°C
Time	Second	S

The Skeleton

Always very popular: "What is the medical name for the breast-bone?", "What is the common name for the scapula?". Learning the names of various bones will always stand the quiz player in good stead.

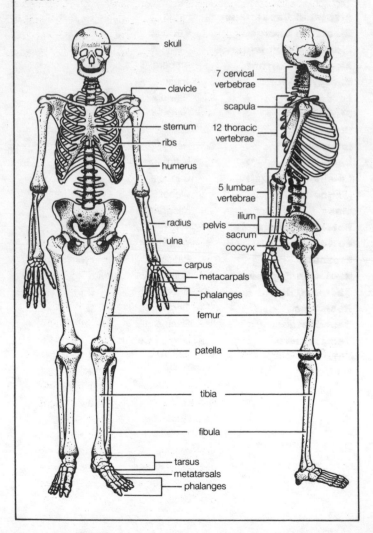

....

Soap Operas

Questions on TV soap operas are generally confined to a handful of the popular soaps which are shown two or three times a week. They are almost always of the "Who plays Mr X in Coronation Street?" or "Which Eastenders' character is played by Miss Y?" variety. Consequently this list confines itself to listing some of the major characters in popular soaps and the actors or actresses who play them. Even so, this is a minefield; by the time you have read this section some of the characters may have been "killed off", married, jailed or just drifted from the scene. Apologies in advance for information which may already be outdated or inaccurate.

Soap	Character	Real Name
Brookside	David Crosby	John Burgess
	Jean Crosby	Marcia Ashton
	Jacqui Dixon	Alex Fletcher
	Mike Dixon	Paul Byatt
	Ron Dixon	Vince Earl
	Max Farnham	Steven Pinder
	Patricia Farnham	Gabrielle Glaister
	Barry Grant	Paul Usher
	Mick Johnson	Louis Emerick
	Beth Jordache	Anna Friel
	Mandy Jordache	Sandra Maitland
	Rachel Jordache	Tiffany Chapman
	Bev McLoughlin	Sarah White
	Sinbad	Michael Starke
Coronation Street*	Alma Baldwin	Amanda Barrie
	Mike Baldwin	Johnny Briggs
	Deirdre Barlow	Anne Kirkbride
	Ken Barlow	William Roache
	Tracy Barlow	Dawn Acton
	Des Barnes	Philip Middlemiss
	Emily Bishop	Eileen Derbyshire
	Jack Duckworth	William Tarmey
	Vera Duckworth	Elizabeth Dawn
	Bet Gilroy	Julie Goodyear

Soap	Character	Real Name
	Reg Holdsworth	Ken Morley
	Gail Platt	Helen Worth
	Martin Platt	Sean Wilson
	Alf Roberts	Bryan Mosley
	Audrey Roberts	Sue Nicholls
	Percy Sugden	Bill Waddington
	Rita Sullivan	Barbara Knox
	Sally Webster	Sally Whittaker
	Curly Watts	Kevin Kennedy
	Derek Wilton	Peter Baldwin
	Mavis Wilton	Thelma Barlow
	Raquel Wolstenholme	Sarah Lancashire

*Because 'the Street' has been running for so long and over the course of years has involved so many different actors and actresses it is well worthwhile committing the following to memory, they have cropped up from time to time.

Michael Elphick	Appeared as a character called Douglas Wormold
Gorden Kaye	(of Allo Allo fame) played a character called Bernard Butler
Ben Kingsley	(Well worth remembering, this one) played Ron Jenkins
Arthur Lowe	(Captain Mainwaring in a later incarnation) played Leonard Swindley
Joanna Lumley	Played a girlfriend of Ken Barlow - Eileen Perkins
Peter Noone	(of Herman's Hermits fame) played Stanley, Len Fairclough's son
Kathy Staff	(aka Nora Batty) played Vera Hopkins
Molly Sugden	(later to gain fame in Are You Being Served) played Nellie Harvey

Soap	Character	Real Name
Eastenders	Pat Butcher	Pam St Clement
	Arthur Fowler	Bill Treacher
	Michelle Fowler	Susan Tully
	Pauline Fowler	Wendy Richard
	Cathy Mitchell	Gillian Taylforth
	Grant Mitchell	Ross Kemp
	Phil Mitchell	Steve McFadden
Home And Away	Donald Fisher	Norman Coburn
	Sally Keating	Kate Ritchie
	Michael Ross	Dennis Coard
	Pippa Ross	Debra Lawrance
	Alf Stewart	Ray Meagher
	Ailsa Stewart	Judy Nunn
Neighbours	Rick Alessi	Dan Falzon
	Lou Carpenter	Tom Oliver
	Helen Daniels	Anne Haddy
	Mark Gottlieb	Bruce Samazan
	Annalise Hartman	Kimberley Davies
	Debbie Martin	Marnie Reece-Wilmore
	Hannah Martin	Rebecca Ritters
	Julie Martin	Julie Mullins
	Michael Martin	Troy Beckwith
	Phillip Martin	Ian Rawlings
	Brett Stark	Brett Blewitt
	Cheryl Stark	Caroline Gilmer
	Danni Stark	Eliza Szonert
	Cody Willis	Peta Brady
	Doug Willis	Terence Donovan
	Gaby Willis	Rachel Blakely
	Pam Willis	Sue Jones

Space Exploration

This subject is a firm favourite with question setters as it involves dates, names and achievements, in other words all the prime ingredients for a question.

Date	Space Project
October 1957	**Sputnik 1** The first earth satellite
November 1957	**Sputnik 2** The dog Laika in space
January 1959	**Luna 1** First craft to escape the earth's gravity
September 1959	**Luna 2** First craft to reach the moon
April 1960	**Tiros 1** First weather satellite
August 1960	**Echo 1** First communications satellite
August 1960	**Sputnik 5** Two dogs returned alive
April 1961	**Vostok 1** First manned space flight by Yuri Gagarin
May 1961	**Freedom 7** First American in space (Alan Shepard)
February 1962	**Friendship 7** First American to orbit the earth (John Glenn)
August–December 1962	**Mariner 2** To Venus
June 1963	**Vostok 6** First woman in space (Valentina Tereshkova)
March 1965	**Voskhod 2** First walk in space by Alexei Leonov

Date	Space Project
December 1965	**Gemini 6 and Gemini 7** First rendezvous in space
January–February 1966	**Luna 9** First soft lunar landing
March/April 1966	**Luna 10** First orbit of the moon
January 1967	**Apollo 1** Astronauts Grissom, White and Chaffee killed in fire in spacecraft
December 1968	**Apollo 8** Borman, Lovell and Anders make 10 lunar orbits
July 1969	**Apollo 11** Armstrong and Aldrin became the first men to walk on the moon (17th July 1969). Collins remained in control module
November 1969	**Apollo 12** Conrad and Bean walk on the moon (Gordon remained in command module)
April 1970	**Apollo 13** Service module exploded. Crew (Lovell, Swigert and Haise) return home in lunar module
January/February 1971	**Apollo 14** Moon landing by Shepard and Mitchell (Roosa remained in command module)
July/August 1971	**Apollo 15** Scott and Irwin landed on moon (Worden remained in module)
April 1972	**Apollo 16** Young and Duke landed on moon (Mattingly remained in module)

Date	Space Project
December 1972	**Apollo 17**
	Cernan and Schmitt became the last Apollo astronauts to walk on the moon (Evans remained in command module)
May–November 1971	**Mariner 9**
	Orbit of Mars
March 1972–June 1983	**Pioneer 10**
	Flew past Jupiter; crossed the orbit of Pluto and escaped the solar system
April 1973– September 1979	**Pioneer 11**
	Flew past Jupiter and Saturn
September 1977– August 1989	**Voyager 2**
	Flew past Jupiter, Saturn, Uranus and Neptune
September 1977– November 1980	**Voyager 1**
	Flew past Jupiter and Saturn
March 1978	**Soyuz 28**
	First non-Soviet non-American in space (Vladimir Remek, a Czech)
April 1981	**Columbia 1**
	Maiden flight of space shuttle with crew of Young and Crippin
August 1982	**Soyuz 7**
	Second woman in space (Svetlana Savitskaya)
June 1983	**Challenger 7**
	First American woman in space (Sally Ride)
	Soyuz 12
	First space walk by a woman (Svetlana Savitskaya)
October 1984	**Challenger 41**
	First American woman to spacewalk (Kathy Sullivan)

Date	Space Project
July 1985	**Giotto** Space probe built by the European Space Agency to study Halley's Comet
January 1986	**Challenger 52** Craft exploded at 47,000 ft. All the crew were killed. Crew: Dick Scobee, Mike Smith, Judith Resnik, Ronald McNair, Ellison Onizuka, Christa McAuliffe and Gregory Jarvis
February 1986	**Mir 1** First attempt to build a space station

Sporting Trophies

Another old favourite of question setters. Usually the question asks "At which sport is a certain trophy awarded?" It is possible that this type of question is an endangered species; commercial sponsorship of sport will inevitably lead to the renaming of many of the trophies. Perhaps in years to come the Nintendo Bowl or the MacDonald's Plate will form the basis of quiz questions; but somehow I cannot imagine the massed ranks of the Stretford End, the Kop, or the North Bank chanting "We're going to win the Durex Cup again." The following is a list of sporting trophies which have long been favourites with question setters.

Sport	Trophy	
Badminton	Thomas Cup	Men's World Team Championship
	Uber Cup	Women's World Team Championship.
Bowls	Middleton Cup	Competed for by English counties.
Croquet	MacRobertson Shield	
Equestrianism	King George V Gold Cup	
	Queen Elizabeth II Cup	
	Nations Cup	
Golf	Ryder Cup	Contested every two years between professional teams from the United States and Europe.
	Walker Cup	Contested every two years by amateur teams on the same basis.
	Curtis Cup	Contested every two years by lady golfers of the United States and Europe.

Sport	Trophy	
Ice Hockey	**Stanley Cup**	Contested by professional teams from the National Hockey League of North America.
Lacrosse	**Iroquois**	Contested annually by English Lacrosse clubs.
Real Tennis	**Henry Leaf Cup**	
Rowing	**Ladies' Plate**	
	Visitors' Cup	
	Thames Cup	
	Prince Philip Cup	
	Wyfold Cup	Trophies awarded at the Henley Royal Regatta.
	Britannia Cup	
	Stewards' Cup	
	Grand Challenge Cup	
	Princess Elizabeth Cup	
	Queen Mother Cup	
	Silver Goblets & Nickalls'	
Table Tennis	**Swaythling Cup**	Men's Team World Championship
	Corbillon Cup	Women's Team World Championship.
Walking	**Lugano Cup**	International Team Championship – staged every two years.

I have excluded from this list all the sporting trophies which take their name solely from sponsors; the sponsors could change at any time.

Stock Exchange Terms

Bear   Selling stock in the hope of encouraging a fall in price, and then buying the stock back at a profit.

Bull   Buying stock to encourage a rise in market price, then selling at a higher price than originally paid.

Stag   Buying a new share issue in the hope of a quick sale at a profit.

Symphonies

The nicknames of various well-known symphonies have always been a source of inspiration for quiz setters. Whether many of the people who set the questions or even answer them could hum any three notes from many of these works is debatable, but the following are well worth remembering.

Nickname	*Name of Symphony*
Antarctica Symphony	Vaughan Williams's Symphony No. 7
Choral Symphony	Beethoven's Symphony No. 9 in D minor
Clock Symphony	Symphony No. 101 in D by Haydn
Eroica Symphony	Symphony No. 3 in E flat by Beethoven
From the New World Symphony	Symphony No. 9 in E by Dvorak
Imperial Symphony	Symphony No. 53 in D by Haydn
The Italian Symphony	Symphony No. 4 in A by Mendelssohn
Jupiter Symphony	Symphony No. 41 in C by Mozart
Leningrad Symphony	Symphony No. 7 in C by Shostakovich
Linz Symphony	Symphony No. 36 in C by Mozart
Little Symphony	Symphony No. 6 in C major by Schubert

Nickname	Name of Symphony
Little Russian Symphony	Symphony No. 2 in C minor by Tchaikovsky
London Symphony	Symphony No. 4 in D by Haydn
Mercury Symphony	Symphony No. 43 in E flat by Haydn
1917 Symphony	Symphony No. 12 in D minor by Shostakovich
October Symphony	Symphony No. 2 in C by Shostakovich
Organ Symphony	Symphony No. 3 in C minor by Saint-Saëns
Oxford Symphony	Symphony No. 92 in G by Haydn
Paris Symphony	Symphony No. 31 in D by Mozart
Pastoral Symphony	Symphony No. 6 in F by Beethoven
Pathetique Symphony	Symphony No. 6 in B minor by Tchaikovsky
Polish Symphony	Symphony No. 3 in D by Tchaikovsky
Prague Symphony	Symphony No. 38 in D by Mozart
Reformation Symphony	Symphony No. 5 in D minor by Mendelssohn
Scottish Symphony	Symphony No. 3 in A minor by Mendelssohn
Sea Symphony	Symphony No. 1 by Vaughan Williams
Surprise Symphony	Symphony No. 94 in G by Haydn
Tragic Symphony	Symphony No. 4 in C minor by Schubert
Unfinished Symphony	Symphony No. 8 in B minor by Schubert
Wagner Symphony	Symphony No. 3 in D minor by Bruckner

....

The Ten Commandments

Usually questions relating to the Ten Commandments call for a brief description of the third or fourth or sixth Commandment, or sometimes they are phrased in the "Which of the Commandments says 'Thou Shalt not Steal'?" style. Here, in full, are the Ten Commandments.

1   Thou shalt have no other gods before me.

2   Thou shalt not make unto thee any graven image, or any
    likeness of any thing that is in heaven above, or that is in the
    earth beneath, or that
    is in the water under the earth;
    Thou shalt not bow down thyself to them, nor serve them;
    For I the Lord thy God am a jealous God, visiting the iniquity of
    the fathers upon the children unto the third and fourth
    generation of them that hate me;
    And showing mercy unto thousands of them that love me, and
    keep my commandments.

3   Thou shalt not take the name of the Lord thy God in vain;
    for the Lord will not hold him guiltless that taketh his name in
    vain.

4   Remember the sabbath day, to keep it holy.
    Six days shalt thou labour, and do all thy work;
    But the seventh day is the sabbath of the Lord thy God;
    in it thou shalt not do any work, thou, nor thy son, nor thy
    daughter,
    thy manservant, nor thy maidservant, nor thy cattle, nor thy
    stranger
    that is within thy gates:
    For in six days the Lord made heaven and earth, the sea, and
    all that in them is, and rested the seventh day:
    wherefore the Lord blessed the sabbath day and hallowed it.

5   Honour thy father and thy mother: that thy days may be long
    upon the land which the Lord thy God giveth thee.

6   Thou shalt not kill.

7   Thou shalt not commit adultery.

8   Thou shalt not steal.

9   Thou shalt not bear false witness against thy neighbour.

10 Thou shalt not covet thy neighbour's house, thou shalt not covet thy neighbour's wife, nor his manservant, nor his maidservant, nor his ox, nor his ass, nor any thing that is thy neighbour's.

Underground Lines – London

Second nature to those who live and work in the capital but the colours used to represent the various underground lines on maps of the network are still popular out in the sticks.

Underground Line	Colour
Bakerloo	Brown
Central	Red
Circle	Yellow
District	Green
East London	Orange
Hammersmith & City	Pink
Jubilee	Grey
Metropolitan	Purple
Northern	Black
Piccadilly	Dark blue
Victoria	Pale blue
Docklands Light Railway	White within blue

Universities – British

Obviously Bristol University is in Bristol and Durham University is in Durham but the location of Universities with nongeographic names has always been a popular source of quiz questions. In 1992 many polytechnics were granted full university status thus some of these "new" universities will start to appear in quiz questions. The following is a list of universities and their locations.

University	Location
Brunel	Uxbridge
University of Central England	Birmingham (formerly Birmingham Polytechnic)
University of Central Lancashire	Preston (formerly Lancashire Polytechnic)
DeMontfort	Leicester (formerly Leicester Polytechnic)
University of East Anglia	Norwich
University of Essex	Colchester
Glamorgan	Pontypridd (formerly Polytechnic of Wales)
University of Greenwich	Formerly Thames Polytechnic
Heriot-Watt	Edinburgh
University of Hertfordshire	Hatfield (formerly Hatfield Polytechnic)
Leeds Metropolitan	Formerly Leeds Polytechnic
Liverpool John Moores	Formerly Liverpool Polytechnic
Manchester Metropolitan	Formerly Manchester Polytechnic
Napier	Edinburgh (formerly Napier Polytechnic)
University of Northumbria	Newcastle (formerly Newcastle Polytechnic)
Robert Gordon University	Aberdeen (formerly Robert Gordon Institute of Technology)

University	Location
Thames Valley University	London (formerly Polytechnic of West London)
University of Ulster	Coleraine
University of Warwick	Coventry
West of England University	Bristol (formerly Bristol Polytechnic)
Westminster University	Formerly the Central London Polytechnic

Universities – American

Some long established American universities are sometimes the subject of quiz questions. Here a few which are worth remembering.

University	Location
Brown	Providence, Rhode Island
Columbia	New York (there are several Columbia Universities in the USA but this is the one which was founded in 1754)
Cornell	Ithaca, New York
Harvard	Cambridge, Massachusetts (the USA's oldest university founded in 1636)
Johns Hopkins	Baltimore, Maryland
Princeton	Princeton, New Jersey
Stanford	Stanford, California
Yale	Newhaven, Connecticut

Whilst we are in the USA we may as well have the academies for the American armed forces.

Academy	Location
US Air Force	Colorado Springs
US Military	West Point, New York
US Naval	Annapolis, Maryland

Vegetables – Scientific Names

As with the section on fruit the question usually asks you to identify a common vegetable by its scientific name. Here are the ones you are most likely to be asked.

Bean (Broad)	Vicia faba
Bean (Green)	Phaseolus vulgaris
Bean (Runner)	Phaseolus vulgaris
Broccoli	Brassica oleracea italica
Brussels Sprout	Brassica oleracea gemmifera
Cabbage	Brassica oleracea capitata
Carrot	Daucus carota
Cauliflower	Brassica oleracea botrytis
Celery	Apium graveolens
Courgette	Cucurbita pepo
Cucumber	Cucumis sativus
Garlic	Allium sativum
Leek	Allium porrum
Lettuce	Lactuca sativa
Onion	Allium cepa
Pea	Pisium sativum
Potato	Solanum tuberosum
Radish	Raphanus sativus
Spinach	Spinacia oleracea
Swede	Brassica napobrassica
Tomato	Lycopersicon esculentum
Turnip	Brassica rapa
Watercress	Nasturtium officinale

Vegetables – Varieties

Possibly more popular than fruit varieties – this may be because of some of their names. Questions about "Worcester Whoppers" or "Droitwich Droopers" and exotic names such as these always cause a titter in quizzes. However, the following are worth remembering.

Vegetable	*Varieties*
Broad Bean	Bonny Lad, Bunyard's Exhibition, Express, Green Windsor, Red Epicure, Sutton, White Windsor.

Vegetable	Varieties
Brussels Sprout	Bedford-Fillbasket, Bedford Winter Harvest, Cambridge No. 5, Early Half Tall, Fortress, Huizer's Late, Pocr Gynl, Predora, Widgen, Welland, Wellington.
Cabbage	April, Derby Day, Durham Early, Golden Acre, Greyhound, Hargenger, Hispy, January King, June Star, Ormskirk, Quickstep, Rear Guard, Spivoy, Spring Hero, Winnigstadt, Wivoy.
Carrot	Autumn King, Early Giant, Favourite, Figaro, Regulus Imperial, St Valery.
Cauliflower	Alpha, Snow Crown, Dominant, Nevada, Canberra, Snow Cap.
Cucumber	Bushcrop, King of the Ridge, Pacer, Pepita, Tokyo Slicer.
French Bean	Cordon, Loch Ness, Long Bow, Masterpiece, Remus, Sprite, Tendergreen.
Leek	Early Market, Lyon Prizetaker, Catalina, Musselburgh, Walton Mammouth, Giant Winter-Wila, Royal Favourite.
Lettuce	Fortune, Lakeland, Little Gem, Lobjoit's Green, Paris White, Sabine, Saladin, Sigmaball, Tom Thumb, Unrivalled, Webb's Wonderful, White Density.
Onion	Ailsa Craig, Bedfordshire Champion, Brunswick, Dobies Allrounder, Lancastrian, Marshall's Giant Fenglobe, North Holland Blood Red, Ricardo, Southport Red Globe, Stuttgarter Giant, Sturon, Turbo.
Parsnip	Improved Hollow Crown, Tender and True, The Student, White Gem.
Pea	Feltham First, Histon Mini, Hurst Beagle, Hurst Green, Kelvedon Wonder, Little Marvel, Shaft, Meteor, Onward, Semitar.
Potato	Craig's Royal, Catriona, Desiree, Esteema, Majestic, Romano, Vanessa, Wilja.

Vegetable	Varieties
Runner Bean	Butler, Kelvedon Marvel, Mergoles.
Tomato	Alfresco, Alicante, Big Boy, Dombito, Eurocross, Golden Boy, Herald, Marmande, Minibel, Piranto, Red Alert, Shirley, Sigmabush, Sioux, Sleaford Abundance, Sonato.
Turnip	Golden Ball, Green Globe, Model White, Veitch's Red Globe.

Vehicle Registration Letters (International)

Most people will know that the international vehicle registration letter for Germany is "D" and Spain is "E", so this list does not include the vehicle registration letters which are widely known or can be reasonably guessed at (for example, "NZ" is New Zealand). The list comprises international registration letters which are sometimes confused with each other and those which are not obvious but are frequently asked.

International Registration Letter	Country	International Registration Letter	Country
A	Austria	**FL**	Liechtenstein
AUS	Australia	**GBZ**	Gibraltar
B	Belgium	**H**	Hungary
BD	Bangladesh	**HK**	Hong Kong
BG	Bulgaria	**HKJ**	Jordan
BR	Brazil	**I**	Italy
C	Cuba	**IL**	Israel
CDN	Canada	**IND**	India
CH	Switzerland	**IR**	Iran
CY	Cyprus	**IRL**	Republic of Ireland
DK	Denmark	**IRQ**	Iraq
DZ	Algeria	**IS**	Iceland
EAK	Kenya	**M**	Malta
EAT	Tanzania	**MA**	Morocco
EAU	Uganda	**MC**	Monaco
ET	Egypt	**PA**	Panama
ETH	Ethiopia	**PAK**	Pakistan

International Registration Letter	Country	International Registration Letter	Country
RA	Argentina	SF	Finland
RC	Taiwan	V	Vatican City
RCA	Central African Republic	VN	Vietnam
RCB	Congo	WAG	Gambia
RCH	Chile	WAL	Sierra Leone
RH	Haiti	WAN	Nigeria
RI	Indonesia	Z	Zambia
RL	Lebanon	ZA	South Africa
RN	Niger	ZRE	Zaire
ROK	Korea	ZW	Zimbabwe
ROU	Uruguay		

Wars

Questions on wars are confined almost exclusively to those campaigns in which Britain was involved (or before the Union, England or Scotland). The following are the wars which frequently crop up in quiz questions.

Name of War	
Anglo-Afghan Wars	1. 1839–1842
	2. 1878–1880
	3. 1919
American Revolutionary War (or War of Independence as they call it)	From 1776–1783 was concluded by the Treaty of Versailles.
American War Of 1812	1812–1815 – was concluded by the signing of the Treaty of Ghent.
War Of The Austrian Succession	1740–1748 – was concluded by the Treaty of Aachen (Aix–la–Chapelle).
Barons' Wars	1. 1215–1217
	2. 1264–1267

Name of War

Boer Wars

There were actually two Boer Wars (more properly called The South African Wars) the first between 1880 and 1881, but the one that everybody remembers is:
The second Boer War, 1899–1902 ended by the Treaty of Vereeniging

Civil War (English Civil War)

1642–1649 – the first battle of the Civil War was Edgehill.

Crimean War

1854–1856 – concluded by the Congress of Paris.

Crusades

The first Crusade was led by Robert, Duke of Normandy (eldest son of William I which set off in 1096 and culminated with the capture of Jerusalem in 1099.
Richard I led the third Crusade (1190–1192).
The last real Crusade was led by Louis IX of France in 1248.

Falklands War

2nd April – 14th June, 1982 – Argentinian forces led by Major General Menendez British Task Force Commander: Admiral Sandy Woodward. British Land Force commanded by Major General Jeremy Moore.

Forty-Five Rebellion

1745–1746. Charles Edward Stuart, the Young Pretender, raised his standard at Glenfinnan on 19th August 1745. His forces were finally routed by an English Army led by the Duke of Cumberland at Culloden on 16th April 1746.

Hundred Years War

Really a series of wars fought between England and France between 1337 and 1453.

Indian Mutiny

1857–1858.

Name of War	
Monmouth Rebellion	1685. Duke of Monmouth landed at Lyme Regis on 11th June and was finally routed at Sedgmoor on 6th July. Monmouth was executed on 14th July.
Napoleonic Wars	Intermittently between 1793 and 1815. Concluded by the Congress of Vienna.
Opium Wars	1. 1839–1842; 2. 1856–1860. Ended by the Treaty of Nanjing which ceded Hong Kong to Britain.
Peninsular War	1808–1814. British forces led by Sir Arthur Wellesley (the Duke of Wellington).
War Of The Roses	1455–1485. By general consensus the first battle fought in the War of the Roses was St Albans and the final one was Bosworth; but the main phase of the War of the Roses was over by 1471 and it is probably more accurate to say that the Battle of Tewkesbury was the last real engagement.
Seven Years War	1756–1763. Ended by the Treaty of Paris.
War Of The Spanish Succession	1701–1713. Ended by the Treaty of Utrecht (which established Gibraltar as a British colony).
Thirty Years War (One of the few wars which occur in quizzes which did not involve British combatants)	1618–1648. War was ended by the Treaty of Westphalia.

It is assumed that everybody will know the dates of the First and Second World Wars.

Wedding Anniversaries

We all know the important ones: 25th, 50th, etc, but the 'minor' anniversaries are frequently asked. Does anybody still give the appropriate gift on their wedding anniversary? If so, how many people really celebrate their third wedding anniversary in appropriate style? A word of caution; there are slight differences between the names of wedding anniversaries in the UK and the USA. These are British wedding anniversaries.

First	Cotton
Second	Paper
Third	Leather
Fourth	Fruit and flowers
Fifth	Wood
Sixth	Sugar or iron
Seventh	Wool
Eighth	Bronze
Ninth	Copper (or pottery)
Tenth	Tin
Eleventh	Steel
Twelfth	Silk and fine linen
Thirteenth	Lace
Fourteenth	Ivory
Fifteenth	Crystal
Twentieth	China
Twenty-Fifth	Silver
Thirtieth	Pearl
Thirty-Fifth	Coral
Fortieth	Ruby
Forty-Fifth	Sapphire
Fiftieth	Gold
Fifty-Fifth	Emerald
Sixtieth	Diamond
Seventieth	Platinum

Writers and their Books

These are the authors and titles which I have encountered most frequently in quizzes.

Harrison Ainsworth	Rookwood
Kingsley Amis	Lucky Jim
	That Uncertain Feeling
	Take a Girl Like You
	One Fat Englishman
	Jake's Thing
	Stanley and the Women
	The Old Devils
Jane Austen	Sense and Sensibility
	Pride and Prejudice
	Mansfield Park
	Emma
	Northanger Abbey
	Persuasion
James Baldwin	Go Tell it on the Mountain
	Giovanni's Room
	Another Country
	Just Above my Head
J. G. Ballard	The Drowned World
	High Rise
	Empire of the Sun
H. E. Bates	The Darling Buds of May
Saul Bellow	The Victim
	Seize the Day
	Herzog
	Humboldt's Gift
Arnold Bennett	Anna of the Five Towns
	Clayhanger
R. D. Blackmore	Lorna Doone
Giovanni Boccaccio	The Decameron
Malcolm Bradbury	Eating People is Wrong
	The History Man

John Braine	Room at the Top
	Life at the Top
Anne Brontë	Agnes Grey
	The Tenant of Wildfell Hall
Charlotte Brontë	Jane Eyre
Emily Brontë	Wuthering Heights
John Buchan	The Thirty-Nine Steps
	Greenmantle
Anthony Burgess	Time for a Tiger
	A Clockwork Orange
	Earthly Powers
Frances Hodgson Burnett	Little Lord Fauntleroy
	The Secret Garden
Samuel Butler	Erewhon
Albert Camus	The Plague
Truman Capote	Breakfast at Tiffany's
Raymond Chandler	The Big Sleep (and many other "Philip Marlowe" stories)
G. K. Chesterton	The Napoleon of Notting Hill
	The Man who was Thursday
	Father Brown Stories
Agatha Christie	The Mysterious Affair at Styles
	The Murder of Roger Ackroyd
Arthur C. Clarke	The City and the Stars
	The Nine Billion Names of God
	2001: A Space Odyssey
John Cleland	Memoirs of a Woman of Pleasure (Fanny Hill)
William Cobbett	Rural Rides
Wilkie Collins	The Woman in White
	The Moonstone
Joseph Conrad	An Outcast of the Islands
	The Nigger of the Narcissus
	Lord Jim
	Nostromo
James Fenimore Cooper	The Last of the Mohicans
A. J. Cronin	The Citadel

Dante Alighieri	The Divine Comedy
Daniel Defoe	Robinson Crusoe
	Moll Flanders
	A Journal of the Plague Year
Benjamin Disraeli	Vivian Grey
	Coningsby
	Sybil
	Endymion
J. P. Donleavy	The Ginger Man
Fyodor Dostoevsky	Notes from the House of the Dead
	Notes from Underground
	Crime and Punishment
	The Brothers Karamazov
Arthur Conan Doyle	The White Company
	The Exploits of Brigadier Gerard
	The Lost World
Alexandre Dumas	The Three Musketeers
	The Count of Monte Cristo
Daphne du Maurier	Rebecca
	Jamaica Inn
George du Maurier	Trilby
George Eliot	Adam Bede
	The Mill on the Floss
	Silas Marner
	Middlemarch
	Daniel Deronda
William Faulkner	The Sound and the Fury
Henry Fielding	Tom Jones
	Joseph Andrews
F. Scott Fitzgerald	The Great Gatsby
	Tender is the Night
	The Last Tycoon
Gustave Flaubert	Madame Bovary
C. S. Forester	Hornblower novels
	The African Queen
E. M. Forster	A Room with a View
	Howard's End
	A Passage to India

John Fowles	The Collector
	The Magus
	The French Lieutenant's Woman
John Galsworthy	The Forsyte Saga
Elizabeth Gaskell	Cranford
	North and South
William Golding	Lord of the Flies
	The Inheritors
	Pincher Martin
	Free Fall
	Rites of Passage
Oliver Goldsmith	The Vicar of Wakefield
Kenneth Grahame	The Wind in the Willows
Graham Greene	Stamboul Train
	The Confidential Agent
	The Power and the Glory
	England Made Me
	The Heart of the Matter
	The End of the Affair
	The Quiet American
	The Honorary Consul
	Our Man in Havana
	The Third Man
	The Human Factor
Walter Greenwood	Love on the Dole
George and Weedon Grossmith	The Diary of a Nobody
H. Rider Haggard	King Solomon's Mines
	She
Dashiell Hammett	The Maltese Falcon
	The Thin Man
Thomas Hardy	Desperate Remedies
	Under the Greenwood Tree
	A Pair of Blue Eyes
	Far from the Madding Crowd
	Tess of the D'Urbervilles
	Jude the Obscure

	The Mayor of Casterbridge
	The Return of the Native
	The Trumpet Major
Joel Chandler Harris	Uncle Remus stories
L. P. Hartley	The Go-Between
Nathaniel Hawthorne	The Scarlet Letter
Joseph Heller	Catch-22
Ernest Hemingway	The Sun Also Rises
	A Farewell to Arms
	Death in the Afternoon
	For Whom the Bell Tolls
	The Old Man and the Sea
	A Moveable Feast
Herman Hesse	Der Steppenwolf
	The Glass Bead Game
James Hilton	Lost Horizon
	Good-bye Mr Chips
Homer	The Iliad
	The Odyssey
Anthony Hope	The Prisoner of Zenda
E. W. Hornung	Raffles books
Thomas Hughes	Tom Brown's Schooldays
Victor Hugo	Notre Dame de Paris
	(The Hunchback of Notre Dame)
	Les Misérables
Aldous Huxley	Crome Yellow
	Point Counter Point
	Brave New World
	Eyeless in Gaza
	The Doors of Perception
Washington Irving	The Legend of Sleepy Hollow
Christopher Isherwood	Goodbye to Berlin
Henry James	The Ambassadors
	The Turn of the Screw
	Washington Square
Jerome K. Jerome	Three Men in a Boat
James Joyce	Dubliners

	A Portrait of the Artist as a Young Man
	Ulysses
	Finnegans Wake
Franz Kafka	The Trial
	The Castle
Jack Kerouac	On the Road
Charles Kingsley	Westward Ho!
	The Water Babies
Rudyard Kipling	Stalky & Co.
	Plain Tales from the Hills
	Soldiers Three
	Barrack-Room Ballads
	The Jungle Book
	Just So Stories
	Puck of Pook's Hill
D. H. Lawrence	Sons and Lovers
	The White Peacock
	The Rainbow
	Women in Love
	The Plumed Serpent
	Lady Chatterley's Lover
Edward Lear	A Book of Nonsense
John le Carré	Call for the Dead
	The Spy Who Came in from the Cold
	The Looking Glass War
	A Small Town in Germany
	Tinker, Tailor, Soldier, Spy
	The Honourable Schoolboy
	Smiley's People
Laurie Lee	Cider with Rosie
C. S. Lewis	Out of the Silent Planet
	The Lion, the Witch and the Wardrobe
Jack London	The Call of the Wild
	The Sea-Wolf
	White Fang
Niccolò Machiavelli	The Art of War
	The Prince

Compton Mackenzie	Whisky Galore
Norman Mailer	The Naked and the Dead
Thomas Malory	Le Morte D'Arthur
Thomas Mann	Death in Venice
Captain Marryat	Children of the New Forest
	Mr Midshipman Easy
Ngaio Marsh	Inspector Alleyn stories
Somerset Maugham	Of Human Bondage
	The Moon and Sixpence
	The Razor's Edge
Gavin Maxwell	Ring of Bright Water
Herman Melville	Moby-Dick
	Billy Budd, Foretopman
Henry Miller	Tropic of Cancer
	Tropic of Capricorn
A. A. Milne	Winnie-the-Pooh
Margaret Mitchell	Gone with the Wind
Nicholas Monsarrat	The Cruel Sea
Michael Moorcock	The Final Programme
	A Cure for Cancer
	The English Assassin
George Moore	Esther Waters
Thomas More	Utopia
John Mortimer	Rumpole of the Bailey books
Iris Murdoch	Under the Net
	The Time of the Angels
	The Sea, The Sea
Vladimir Nabakov	Lolita
V. S. Naipaul	In a Free State
	A Bend in the River
	The Middle Passage
Edna O'Brien	The Country Girls
Baroness Orczy	The Scarlet Pimpernel
George Orwell	Nineteen Eighty-four
	The Road to Wigan Pier
	Coming up for Air
	Animal Farm

Boris Pasternak	Doctor Zhivago
Thomas Love Peacock	Nightmare Abbey
	Headlong Hall
Sylvia Plath	The Bell Jar
Edgar Allan Poe	The Fall of the House of Usher
	The Murders in the Rue Morgue
	The Pit and the Pendulum
Stephen Potter	The Theory and Practice of
	Gamesmanship
	Some Notes on Lifemanship
	One-Upmanship
Anthony Powell	A Dance to the Music of Time
J. B. Priestley	The Good Companions
Marcel Proust	Remembrance of Things Past
François Rabelais	Gargantua
	Pantagruel
Arthur Ransome	Swallows and Amazons
Erich Remarque	All Quiet on the Western Front
	The Road Back
Frank Richards	Billy Bunter stories
Samuel Richardson	Pamela
	Clarissa
Philip Roth	Portnoy's Complaint
J. D. Salinger	The Catcher in the Rye
Sapper	Bull-dog Drummond
Siegfried Sassoon	Memoirs of a Fox-Hunting Man
Dorothy L. Sayers	Lord Peter Wimsey books
Paul Scott	The Raj Quartet (including "The
	Jewel in the Crown")
	Staying On
Walter Scott	Waverley
	Rob Roy
	The Heart of Midlothian
	Kenilworth
	Quentin Durward
	Tales of my Landlord
	Castle Dangerous

Anna Sewell	Black Beauty
Mary Shelley	Frankenstein, or the Modern Prometheus
Mikhail Sholokhov	And Quiet Flows the Don
Alan Sillitoe	Saturday Night and Sunday Morning
	The Loneliness of the Long Distance Runner
Georges Simenon	Maigret books
Tobias Smollett	The Adventures of Roderick Random
	The Adventures of Peregrine Pickle
	The Expedition of Humphry Clinker
C. P. Snow	Strangers and Brothers
	Corridors of Power
Alexander Solzhenitsyn	One Day in the Life of Ivan Denisovich
	Cancer Ward
	The Gulag Archipelago
Muriel Spark	The Prime of Miss Jean Brodie
	The Ballad of Peckham Rye
Howard Spring	Fame is the Spur
John Steinbeck	Tortilla Flat
	Of Mice and Men
	The Grapes of Wrath
	East of Eden
Laurence Sterne	The Life and Opinions of Tristram Shandy
Robert Louis Stevenson	Treasure Island
	The Strange Case of Dr Jekyll and Mr Hyde
	Kidnapped
	Catriona
	The Master of Ballantrae
	Weir of Hermiston
Bram Stoker	Dracula
Harriet Beecher Stowe	Uncle Tom's Cabin
Robert Surtees	Jorrocks's Jaunts and Jollities
Jonathan Swift	A Tale of a Tub
	Gulliver's Travels

William Makepeace Thackeray	Vanity Fair
	Pendennis
	The History of Henry Esmond
J. R. R. Tolkien	The Hobbit
	Lord of the Rings
	The Silmarillion
Leo Tolstoy	War and Peace
	Anna Karenina
B. Traven	The Treasure of Sierra Madre
Robert Tressell	The Ragged Trousered Philanthropists
Anthony Trollope	The Barchester Chronicles
Mark Twain	Tom Sawyer and Huckleberry Finn stories
	The Prince and the Pauper
	A Connecticut Yankee in King Arthur's Court
Jules Verne	Journey to the Centre of the Earth
	Twenty Thousand Leagues under the Sea
	Around the World in Eighty Days
Voltaire	Candide
Horace Walpole	The Castle of Otranto
Keith Waterhouse	Billy Liar
Evelyn Waugh	Decline and Fall
	A Handul of Dust
	Scoop
	Sword of Honour
	Brideshead Revisited
H. G. Wells	The Time Machine
	The Island of Doctor Moreau
	The Invisible Man
	The War of the Worlds
	The First Men in the Moon
	Love and Mr Lewisham
	Kipps
	The History of Mr Polly
	The Shape of Things to Come

T. H. White	The Once and Future King
	The Sword in the Stone
Oscar Wilde	The Picture of Dorian Gray
Henry Williamson	Tarka the Otter
P. G. Wodehouse	Jeeves and Wooster books
Virginia Woolf	The Voyage Out
	Mrs Dalloway
	To the Lighthouse
	The Waves
	Between the Acts

Zodiac Signs

Easy if you are asked questions about zodiac signs around your own birthday, but it can be infuriating if you do not know, for example, which birth sign you would be if you were born on 1st January. Here they are:

Aries – The ram	21 March–19 April
Taurus – The bull	20 April–20 May
Gemini – The twins	21 May–21 June
Cancer – The crab	22 June–22 July
Leo – The lion	23 July–22 August
Virgo – The virgin	23 August–22 September
Libra – The balance	23 September–23 October
Scorpio – The scorpion	24 October–21 November
Sagittarius – The archer	22 November–21 December
Capricorn – The goat	22 December–19 January
Aquarius – The water carrier	20 January–18 February
Pisces – The fishes	19 February–20 March